NetWare 5 CNE:
Update to NetWare 5
Study Guide

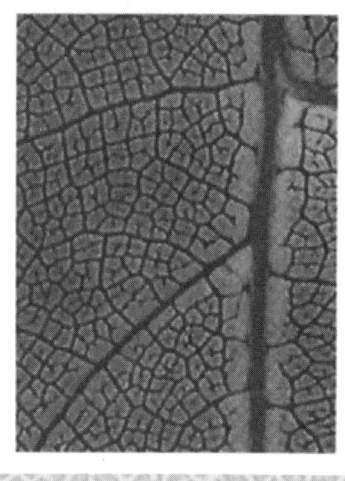

NOVELL OBJECTIVE	COVERED IN
25. List the benefits and components of Z.E.N.works and describe the function of each.	Chapter 6,7
26. Install Z.E.N.works and the Z.E.N.works NetWare Client.	Chapter 6
27. Describe Z.E.N.works policy packages and explain how policies are used to manage workstations.	Chapter 6
28. Explain how to register workstations and import them into NDS using NetWare Administrator.	Chapter 6
29. Configure desktop environments throughout the network.	Chapter 7
30. Distribute applications using the Novell Application Launcher.	Chapter 7
31. Manage workstations using the Z.E.N.works Remote Control utility.	Chapter 7
32. Set up the HelpRequester application so users can report workstations problems.	Chapter 7
33. Describe transitive synchronization.	Chapter 4
34. Describe WAN Traffic Manager and its use to manage synchronization traffic.	Chapter 4
35. Describe Network Time Protocol.	Chapter 4
36. Configure Network Time Protocol (NTP) to synchronize time in an IP or mixed IP/IPX environment.	Chapter 4
37. Describe contextless login.	Chapter 11
38. Set up the network to allow contextless login.	Chapter 11
39. Describe NetWare 5 licensing, including license container objects and license certificate objects.	Chapter 2
40. Manage NetWare user licenses.	Chapter 2
41. Describe compatibility mode.	Chapter 4
42. Describe the Migration Gateway.	Chapter 4
43. Configure and maintain compatibility mode on a NetWare 5 server.	Chapter 4
44. Describe Service Location Protocol (SLP).	Chapter 11
45. Describe Novell's Public Key Infrastructure (PKI).	Chapter 11
46. Describe Novell International Cryptography Infrastructure (NICI).	Chapter 11
47. Configure and maintain PKI.	Chapter 11
48. Describe the features and benefits of NetWare 5.	Chapter 1
49. Describe the process of migrating to NetWare 5 in an IP only environment.	Chapter 4

NOTE   The exam objectives listed above were current at the time of this book's printing. Objectives are subject to change at any time without prior notice and at Novell's sole discretion. Please visit Novell's web site (www.novell.com) for the most current exam objectives.

NetWare® 5 CNE®: Update to NetWare® 5 Study Guide

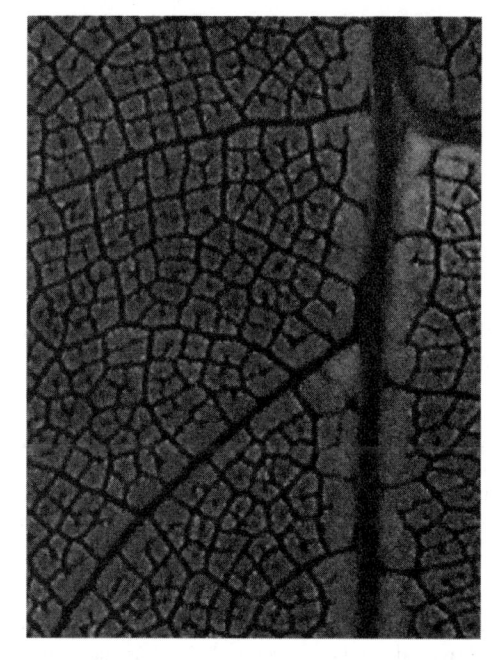

Michael G. Moncur
John Wm. Jenkins, Jr.
with James Chellis

San Francisco • Paris • Düsseldorf • Soest • London

Associate Publisher: Guy Hart-Davis
Contracts and Licensing Manager: Kristine O'Callaghan
Acquisitions & Developmental Editors: Bonnie Bills, Neil Edde
Editor: Kathy Grider-Carlyle
Project Editor: Rebecca Rider
Technical Editor: Mark Kovach
Book Designer: Bill Gibson
Graphic Illustrators: Patrick Dintino, Bill Gibson
Electronic Publishing Specialist: Franz Baumhackl
Production Coordinator: Julie Sakaue
Indexer: Lynnzee Elze
Cover Designer: Archer Design
Cover Illustrator/Photographer: The Image Bank

Library of Congress Card Number: 98-88909
ISBN: 0-7821-2390-2

Manufactured in the United States of America

10 9 8 7 6 5 4 3 2 1

We dedicate this book to our families and friends.

Acknowledgments

We would all like to thank Guy Hart-Davis for getting the ball rolling and Bonnie Bills for her constant guidance and feedback throughout the project. Thanks go to Rebecca Rider for managing the day-to-day details and keeping this book moving along. We would also like to thank Kathy Grider-Carlyle for clarifying confusion and Mark Kovach for eliminating errors. Thanks to Kristine O'Callaghan for spelling out the deal. Thanks also to Electronic Publishing Specialist Franz Baumhackl and to Production Coordinator Julie Sakaue for all their hard work in putting together the pieces of this book.

Michael Moncur: I would like to thank my family and friends, particularly my wife, Laura, and my parents, Gary and Susan Moncur. Thanks again to everyone at Sybex for their help with this project.

John Jenkins: I would like to thank my family and friends including John Wm. Jenkins, Sr., Linden Mitchell, Loretta Greaves, Kristen Eggertsen, Star Place, JoAnn Garcia, Donise Davidson, Allisone Weiss, Janit London, James Chellis, Bill Clark, James M. Jenkins, Julia Loughran, James Sullivan, Bonnie Phillips, Ralph Edwards, James Chavez, Doug Vest, Peggy Cronin, Jeff Ward, and the Arica School.

James Chellis: Thanks to my family—Kiki, Mary Jo, Gayle, David, Paul, Aaron, Ray, and Bill—as well as Sibylla, Matt, John, Lisa, Salman, Jairo, Bo, Oscar, Arica, Kewei, Gin, Donese, Mike, Laura, Howarth, Jenny, Travis, Heidi, Stefene, Rick, Esmerelda La Cat, Guy, Kristine, and Neil.

Contents at a Glance

Table of Contents

Table of Procedures

Introduction

With over 81 million users and 4 million servers worldwide, NetWare is by far the most popular server operating system in the world. According to a report released by International Data Corporation (IDC) in June of 1998, NetWare servers comprise 38 percent of all servers out there, while the various UNIX operating systems together rank second at 21 percent, Windows NT Server third at 16 percent, OS/2 fourth at 11 percent, and several others comprising the last 14 percent. Clearly, there is a demand for professionals capable of managing NetWare. With the release of NetWare 5, the opportunity for professional NetWare administrators trained in Novell's latest product has risen again.

Why You Should Buy This Book

So you're standing in the bookstore with this book in your hand. Should you buy it?

YES—if you just want to learn to work with Novell's latest and greatest operating system. Building on your basic understanding of previous versions of NetWare, this book will quickly and directly update your knowledge and skills.

or

YES—if you are a CNE and want to upgrade your certification to the most current level. This book gives you an affordable, efficient means of learning NetWare 5 and preparing for the CNE certification upgrade exam.

or

YES—if you are with a training company, because this book offers the best alternative to the very expensive Novell Education training manuals.

What Subjects Are Covered in This Book?

The short answer to this question is: the information you need for the CNE update test and much more. To be more specific, the information presented in this book can help you in two distinct areas:

- The realm of Novell Education, with its unique perspective on how things are and what you should know about networking.

- The real world, where tough demands on your time and energy require you to focus on only the most important information.

This book contains not only the information you need to achieve success on the CNE update test, but also the information that will enable you to implement actual networks under real-world conditions. We know that you don't want materials that will be of little use to you once you've taken the test, so we've packed this book with information that will genuinely help you in your work with NetWare networks.

Specifically, the following topics are covered in this book:

- Understanding NetWare 5's new features and components

- Upgrading a NetWare 3.1*x* or 4.*x* server to NetWare 5

- Using the Java console and ConsoleOne to manage the NetWare 5 server

- Configuring and using TCP/IP with NetWare 5 servers and clients

- Installing and configuring DNS and DHCP services

- Implementing and managing Novell Distributed Print Services (NDPS)

- Creating and managing NSS (Novell Storage Services) volumes on a NetWare 5 server

- Installing Z.E.N.works

- Managing workstations with Z.E.N.works

- Installing, configuring, and using Netscape FastTrack Server for NetWare

How Do I Update My CNE to NetWare 5?

If you are a CNE and are considering updating your certification, there are two possibilities:

Option 1: If you are a NetWare 4 or intraNetWare CNE, pass the following exam:

50-638: NetWare 4.11 to NetWare 5 Update

Option 2: If you are a NetWare 3, GroupWise, or Classic CNE, pass the following exam:

50-640: NetWare 5 Advanced Administration

This book deals with Option 1, the choice for NetWare 4 or intraNetWare CNEs.

If you don't already have a CNE-4 and would like to study for the NetWare 5 CNE program from scratch, we recommend these Sybex titles: *NetWare 5 CNA/CNE: Administration and Design Study Guide; NetWare 5 CNE: Core Technologies Study Guide;* and *NetWare 5 CNE: Integrating Windows NT Study Guide.*

Novell's tests are administered by Sylvan Prometric and VUE, both independent testing companies. At the time of writing, the tests are $95.00 each. For more information on testing, you can reach Sylvan at 1-800-RED-EXAM and VUE at 1-800-511-8123. You can also register for tests online at the Sylvan Prometric or VUE Web site:

```
http://www.prometric.com/
http://www.vue.com/novell/
```

How to Use This Book

The best way to prepare for the test is:

- Study a chapter carefully, making sure that you fully understand the information.

- Consider setting up a practice network to help you work through the procedures and to review as you study for the test.

- Answer the Practice Questions related to that chapter. (The answers to the Practice Questions are located in the Appendix.)

- Notice which questions of the test you did not understand, and study those sections of the book again.

- Review the Practice Questions until you have mastered the appropriate material.

- Study the next section, and repeat the process described in the three previous tips.

- Once you have read all of the chapters, go to Sybex's Web page at http://www.sybex.com. Once there, click Catalog. Under Browse by Category and the subsection Certification, select CNE/CNA. Find the title to this book, and select that link. This will take you to a page where you can access the most recent updates to the book, as well as take an online test, The Sybex CNA EdgeTest for NetWare 5.

- If you prefer to learn in a classroom setting, you have many options. Both Novell-authorized and independent training are widely available.

- Having access to a NetWare 5 network on which you may practice is definitely an advantage in the process of studying. If you are practicing on a network used by others, be sure you do not try anything that may influence their data in any way.

- The following pages contain a lot of information. To learn all of it, you will need to study regularly and with discipline. Try to set aside the same time every day to study, and select a comfortable and quiet place in which to do it. If you work hard, you will be surprised at how quickly you learn this material. Good luck.

Obtaining a Trial Copy of NetWare 5

At the time of publication of this book, Novell is offering a three-user demo of NetWare 5, with no expiration date, for only $15.00 dollars plus shipping. (This is a full version of the NetWare 5 operating system, but it includes licenses for only three clients.) This can be an excellent support tool in your efforts to become skilled with NetWare 5.

The world-wide price is $15.00 (U.S. dollars) plus shipping. Orders take approximately two weeks to arrive.

To order:

- In the United States, call 1-800-395-7135, Monday–Friday, 7 A.M.–5 P.M. U.S. PST.

- In Latin American and Asian Pacific regions, call 925-463-7391, Monday–Friday, 6 A.M.–5 P.M. U.S. PST.

- In Europe, the Middle East, and Africa, call 353-1-8037035.

Conventions Used in This Book

Where possible, we have tried to make things clearer and more accessible by including Notes, Tips, and Warnings based on our personal experiences in the field of networking. Each has a special margin icon and is set off in special type.

Notes provide you with helpful asides, reminders, and bits of information that deserve special attention.

Tips provide you with information that will make the current task easier. Tips include shortcuts and alternative ways to perform a task.

Warnings help so you can avert a possible disaster. The Warnings will help you avoid making mistakes that could require a tremendous effort to correct.

How to Contact the Authors

If you have questions or comments about the content of this book, you can contact the authors. This e-mail address will reach John Wm. Jenkins, Jr., Michael G. Moncur, and James Chellis:

nw5update@starlingtech.com

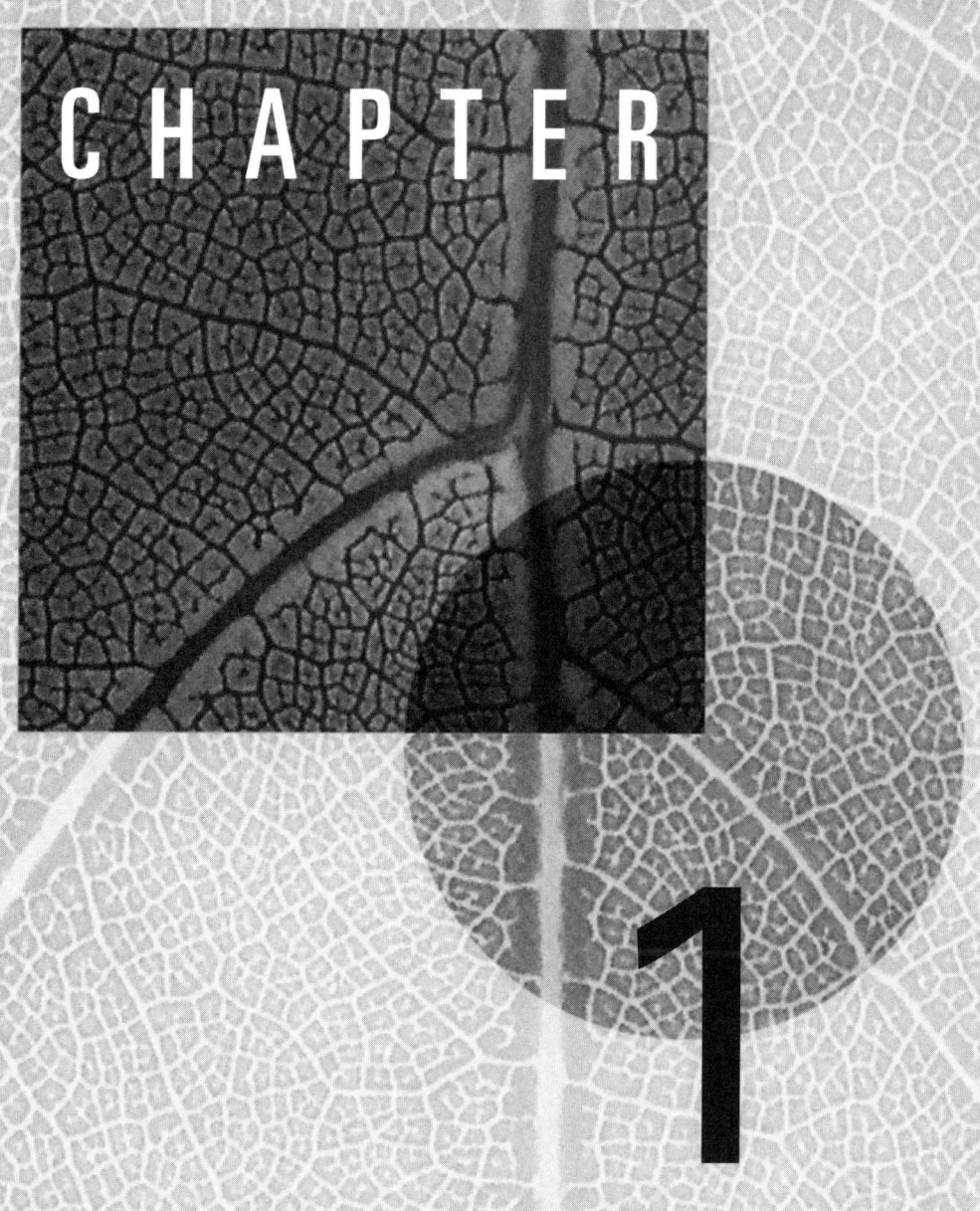

CHAPTER

1

What's New in NetWare 5?

Roadmap

This chapter introduces NetWare 5. Some very exciting features in NetWare 5 are briefly covered in this chapter; other features are introduced here and then covered in depth later in the book.

Topics Covered

- A concise introduction and overview of the new features in NetWare 5

- An expanded introduction to the central features that will be covered in detail in this course, particularly:
  - NetWare 5 installation
  - Z.E.N.works
  - Novell Distributed Printing Services
  - TCP/IP features
  - Novell DNS/DHCP Services
  - FastTrack Server
  - Other NetWare 5 features you'll want to know about

Skills You'll Learn

- Install, upgrade, and migrate to a NetWare 5 network

- Understand, configure, and manage DNS/DHCP Services

- Understand and use the Java-based ConsoleOne on the NetWare 5 Server

- Manage and use the workstation and application management and reporting features in Z.E.N.works suite

- Understand and manage the Netscape FastTrack Server

- Implement and manage NDPS

- Understand, manage, and benefit from NetWare 5's Pure IP environment

- List and understand the new features present in NetWare 5

NetWare 5 is the latest entry in the network wars that have been brewing for some years now between Novell's NetWare and Microsoft's Windows NT. With NT 5 due in 1999, Novell's latest version seems to keep NetWare solidly out front with its technological advances that extend the power and reach of the network. Novell has shipped ten times more beta copies of NetWare 5 than any previous NetWare beta program. NetWare 5 has many exciting new features that have stimulated this demand.

With NetWare 5, new management utilities have been added to extend the reach of a network administrator from client workstations to applications to remote functionality. Its Java-friendly platform base and open standards and protocols make it easy for developers to join in the fun. NDS (Novell Directory Services) is Novell's X.500-based global directory, which has been leveraged to fulfill its promise as an information-laden hierarchical directory structure with a great capacity to extend the functional power the network provides.

Course Overview

To upgrade to a NetWare 5 CNE, you must fully understand the details covered in this book. We will look at the many new features present in NetWare 5. Then we will go into more depth regarding the features that CNE test 50-638 or CNI test 50-838 will test you on to upgrade your CNE to NetWare 5. Because we will perform many hands-on procedures in this book, you will need to have NetWare 5 installed. Some NetWare 5 features will not be explored in detail and will be included only in this chapter. However, you may need to know these details for the test.

Some of the new features we will look at are:

- Pure IP environment or a mixed IP/IPX environment
- Novell DNS/DHCP Services

- Novell Z.E.N.works suite
- Novell Distributed Print Services (NDPS)
- Netscape FastTrack Server for NetWare
- Novell Storage Services (NSS)
- Novell Replication Services (NRS)
- ConsoleOne
- Modified console commands
- NDS
- Installation utilities
- New NetWare 5 kernel features
- New NetWare 5 disk driver system
- Oracle8 for NetWare
- Intelligent I/O Support (I_2O)
- Cryptographic Services
- Open Solutions Architecture SDK
- Hot Plug PCI

Let's take a quick look at these exciting new features and functions in NetWare 5.

With Novell/IP, NetWare 5 allows a Pure IP environment or a mixed IP/IPX environment. (NetWare 5 is backward-compatible with IPX/SPX.) When IP is chosen as a core protocol, it requires less hardware and software in routed environments, saves bandwidth, and can increase remote user opportunities while providing a smooth IP environment with the sure network winner—the Internet. Compatibility Mode allows IPX applications to run in an IP-only environment, while the Migration Gateway links IPX and IP network segments seamlessly, allowing IP and IPX parts of the network to communicate and function together. Service Location Protocol (SLP) provides plug-and-play capability with automatic resource registration and discovery and is much more bandwidth efficient than the repetitive messages of Service Advertisement Protocol (SAP).

Novell DNS/DHCP Services is standards-based software that integrates DNS (Domain Name System) and DHCP (Dynamic Host Configuration Protocol) into NDS (Novell Directory Services). DNS/DHCP Services also supports Dynamic DNS (DDNS), which allows for dynamic updates of host names with changing IP addresses. The DNS server translates network node IP addresses to user-friendly appellations like www.company.com. The administration time for IP addresses is, therefore, automated and linked to the benefits of NDS (fault tolerance, replication, and centralized management). NetWare 5 includes the DNS/DHCP Management Console, a Java-based utility that allows you to manage and administer DNS and DHCP services.

The Novell Z.E.N.works suite is a collection of network management tools that aim to make the administrator's job easier. The Z.E.N. acronym is short for Zero Effort Networking, representing the lack of effort needed on the part of the NetWare 5 user. Z.E.N.works creates workstation objects in the NDS tree, thereby allowing information retrieval, repair, software manipulation, and automated processes on all workstations (which limits physical visits that can be so costly in time and energy). This valuable application and utility suite also facilitates remote control of the workstation, application installation, management at the desktop, and help desk communications. (NetWare 5 will ship with the Z.E.N.works Starter Pack, which includes software distribution and workstation management components. The missing Z.E.N.works components are available as an add-on.)

Novell Distributed Print Services (NDPS) is a flexible, new approach to printing that lowers administrative costs, reduces printing problems on the network, and should improve network performance. NDPS replaces queue-based systems and includes plug-and-print automatic printer detection, automatic print driver download and installation, and bidirectional control and feedback in real-time. It facilitates single point of administration for all network printers and will perform automatic printer discovery and configuration. NDPS reduces both job polling time and SAP traffic.

Netscape FastTrack Server for NetWare is a quick, reliable Web server that ships with NetWare 5. FastTrack Server can also be easily upgraded for more complex Web needs to Netscape's Enterprise Server.

Novell Storage Services (NSS) is a 64-bit, indexed, scalable file system that improves on the standard NetWare file system by adding speed and the capability to handle large storage devices.

Novell Replication Services (NRS) is a new tool that enables you to easily access replicated files and data while coordinating their WAN dispersal during replication. Your network retains all security and location optimization with NRS.

Novell's Java Console is billed as "the fastest virtual machine on any server." Novell CEO Eric Schmidt is well known for the Java genius he displayed in his former position with Sun Microsystems. Now he brings that Java orientation to Novell. NetWare 5's GUI management with ConsoleOne situates 100 percent Java-based GUI (Graphics User Interface) management on the server. It is based on the X Windows environment found on UNIX platforms. This mouse-friendly management tool is just what many Novell administrators have been waiting for. NetWare 5 allows Java applets to run on any server console while Java applications are multitasked on a busy server. ConsoleOne supports file copying, local volume browsing, and graphical server monitoring, as well as basic server management and administration. ConsoleOne also supports the server-based remote console functions.

The console commands have been modified slightly. The LOAD command is now optional. NWCONFIG.NLM replaces INSTALL .NLM. MONITOR.NLM now includes SERVMAN.NLM's functionality. SCRSAVER.NLM now secures the console. RESTART SERVER replaces the cumbersome two-step process of DOWN and RESTART SERVER. DOWN replaces the two-step DOWN and EXIT commands. RESET SERVER initiates a warm server reboot. Finally, SET commands that you enter at the console are remembered after restarting the server.

NDS, the hierarchical global directory service, remains an industry leader. NDS improvements include:

- WAN Traffic Manager, which improves WAN traffic
- LDAP support for the interface between NDS and applications and to access and query any directory
- Catalog Services that enables a "contextless" login and allows a catalog of information to be stored in NDS
- New diagnostics module functionality
- New password administration
- Transitive synchronization
- DSbacker
- Full IP support

Installation utilities are included with NetWare 5 to make transitions from past versions of NetWare smooth and rewarding. Install, Novell Upgrade Wizard, Rexxware Migration Toolkit (RMT), and Automatic Client Update facilitate the transition for across-the-wire and in-place moves to NetWare 5.

New NetWare 5 kernel features include virtual memory for better performance, memory protection to increase fault tolerance, an integrated debugger, and multiprocessor support (which works with single processor machines and with as many as 32 processors). It also includes a new application preemption feature that enables you to prioritize applications running on the server.

NetWare 5 includes a new disk driver system based on NetWare Peripheral Architecture (NPA), first introduced with NetWare 4.1. Unlike NetWare 4.1, NetWare 5 does not support older disk drivers with .dsk extensions. NPA divides NetWare driver support into two components: a HAM (Host Adapter Module) that controls the host bus adapter, and one or more CDMs (Custom Device Modules) that control the hardware devices attached to the host bus adapter. New

NetWare 5-compatible disk drivers may be available in the future, as other companies develop them.

Oracle8 for NetWare, which ships with NetWare 5, provides maximum performance and scalable database support with the NetWare multithreaded architecture. Oracle8 is a universal data server that provides network database servers to NetWare 5-equipped companies. Oracle8 for NetWare offers tight integration with NDS and will permit a single sign-on and NDS management through a GUI snap-in to NetWare Administrator. Oracle8's preconfigured and pretuned database is easy and quick to bring up. A GUI snap-in for NetWare Administrator allows a single database server sign-on and privilege management through NDS. Oracle8 also includes Memory Protection Module (MPM), Support for Oracle Enterprise Manager, and major improvements with support of high-end online transaction processing (OLTP) and decision support systems.

Intelligent I/O Support (I$_2$O) provides support for LAN and block storage I/O traffic. It allows the server to offload the I/O traffic from the host processor to other processors. This can reduce your host processor utilization, thereby allowing more applications to be supported without a loss to performance.

Novell's security leadership is extended on NetWare 5. Cryptographic Services situates an international cryptographic infrastructure on the NetWare platform that delivers fundamental security features including authentication, nonrepudiation, confidentiality, and integrity. Cryptographic Services includes an interface manager and a secure loader to confirm that only signed modules are used. Secure Authentication Services (SAS) expands the security of NetWare 4.11, previously the only C2-certified network on the market. SAS will authenticate users to NDS secure files and server-based applications. SAS can discriminate between the qualities of different authentication mechanisms, and it allows third-party authentication services to be introduced. The Public Key Infrastructure (PKI) allows Public Key Cryptography and digital certificates to be used in the NetWare environment. A Certificate Authority (CA) domain is established within NDS to enable administrators to manage certificate and key security services such as

Secure Socket Layer (SSL) security for LDAP servers. The expanded audit services enhance the NetWare 5 standard. Audit log files are represented, managed, and secured as an NDS object.

Open Solutions Architecture SDK for developers receives its official release with NetWare 5. This package encourages developers to write useful programs for NetWare 5. Enhanced Loader support in NetWare 5 allows developers to use other compilers such as C++ and Microsoft Visual Studio to create programs for the NetWare environment. This is achieved by allowing loader extensions to be registered for non-NLM object types.

Hot Plug PCI allows you to replace or add network cards with the server running. This can decrease server downtime and facilitate expansion.

Now let's take a closer look at some of these exciting new capabilities!

Installation Wizard and Licensing Services

NetWare 5 is the first version of NetWare that allows you to install all of the Novell products and third-party applications with the new common installation architecture, Novell Installation Services. In previous versions, each product had its own installation process. This new install is a Java-based, data-driven object design that Novell eventually plans to use for all of its future product installations. A simplified pre-Java setup automates the creation of a boot partition, and a Wizard interface walks you through the install. Installation templates can save time and money when you have a large number of servers to install. NetWare 5 is backward-compatible with NetWare versions 3.1*x* and 4.*x*, IntraNetWare, and IntraNetWare for Small Business. You should prepare for a big push from Novell to get NetWare users to upgrade to NetWare 5. Moving from previous versions to NetWare 5 is relatively easy.

Installation Overview

NetWare 5 supports Pure IP (Internet Protocol) and IPX (Internetwork Packet Exchange). You can choose to run either or a combination of both. You can also choose to install in an improved text mode or to install in the Java-based mode with the graphical user interface (the Installation Wizard shown in Figure 1.1), which has increased system requirements. For upgrades from older versions, the Novell Upgrade Wizard includes drag-and-drop modeling for easy transitions, and it will identify problems before the install occurs. It will also migrate user account passwords, thereby avoiding the headaches of changing them all.

FIGURE 1.1

The NetWare 5 Installation Wizard makes installation easier with a clickable GUI.

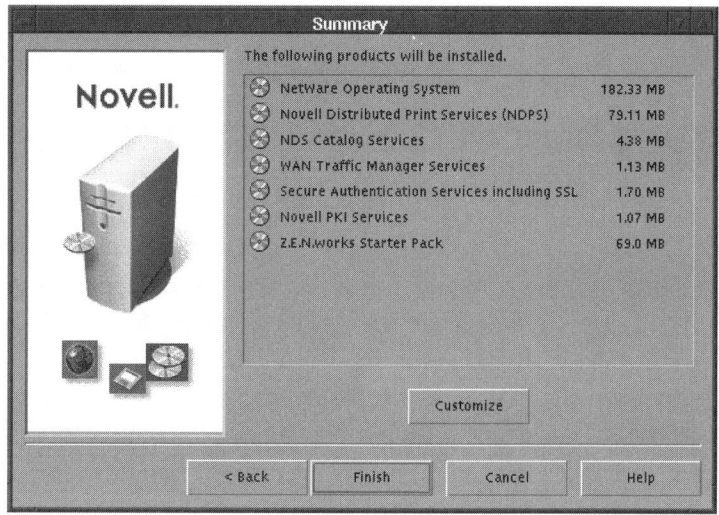

If you have several identical servers, you can use NetWare 5 Batch Support to automate a profile after the first installation. Network and hard disk drivers are programmed automatically, and version checking guarantees that only the latest version of files is copied.

Upgrade Utilities

You may choose between four upgrade utilities to make the move to NetWare 5:

Install   This is the central utility that automatically detects hardware. This utility was developed with Novell Installation Services (NIS), Novell's new common installation architecture. Install first creates the boot partition and then brings the Java-based GUI benefits to the process. Install employs the best configuration and converts users, groups, queues, printers, and print servers to NDS objects and situates them while maintaining all existing passwords. Install has a data-driven object design that allows for easy customization. This utility will work with either NetWare 3.1x or NetWare 4.x for in-place or across-the-wire upgrades.

Novell Upgrade Wizard   This convenient GUI utility (see Figure 1.2) for NetWare 3.1x to NetWare 5 upgrades includes a split window that allows you to see both the NetWare 3.1x source server and the destination NDS tree. This allows you to drag-and-drop all of the volume contents and the bindery to their new NDS locations. Verification checks various potential problems (such as duplicate names, rights problems, improper NLMs, and insufficient disk space) before they manifest.

F I G U R E 1.2

The Novell Upgrade Wizard allows you to create a new Upgrade Wizard project or open an existing one.

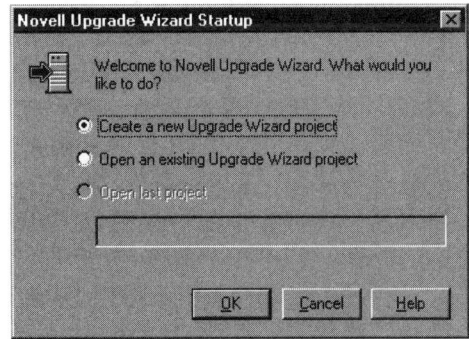

Rexxware Migration Toolkit (RMT)   This across-the-wire upgrade utility comes free for customers with an existing NetWare 3 server and includes enhanced customization and functionality, such as scripting and server consolidation. An interesting feature of RMT allows you to interrupt the process at any time and resume where you left off. Simware Technical Support licenses this product to Novell and provides customer support (go to `http://support.simware.com/index.htm`).

Automatic Client Upgrade   This utility is used to automatically upgrade NetWare clients. Whenever a client logs in or clicks the NetWare Application Launcher (NAL), he or she is upgraded automatically to the specific NetWare 5 client that supports whatever desktop operating system the client is running. (All major desktop operating systems are supported.) You can specifically customize each user if desired.

Novell Licensing Services

Novell Licensing Services is a distributed enterprise network service that allows you to administer licensed applications on the network by incorporating Licensing Service Programming Interface (LSAPI). NLS provides a single utility to license all current and future Novell products. Previous NetWare versions were specific to the number of servers installed. Licenses could be expensive and could include large user increments. While on NetWare 5, each server has a certificate and is configured for the number of network users present at any one time, which saves time and provides a more scalable solution.

Z.E.N.works

Z.E.N.works is a directory-enabled desktop management suite. Z.E.N.works leverages NDS and provides features that reward those who have invested in that directory structure. Z.E.N.works keeps information about the network and users in NDS (including information about printers, users, workstations, desktop and configuration preferences, applications, and context and error information to help the help desk). Z.E.N.works also creates what Novell CEO Eric Schmidt dubbed the *virtual persona* (a network identity that can move to whatever workstation a user uses to log on to the network).

Workstation objects, workstation group objects, and NDS management also automate software installation, maintenance, and updates. These automated features will be very important to the many companies planning to include Year 2000 (Y2K) fixes across their networks. This one-point management eliminates the high cost of duplicating physical administration at user desktops.

With Z.E.N.works installed on their NetWare 4.11 or 5 network, administrators can automate many tasks that were traditionally very time consuming. These tasks include application management, desktop management, remote control workstation maintenance, and scheduling. A Scheduler utility runs programs on Windows NT or Windows 95.

Users on Z.E.N.works-equipped networks can send help requests with error messages and their workstation's address information to a help desk. Users can revel in the Zero Effort Networking that results in fewer application problems. They will benefit from having their applications, printer configurations, and desktop configurations follow them around the company to wherever they log in with their *virtual personas*.

Z.E.N.works suite contains the following utilities and applications:

- Novell Workstation Manager extends the administrators dominion over the workstation and makes a new workstation object for NDS.

- NetWare Application Launcher existed in NetWare 4 versions; however, application distribution and upkeep was not fully automated across the network or enterprise. They are accomplished in the new Application Launcher with snAppShot and the Z.E.N.works Application Launcher Snap-in for NetWare Administrator.

- Remote control has always been an attractive idea; however, it has had its problems. Traversing the network to find the workstations you were looking for and interacting with those workstations was difficult. With NetWare 5, these problems are now gone.

- By taking advantage of the information stored in NDS, Help Requester creates clearer communications between problem reporters and problem solvers across the network.

Let's take a closer look at these utilities and their functionality.

Desktop Management

The Desktop Management component of Z.E.N.works allows you to configure desktop policies for Windows clients in NDS. NDS objects called *policy packages* are sets of rules or policies that control various workstation configuration parameters. Policy packages refer to desktop operating systems, workstations, and users. By including these policy packages on NDS, you eliminate the need to copy these policies to the PUBLIC directory of various servers.

By creating workstation and user objects, policy package rules can be delegated and implemented specifically to the workstation location, or they can follow the location of the user. Workstation and user group objects can accomplish this for large numbers of workstations and users. This allows standard, user, or group interfaces and desktops to be implemented across the network. In addition, you can manage print driver, client, and application upgrades and installations from a remote location.

The Z.E.N.works client also includes a Scheduler component, shown in Figure 1.3. This can be used to run the registration program automatically or perform other maintenance tasks, and it can be managed within NDS.

Application Launcher

Z.E.N.works includes NAL 2.5, the latest version of the Application Launcher. The Application Launcher, as shown in Figure 1.4, gives an administrator increased power to manage applications across the network and allows users to take better advantage of those managed resources.

FIGURE 1.3

The Z.E.N.works
Scheduler allows
scheduled tasks to be
managed from NDS.

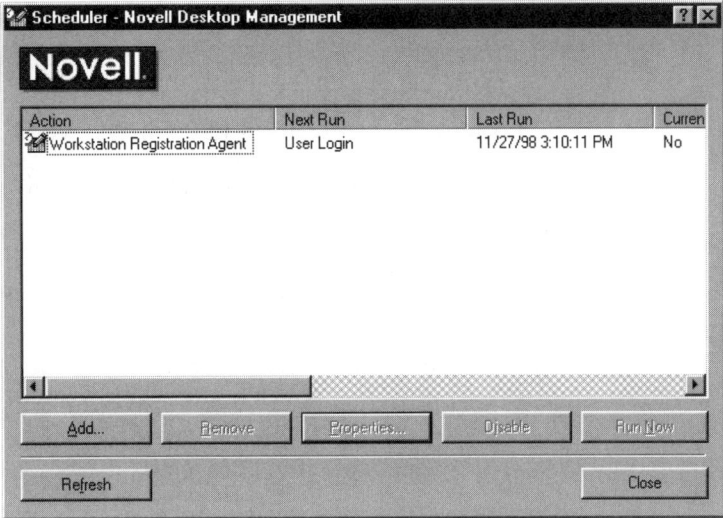

FIGURE 1.4

The NetWare
Application Launcher
allows you to manage
applications across
the network.

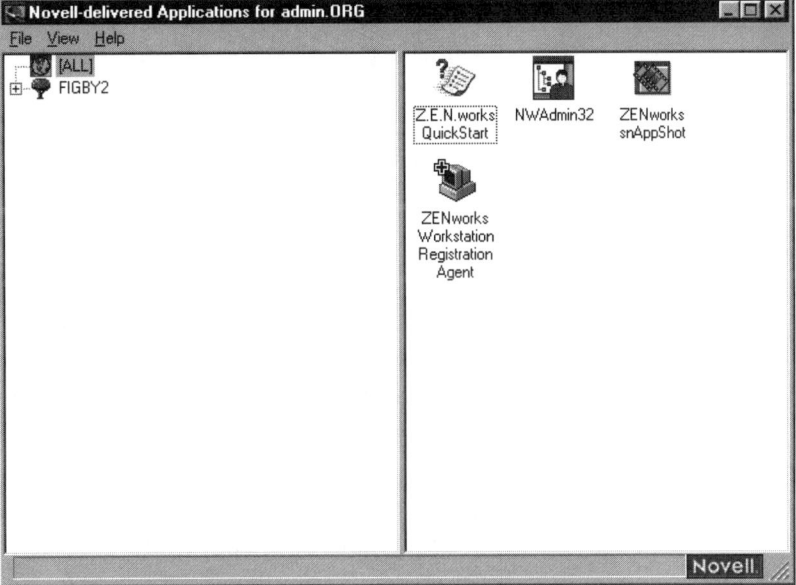

NetWare 5 users can access applications from the Application Launcher window or from the Application Launcher Explorer. They don't need to be concerned with application upgrades, drive letters, or their workstation's configuration. These processes are all managed through the Application Launcher's two administrative components:

- The Application Launcher snap-in for NetWare Administrator
- snAppShot

The Application Launcher snap-in is a Windows DLL file, APPSNP32 .DLL, that adds new functionality by creating application objects for NDS (NetWare Directory Services). It adds properties pages on NDS where properties can be set at the container, group, or individual level. Applications pages also provide for the container and user objects on NDS. Other tools that are added with the Application Launcher snap-in for NetWare Administrator are:

- Migrate Application Objects
- Show All Inherited Applications
- Export Application Object
- Search and Replace
- Sync Distribution GUIDs
- Generate new GUIDs
- AOT/AXT File Tools

New Application Distribution functionality is provided by snApp-Shot. This simple but powerful tool builds an application object template (AOT) that determines the differences between "before" and "after" snapshots of your workstation's configuration when an application has been installed on it. This allows the new template (AOT), Registry changes, INI file changes, DLLs, and any new application files to become part of the application object.

All of this makes installing or upgrading from the network a breeze. The Application Launcher leverages NDS by taking advantage of all the information stored on NDS and adding more objects. Thousands of users can have software installed, and individual parameters from NDS can be included in those installations. For example, a new browser can be installed with all of the individual workstation mail parameters included on each individual workstation.

Remote Control

Remote control of workstations on the network has traditionally been beset with three problems:

- The security hierarchy problems of who controls whom
- Traffic problems on the network due to remote control agents that must constantly advertise their availability
- Navigation problems

NetWare 5's new remote control functionality leverages NDS by taking advantage of the hierarchical directory structure and the informational power of NDS.

Security problems are lessened because NDS allows scalability. A single user can have remote access over a single workstation, or an administrator can access remote control capability over the entire network. Traffic and navigation problems are eliminated because remote control agents are not needed to advertise availability. NDS knows the IP and IPX addresses of all workstations and how to navigate to them.

Remote control of workstations with NetWare 5 is easy. You just go to the workstation's NDS object, enter the workstation's details, and click Remote Control. If you have the right to control that workstation, the user is notified (with visual and audio alerts) that a remote control session is imminent or his or her consent to a remote session is requested.

Help Requester

This new Z.E.N.works feature enables efficient and pertinent communications to take place between users and help desk personnel (or whoever is empowered to help with user problems). Help Requester (see Figure 1.5) includes information about user location and configuration. This information is sent to the correct location for help without requiring the user or the helper to leave their seats. With these kinds of improvements, NetWare 5 can pay its own way for many companies.

FIGURE 1.5

The Z.E.N.works Help Requester screen includes the user's IPX address and the error message received by the user.

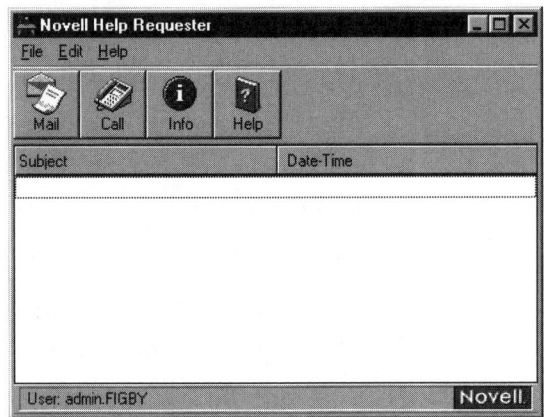

Novell Distributed Print Services (NDPS)

Novell Distributed Print Services (NDPS) is a new generation printing solution developed by Novell in cooperation with Hewlett Packard (the leader in printing hardware) and Xerox (the leader in enterprise printing). NDPS is a fully scalable printing process that facilitates plug-and-print solutions for the small company and makes big reductions in administrative time, while increasing overall network ease-of-use and productivity. Close integration of NetWare Administrator with NDS allows NDPS to facilitate single-point administration for all network printers. This is accomplished through NDPS Manager (see Figure 1.6).

Gone is the necessity for printing complexity. Print queues, print objects, spoolers, and print servers can all be replaced with the Printer Agent. The Printer Agent can be set up through NetWare Administrator by NDPS Manager (see Figure 1.6) or through the gateway when printers are plugged into the network. Yet, NDPS is fully backward-compatible with NPRINTER and QMS.

NDPS gateways include third-party gateways developed by printer manufacturers to support their printers on the network. The Novell Gateway supports other printers using NPRINTER or any queue-based printer, including those running in PSERVER mode.

NDPS also includes the Print Device Subsystem (PDS), which retrieves printer information and makes the Printer Agent for many local and remote printers. The NDPS port handler assures that the PDS can communicate with the printer regardless of the interface used.

F I G U R E   1.6

NDPS Manager creates and manages printing agents.

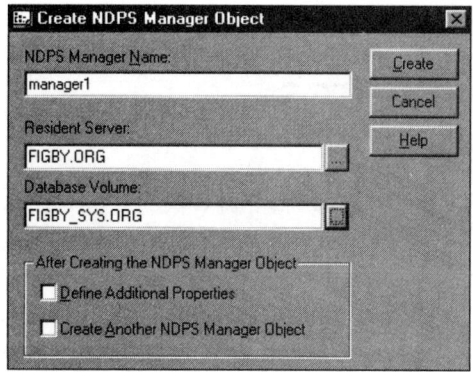

The NDPS Manager is used to create and manage Printer Agents, while the NDPS Broker provides three network support services not previously available in NetWare or IntraNetWare. These services and their functionality include:

- Service Registry Services (SRS) eliminates the previous network SAP (Service Advertising Protocol) traffic created when printers advertised their availability. When a user wants to use a printer, SRS provides a list of all registered printers on the network.

- Resource Management Service (RMS) allows resources to be installed in a location and then downloaded to printers and clients. This method is used to distribute print drivers, banners, fonts, and printer definition (NPD) files. This allows improved resource sharing including the plug-and-print printer option.

- Event Notification Service allows interested parties to be notified of print job events. Without it, only the user who is actually printing can use Novell Printer Manager to configure notifications relating to his or her own jobs.

Novell Distributed Print Services (NDPS) represents a new paradigm for network printing, and printing has always been a sensitive area for network administrators. NDPS means that print management just got easier. Here again NetWare 5 takes advantage of NDS to centralize administration tasks and make life simpler for users.

TCP/IP Features

With NetWare 5, Novell has made the move to a network operating system that works in Pure IP (Internet Protocol) while still retaining backward-compatibility with any applications or segments that still use IPX/SPX encapsulation. This means any company can make the move toward TCP/IP by adapting its transport technology to the advantages inherent in a single TCP/IP protocol. Some of those advantages are:

- Hardware, software, and administration costs diminish when one protocol is used in routed environments.

- Remote user connectivity is enhanced by extension to the Internet.

- Bandwidth use is maximized.

Pure IP

IntraNetWare included the IP/IPX Gateway that enabled IPX to run in an IP environment. NetWare 5 takes this a step further by allowing the network to run in a native or Pure IP environment. The environment is "pure" in the sense that all IPX encapsulation is gone (or all NetBIOS encapsulation is gone for NT Server). A Pure IP environment is not mandatory, however.

The network administrator must be aware of those applications that are IPX dependent and has the option of keeping IPX for them. By using the NetWare 5 Compatibility Mode, the administrator can make the move to IP incrementally over time to maximize the value of IPX-based applications or network segments that are not ready to upgrade to "Pure IP."

Compatibility Mode

For networks where IPX support is still required, the Compatibility Mode feature can be used. Compatibility Mode drivers for the workstation and the server are loaded by default and remain dormant until an IPX service or application needs to be run. This technology includes IP responses that are made to IPX applications or services that request information at the NetWare Core Protocol (NCP) level or from the NetWare 3 bindery. The Migration Gateway and the Bindery Gateway allow seamless communication between NetWare 5 and NetWare 4 or NetWare 3, respectively.

Finally, Compatibility Mode can encapsulate IPX in IP for a small percentage of applications that circumvent normal communications. This maintains a Pure IP environment. The move to TCP/IP has been, in part, motivated by the desire to embrace open standards and de facto industry standards that everyone has settled on through choice or chance.

Novell DNS/DHCP Services

Novell DNS/DHCP Services allows a NetWare server to act as a server for two Internet-standard services. Both DNS (Domain Name Services) and DHCP (Dynamic Host Configuration Protocol) support the IETF standards on the front-end and integrate into NDS on the back-end for network management. DNS is a service that works with the Internet's hierarchical naming scheme. It is essentially a database that matches up computers and other device names with IP addresses and other information. The database hierarchy is listed like an upside down tree with a host's domain specified by the *host domain space*. This makes up the familiar www.whereyouwork.com address form that pervades the media.

DHCP allows client computers to function on an IP network by automatically assigning IP addresses and other information. A DHCP server sends an IP address (along with other configuration data included with the temporary address) from a pool of available addresses. This allows for the most efficient use of scarce IP addresses.

DNS/DHCP Services also includes the DNS/DHCP Management Console utility, which enables you to easily manage and configure the DNS and DHCP Services (see Figure 1.7). The management console has a task-oriented interface to manage the NDS objects related to DNS/DHCP. You can run it from the Tools menu of NetWare Administrator or as a stand-alone program from a client workstation.

DNS/DHCP Services also creates a number of new NDS objects to configure and control their services. NDS tree planning and design considerations are necessary when learning how to manage this new functionality. Because DNS/DHCP is widely available across the network and because the NDS is replicated, virtual DNS and DHCP servers are created across the network.

By joining NDS with DNS/DHCP Services, Novell has combined the power, security, and flexibility of NDS with the standards-based DNS/DHCP solution to protect your network and reduce administration time.

FIGURE 1.7

Java management
with ConsoleOne
facilitates easy
manipulation of
DNS/DHCP Services.

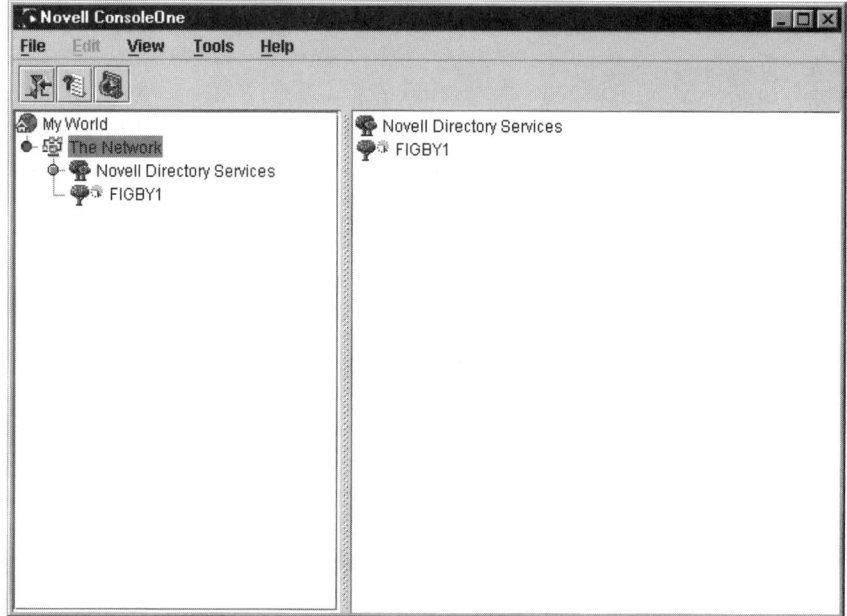

Netscape FastTrack Server

Netscape FastTrack Server is a *Web server* developed by Novell
and Netscape through their joint venture entity, called Novonyx. This
company later became a division of Novell. A Web server operates by
publishing HTML (HyperText Markup Language) or other documents
on the Internet or on a company or enterprise-wide *intranet*. Web servers
function from a client/server format with a browser acting as a client.

A Web server uses HyperText Transfer Protocol (HTTP) to distribute documents that are stored in its files. HTTP is also the protocol used by the browser making the request for files.

The Netscape FastTrack Server is a set of NLMs (NetWare Loadable
Modules) that are loaded on a NetWare 4.11 or NetWare 5 server
resulting in the FastTrack server capacity and functionality. The power

and manageability of NDS allow for management of the FastTrack Web Server, its files, and its administration.

When you install Netscape FastTrack Server, the directories you see will be added to your NetWare Server's file system. The document directory SYS:\NOVONYX\SUITESPOT\DOCS is created and will contain files that Netscape FastTrack Server serves to clients. Any files you want to distribute from the FastTrack Server should be placed either in it or in a subdirectory.

The Administration Server is another series of NLMs running on the NetWare server. NLMs allow the administrator to manage the Netscape FastTrack Server from the Administration server's home page through Server Manager. Any Web browser can access the Administration server after its NLMs are installed, as shown in Figure 1.8.

FIGURE 1.8

The Server Manager page can be accessed from anywhere on the network with a Web browser.

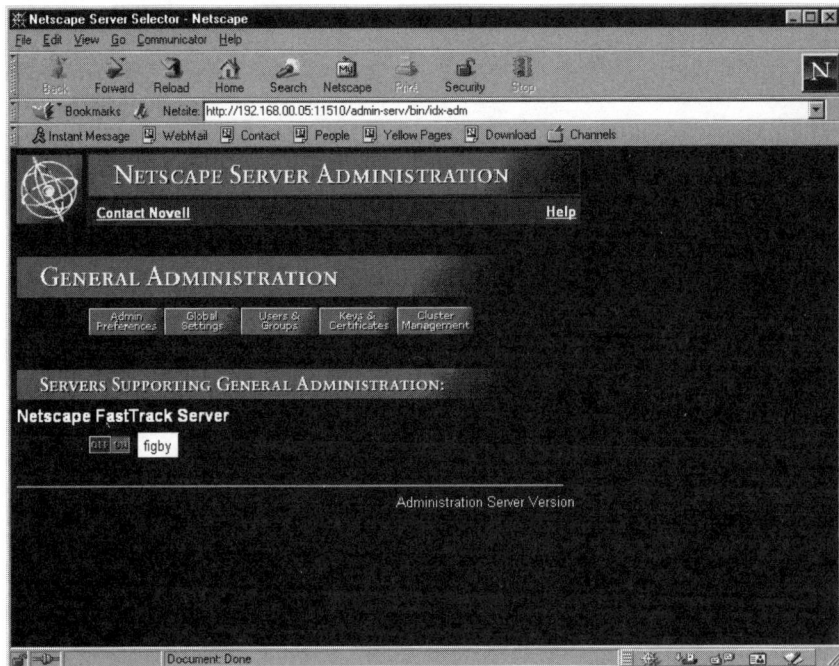

Other NetWare 5 Features

Before we go into detail on all of the new NetWare 5 features, let's briefly look at a few of the other new innovations included with NetWare 5.

Novell Replication Services

Novell Replication Services (NRS) allows local users to access information from a replicated file system without tying up WAN (Wide Area Network) traffic and without manually coordinating the replication and synchronization of the file systems. NRS greatly automates and facilitates the process of transferring the ever-increasing amount of information that needs to be routed from corporate servers through WAN links to end users.

To replicate their files, users only need to save files to servers running NRS. NRS automatically replicates files with changes, and it is administered as a snap-in to NetWare Administrator. For complex enterprise situations, NRS creates master servers, link servers, and replica servers to pass on the information.

Selective replication allows only those files chosen for replication to be copied. NRS is an elegant solution to the serious problems that are being encountered more frequently in enterprise-wide networking.

Novell Storage Services

NetWare 5 brings you Novell Storage Services (NSS), a 64-bit, modular, multipowered file system. NSS works with the previous NetWare file system (NWFS), maintaining perfect backward compatibility. Network administrators can continue to use legacy systems and files for as long as desired. You can use NSS to create NetWare volumes or NSS volumes. Users who don't need NSS can ignore it.

While maintaining a very small memory footprint, NSS increases the NetWare server's capacity to handle files of up to 8 terabytes in size and as many files as will fit on an 8-exabyte volume. That is a lot! (Approximately one thousand gigabytes equals one terabyte. One million gigabytes equals one exabyte.) There is no practical limit to the number of files in a volume or the number of volumes you can mount. The limit extends to the capacities of your storage solutions.

NSS is also very fast. NSS greatly decreases volume mount time and the time necessary to recover data from a file system after a crash. It can perform volume remounting in seconds for any size volume, even up to several terabytes. At the Comdex '97 Show in Las Vegas, a 3-terabyte volume crashed and recovered in 10 seconds.

Only CD-ROMs and hard drives are supported with the initial release of NSS. Additional storage devices will be added in the future. NSS can't be used with older versions of NetWare. NSS can't be used with the SYS volume.

NSS helps manage your storage device's space. Unused free space exists in most storage devices and NetWare volumes. You can combine all the free space accessible to your server into a storage pool and use it to make NSS volumes.

NSS's great capacity and efficiency may guarantee to most companies a solution that their file systems will never outgrow.

Novell Clients

Novell clients are available with NetWare 5 for all major desktop operating systems including DOS, Windows 3.*x*, Windows 95, Windows NT, OS/2, Macintosh, and Unix. Network administrators can use Novell's Automatic Client Update to upgrade the client software to the latest version. A starter pack version of Z.E.N.works is being shipped with every client.

Review

NetWare 5 is moving the bar to a higher level in a number of important areas. By supporting open standards and welcoming developers to its published NDS code, Java platform, and Pure IP environment, Novell is extending the enterprise to the world. By automating a lot of formerly tedious legwork, NetWare 5 has leveraged Novell's investment in NDS and made it pay dividends. Security problems, downtime, and administrative costs should all go down with NetWare 5, although server hardware costs might rise.

In this chapter, we had an overview of the new NetWare 5 features. Although many of these features were just touched on briefly, you will need to know more about many of them for your update test. Here is a list of NetWare 5 features that we covered with a quick overview. See if you remember these features:

- Pure IP environment or a mixed IP/IPX environment
- Novell DNS/DHCP Services
- Novell Z.E.N.works suite
- Novell Distributed Print Services (NDPS)
- Netscape FastTrack Server for NetWare
- Novell Storage Services (NSS)
- Novell Replication Services (NRS)
- ConsoleOne
- Modified console commands
- NDS
- Installation utilities
- New NetWare 5 kernel features
- New NetWare 5 disk driver system

- Oracle8 for NetWare

- Intelligent I/O Support (I_2O)

- Cryptographic Services

- Open Solutions Architecture SDK

- Hot Plug PCI

We looked briefly at these topics in this chapter. We took a more in-depth look at the topics that will make up the bulk of this book. Let's review them now.

NetWare 5 Installation

With NetWare 5, Novell introduces its new Installation Services and works toward a common installation interface for all future products. The clickable GUI interface simplifies and facilitates the installation process. The four upgrade utilities you can use to move to NetWare 5 are:

- Install

- Novell Upgrade Wizard

- Rexxware Migration Toolkit

- Automated Client Update

Z.E.N.works

Z.E.N.works is an exciting multifaceted suite of applications and utilities that extends NDS with workstation and policy package objects. It permits desktop and application management by workstation, user, group, or container. The four components of Z.E.N.works that we will examine more closely are:

- Workstation Manager

- Application Launcher

- Remote Control
- Help Requester

NDPS

Novell Distributed Print Services (NDPS) brings the ease of plug-and-print printers and automatically distributed print drivers to the network. NDPS Manager allows you to manage a single Printer Agent for each printer. Gone are the print server, print queue, and print objects.

The NDPS Broker contains the following three components:

- Service Registry Services (SRS)
- Resource Management Service (RMS)
- Event Notification Service

TCP/IP Features

NetWare 5's "Pure IP" moves on from the IP/IPX Gateway in NetWare 4.11 to allow your network to function in the IP environment. By allowing legacy IPX applications and network segments to remain encapsulated with IPX, NetWare 5 constructs a smooth move to IP. The Compatibility Mode drivers are loaded by default and are ready for IPX whenever needed.

FastTrack Server

FastTrack Server is a Web server that will permit your network to establish a presence on the Internet, in a company-wide intranet, or both. The files that are served to clients through their browsers can be managed from anywhere on the network through the Netscape Administration Server and the forms in Server Manager.

Hands-On Procedures

To gain the fullest advantage from studying this book, you should have a working version of NetWare 5 so you can work through the various hands-on NetWare 5 procedures in the chapters. If you don't have a working NetWare 5 network, at least go through the steps of the hands-on procedures, so you will understand them.

NetWare 5 Practice Test Questions

1. Novonyx, the company that developed the FastTrack Server, is now owned by Netscape. (True or False.)

2. What does the acronym DHCP stand for?

3. From now on, all new Novell products will use a common installation architecture called *Novell Installation Services*. (True or False.)

4. Which of the following security features is not included in Cryptographic Services?

   A. Authentication

   B. Nonrepudiation

   C. Integrity

   D. Digital certificates

   E. Confidentiality

5. In general, if you choose IP as a core protocol, it will not do which of the following? (Choose two.)

   A. Require less hardware in routed environments

   B. Require less software in routed environments

    C. Save bandwidth

    D. Decrease remote user possibilities

    E. Work well with the Internet

    F. Run Compatibility Mode

6. Which Z.E.N.works feature includes snAppShot?

    A. Desktop Manager

    B. Help Requester

    C. Application Launcher

    D. Remote Control

7. What is the maximum size file that NSS (Novell Storage Services) can handle?

8. SRS eliminates the need for SAP (Service Advertising Protocol) by performing which of the following? (Choose one.)

    A. Providing plug-and-print capability

    B. Having the Print Device Subsystem retrieve information about printers

    C. Letting Novell Printer Manager manage all Printer Agents

    D. Keeping a list of all registered printers

9. What new NetWare 5 feature allows you to plug in new network cards while the server is running?

10. Novell Upgrade Wizard will work with either NetWare 3.1*x* or NetWare 4.*x* upgrades for across-the-wire installation. (True or False.)

CHAPTER

2

Installing NetWare 5

Roadmap

This chapter covers the process of installing NetWare 5 on new machines and upgrading or migrating existing servers to NetWare 5.

Topics Covered

- NetWare 5's hardware requirements

- The NetWare 5 installation program

- The Migration Wizard

- NetWare 5 client software

Skills You'll Learn

- Plan a NetWare 5 installation or upgrade

- Install NetWare 5 on a new machine

- Upgrade existing servers to NetWare 5

- Migrate across the network to NetWare 5

- Upgrade clients for NetWare 5 features

One of the first things you'll notice about NetWare 5 is the new installation features. The installation is streamlined and improved from NetWare 4, and it includes a graphical Installation Wizard that guides you through most of the installation process. Whether you're installing NetWare 5 on a new computer or upgrading to NetWare 5, you'll find the process simple.

Although the installation is simplified, there are a wide variety of options to consider when installing a server. In this chapter, we'll examine the issues you should consider before installing or upgrading. We'll also look at the installation process itself and the changes you can make to the server's features after installation.

Planning the Installation

Before you install NetWare 5, you should plan the way the server will be used and the installation options you will choose. Some of the most important items you should consider include:

- If you have an existing NetWare 3.1*x* or 4.*x* server, choose whether to upgrade the existing machine or to move users and data to a new machine.

- Determine memory, disk storage, and other hardware requirements.

- Determine how the NDS tree will be organized or how the server will fit into an existing NDS tree.

The following sections describe how to plan the installation of NetWare 5 for a new or existing server.

Upgrade Methods

There are two basic methods of upgrading to NetWare 5 from an earlier version of NetWare:

- Use the installation program to upgrade the server in place.

- Upgrade to a new server using across-the-wire migration.

Each of these methods has its advantages, which are explained in the following sections.

This chapter focuses on upgrading from NetWare 3.*x* or 4.*x* to NetWare 5; this is also the emphasis of the CNE update exam. If your server is running a version of NetWare prior to 3.1*x*, the easiest way to upgrade is to first upgrade to NetWare 3.1*x* or 4.*x*, and then upgrade to NetWare 5.

The Installation Program

This method is also known as an *in-place upgrade*. Using the installation program is the simplest method of upgrading, and can often be performed in less than an hour. However, it has one major requirement:

- The existing server must meet the hardware requirements for NetWare 5.

NetWare 5 has higher hardware requirements than other versions—most notably, it requires a Pentium processor and 64MB of RAM. Although some older machines may be upgraded to meet these requirements, a new machine is often a better choice for the following reasons:

- CD-ROM drives, disks, and other devices may have compatibility issues on older machines.

- An upgraded older machine often can't be upgraded further. For example, you may not be able to upgrade to more than 64MB of RAM. As the server is used more, you may need to add more RAM or disk storage.

If you choose to upgrade the existing machine to meet NetWare 5's requirements, you should perform the upgrade and verify that the new components function properly before you attempt to upgrade to NetWare 5.

Even if the current machine meets NetWare 5's minimum requirements, you may still want to add more RAM or disk storage. Again, it's usually better to add the new equipment and verify that it works before upgrading to NetWare 5.

Across-the-Wire Migration

If you choose to replace the existing server with a new machine, you can use the *across-the-wire migration* method. To use this method, you must use a new machine for the server and use a workstation to handle the migration process. NetWare 5 includes the Upgrade Wizard, which simplifies this process.

To use this method, you first install NetWare 5 on the new machine, leaving the old server connected to the network. You then install the Upgrade Wizard software on a workstation that can connect to both servers.

After you set the migration options, the Wizard connects to the servers and transfers information between them. The NDS or bindery data and the file system can be migrated.

The across-the-wire method has one major advantage:

- It does not affect the old server.

This means that you can switch back to the old server at any time if the migration process fails. After the migration is complete, you should take the old server down.

For NetWare 2.*x* and earlier versions, you can first perform an across-the-wire migration to a new machine running NetWare 4.*x*, then you can use the installation program to upgrade the server to NetWare 5.

Hardware Requirements

Each new version of NetWare is more sophisticated than the last, so it's no surprise that NetWare 5 has higher hardware requirements than previous versions. Table 2.1 summarizes both the minimum and the recommended hardware requirements for NetWare 5.

T A B L E 2.1 NetWare 5 Hardware Requirements	Component	Requirement	Recommendation
	Processor	Pentium	100Mhz or faster
	RAM	64MB	128MB or more, depending on usage
	Disk Storage	450MB + 50MB for DOS partition	1GB or more depending on usage
	Network Card	Any supported card	Depends on network wiring
	CD-ROM drive	Required to install NetWare 5 (a CD-ROM drive on a remote server can also be used)	IDE or SCSI

T A B L E 2.1 *(cont.)*	Component	Requirement	Recommendation
NetWare 5 Hardware Requirements	Mouse	Not required	Recommended for GUI use
	Monitor	VGA	Super VGA

In the following sections, we'll examine the particular hardware components required by NetWare 5 in more detail.

Memory Options

NetWare 5 officially requires 64MB, but you should think of this requirement as a starting point. Although 64MB will be enough for a server in a small network (fewer than 10 users). For larger networks, more memory will improve performance.

Memory prices vary, but using more than the minimum amount of memory in your server is usually affordable. In a heavily used server, more memory will almost always improve performance, and will allow for future growth.

Be careful when you are purchasing a computer to use as a NetWare server or when you are considering the use of your old server. Many older machines cannot be expanded beyond 64MB of memory, and some newer machines are restricted to 128MB. If possible, choose a machine that supports more than 128MB because you will need to expand the server as network usage increases.

One important addition to NetWare 5 is support for *virtual memory*. This is a system that *swaps* areas of the memory that are not currently in use to a disk volume, allowing applications to run as though much more memory was available. NetWare 5 enables virtual memory by default; you can change these settings after installation.

Disk Storage Options

Because network servers are also known as file servers, you can probably guess that disk storage is an important part of a server.

NetWare 5 improves the use of disk storage with several new features.

NetWare 5 uses a new format for disk drivers. Although previous versions used disk drivers with the extension DSK, NetWare 5 uses a two-part system:

- HAM (host adapter module) drivers support disk adapters in the server (for example, an IDE or SCSI card)

- CDM (custom device module) drivers support individual devices connected to an adapter (for example, a disk drive or CD-ROM drive)

NetWare 4.1 supports HAM and CDM drivers, but it also supports the old DSK format. NetWare 5 supports only the new format, so all of the devices you use must include HAM and CDM drivers.

Another improvement in NetWare 5 is support for a new file system called NSS (Novell Storage Services). You can use either this system or the traditional NetWare file system supported in earlier versions. These systems are explained in the following sections.

The Standard NetWare File System   The standard NetWare file system was used in NetWare 3.1x and (with slight improvements) in 4.1. This system is limited to 2GB per file. It supports only one NetWare partition per physical disk, and it is limited to 16 million directory entries per volume.

Although these limitations are not serious for many networks, 2GB is a rather small file size if your users are dealing with large-storage applications such as CAD and digital video. Additionally, the traditional system uses a large amount of memory and suffers a speed decrease when working with large volumes and large files.

If your needs fit well within these constraints, you may consider using the traditional NetWare system. This system will be the easiest choice if you are upgrading from NetWare 3.12 or 4.1, because the existing partitions and volumes can be used.

NSS (Novell Storage Services)   Novell Storage Services (NSS) is new to NetWare 5. This is a new file system that addresses the limitations of the old system. NSS and traditional volumes can be used in the same server. NSS includes the following improvements:

- The limit for a file's size is increased to 8 terabytes (8,192 gigabytes).

- The limit for directory entries has increased to trillions of files.

- File and volume access is fast, even for large volumes.

- Mounting volumes does not consume nearly as much memory.

The NSS system is also designed to be expandable, and it should support future devices such as DVD (digital versatile disk) drives.

One reason to use NSS is that it probably has a more promising future than the traditional system. Just as NetWare 5 discontinues support for the traditional style of disk drivers, a future version of NetWare may discontinue support for the old file system, forcing you to move to NSS eventually.

Network Adapters

Although you can install NetWare without a network adapter, you'll obviously need one in order to get any use from the server. NetWare 5 supports the same LAN drivers supported by NetWare 4.*x* and earlier versions. These drivers have a LAN extension and are specific to particular network cards.

The NetWare 5 CD-ROM includes drivers for a wide variety of network cards, from Novell's venerable NE-2000 standard to newer 100Mbps cards. However, using the latest driver available from the manufacturer of the card is usually the best choice. When buying a network card, be sure it includes a NetWare driver and has been tested with NetWare 5.

Floppy Drives and CD-ROM Drives

In most cases, your server will need a CD-ROM drive. This drive will be used to install the NetWare 5 operating system and to install applications and other software. It's also possible to mount a CD-ROM in the drive and make it available for sharing by network users.

It's possible to install NetWare 5 on a server without a CD-ROM drive. If you have another NetWare server on the network, you can mount the installation CD-ROM on the old server as a NetWare volume, load DOS client software on the new server, and run the installation program over the network.

A floppy drive, while not strictly necessary, will also aid in installing applications and in debugging or repairing the server. Because floppy drives are very inexpensive and usually included with the machine, you probably don't need to worry much about this component.

Monitor, Mouse, and Keyboard

If you've worked as an administrator for a network running Net-Ware 3.1*x* or 4.*x*, you have probably never given much thought to the choice of monitor for the server. Administrators typically use the cheapest or oldest monitor they have handy or even share a monitor with another computer using a switchbox.

With the release of NetWare 5, monitors have become a more important issue. The NetWare 5 GUI supports high resolutions (up to 1,024 × 768 or higher, depending on the video card). A higher resolution makes the GUI display more readable, and it allows more data to be displayed.

You'll also get more use from the server's monitor with NetWare 5. Although NetWare 4 requires a workstation to perform most administrative tasks, such as creating users, you can use the ConsoleOne feature of NetWare 5 for administration at the server. For more information about this utility, see Chapter 5.

Another component you'll need to add for a NetWare 5 server is a mouse. Although most of the features of the GUI are accessible without a mouse, you won't really enjoy the benefits of the GUI without one. NetWare 5 supports the standard mice used by PCs, either the PS/2 or serial type.

Last but not least, you'll need a keyboard for the server. This is one component that hasn't changed much since the advent of the PC, and just about any reliable keyboard will work for NetWare 5.

Licensing NetWare 5

In order to install NetWare 5, you'll need a server license. Like earlier versions, you can purchase a NetWare 5 license for a set number of users. However, NetWare 5 uses a new licensing format, and licenses from previous versions cannot be used. A license disk is included with the NetWare 5 package.

Unlike previous versions, NetWare 5 licenses include separate server and user licenses. User licenses regulate the number of users connected to an NDS tree, rather than to a particular server. Each server license allows a NetWare server to participate in the network.

NetWare 5 supports NLS (Novell Licensing Services), which allows licensing information to be stored in NDS. This can support application licenses as well as the main NetWare server and user licenses.

NDS Objects

NetWare 5 adds a number of objects related to licensing to the NDS tree. These include the following:

User License Container   A container object that groups together user licenses. This object is created automatically when you install the first NetWare 5 server in a network.

Server License Container   A container object for server licenses, also created automatically when you install NetWare 5.

License Certificate   This object represents an actual group of licenses you purchased and is stored under one of the above container objects. This object is created when you insert the license disk during the NetWare 5 installation process. You can add additional certificates after installation.

Managing Licenses

During the installation of NetWare 5, you can insert one or more license disks to add license certificates. After installation, you can add additional licenses by selecting Tools ➤ Install License ➤ Install License Certificate in the NetWare Administrator utility.

Additionally, you can control which users have access to each license certificate. This allows you to manage and prioritize licenses. For example, you can give an important department access to its own license certificate, while users outside the department share the remaining certificates.

To assign a license certificate to one or more users, open the Properties dialog for the certificate object in NetWare Administrator. Select the Assignments tab, and add one or more users to the list. To simplify administration, you can add Group, Organization, or Organizational Unit objects to the list.

NetWare 5 assigns the Admin account as the owner of License Certificate objects by default. This gives this user access to the licenses, and ensures that a license will always be available for the administrator.

Upgrading NDS

If you plan to install NetWare 5 on a network that includes one or more NetWare 4 servers, you need to plan to avoid NDS incompatibilities. NetWare 5 cannot participate in the same NDS tree as NetWare 4 servers unless the older servers are updated to a new version of NDS.

You can update NDS on NetWare 4 servers using the installation files included on the NetWare 5 CD-ROM. Follow the steps in Procedure 2.1 to upgrade NDS on a NetWare 4 server.

PROCEDURE 2.1

Upgrading NDS on a NetWare 4 Server

1. Insert the NetWare 5 Operating System CD-ROM at the NetWare 4 server, and type **LOAD INSTALL** to begin the installation.

2. From the INSTALL menu, select Product Options.

3. At the Product Options menu, select Install a Product Not Listed.

4. Specify the path on the CD-ROM for the NDS upgrade files, typically \PRODUCTS\411_UPG\NDS.

5. A menu of installation choices is displayed. Select Install NDS Version 5.99.

6. The NDS upgrade files are installed. The actual changes to the NDS database may take several minutes or longer.

You must upgrade all servers to the new version of NDS. If you have a large number of servers, you can upgrade one server, then copy the files to the other servers automatically. To do this, after one server is upgraded, run the NDS Manager utility (NDSMGR32.EXE) at a workstation.

From the NDS Manager menu, select Object ➤ NDS Version ➤ Update. This displays a dialog that allows you to select source and target servers, and it copies the update files to all of the target servers. Depending on the NDS database size, this may take several hours.

Installing NetWare 5 on a New Server

NetWare 5's installation is easier than previous versions, so you should have no trouble getting a new server running. In the following sections, we'll look at the steps you should take to prepare for the installation, and we'll look at the installation process itself.

Preparing for Installation

A bit of preparation will help you choose the best options for installing NetWare 5 on a new server. In the following sections, you'll learn how to choose a machine for the server and how to prepare the machine for the installation process.

Choosing Hardware

You should choose the components of the server to match the hardware requirements presented earlier in this chapter. Additionally, you should choose the components to meet the needs of your network and its users. Here are some items you should consider.

CPU   A NetWare server taxes its disk storage far more than its processor; however, you will get better performance from a faster processor. NetWare 5 is designed to take advantage of the latest Pentium Pro and Pentium II processors, and it supports multiple processors.

Disk Storage   You'll need a minimum of about 1GB of disk storage. The lowest-capacity drives that are currently widely available are about 3GB. Whether or not you need more storage than that depends on the number of users on the server and their application needs.

If you are moving users from another NetWare server or another network operating system, you can estimate the required disk storage based on the amount of storage they are currently using—and of course, you should provide extra room to grow. Network applications can also use a lot of disk storage.

Memory   The general rule for NetWare servers has always been that more memory is better, and this is true of NetWare 5. Despite NetWare 5's virtual memory support, the server will run faster with more memory. Small networks should be able to operate with 64MB; a busy network may need 128MB or more.

If you will be using the NSS file system, you don't need to have a large amount of memory to support disk volumes. For the traditional system, large volumes (bigger than 2GB) will require more than the minimum amount of memory.

Network Card   The choice of network cards largely depends on the network wiring in your building. If you're starting a network from scratch, you can choose a network transmission media. Twisted-pair media (10baseT or 100baseT) is the best choice for most networks, but you may consider fiber or other high-speed alternatives if the network will be heavily used.

Partitioning the Disk

Before installing NetWare 5, you'll need to create a DOS partition on the computer. This partition will be used to start the server and will be useful for diagnostic purposes. The minimum size for the DOS partition is 35MB, but a larger partition can be helpful if you need to install utilities to diagnose hardware problems.

NetWare 5 can perform a memory dump in the event of a server crash, which may be useful in diagnosing server problems. To accommodate this feature, the DOS partition should include 35MB plus the amount of server memory.

To create the DOS partition, use the FDISK utility included with DOS version 3.3 to 6.2. The Windows 95/98 FDISK utility should not be used. The NetWare 5 license disk includes a bootable version of DR-DOS, which can also be used to partition the disk.

You do not need to create a NetWare partition before installation. In fact, you need to leave enough empty space for a NetWare partition when you partition the drive before installation. You'll need a minimum of 1GB for the basic NetWare partition and SYS volume.

Only the first drive (containing the SYS volume) needs a DOS partition. You can leave other drives empty and create NetWare partitions on them during or after the installation.

Connecting to the Network

Last but not least, you should connect the new server computer to the network before installation. This is particularly important if you have other NetWare 4.*x* or NetWare 5 servers on the network and plan to add the new server to an existing NDS tree.

Due to compatibility issues, you should not attach a NetWare 5 server to an existing NetWare 4.*x* network without first updating NDS on the existing servers. This process is explained earlier in this chapter.

The Installation Process

NetWare 5 includes an automated installation program, which you can access from the DOS prompt by typing **INSTALL**. This installation program is more reliable, more automatic, and easier to use than previous NetWare versions.

To begin the installation of NetWare 5 on a new server, boot the server to a DOS prompt. You will also need to load the appropriate CD-ROM drivers. Once you reach the DOS prompt, switch to the drive letter of the CD-ROM drive. Follow the steps in Procedure 2.2 to begin the installation of NetWare 5 on a new machine.

PROCEDURE 2.2

Installing NetWare 5 on a New Machine (Text Portion)

1. Insert the NetWare 5 Operating System CD-ROM, and type **INSTALL** to begin the installation.

2. The NetWare 5 license agreement is displayed. To agree to the conditions of the license and continue, press F10.

PROCEDURE 2.2 (CONTINUED)

---

3. You are prompted to choose whether to install a new server or upgrade an existing server. Choose the new server option. You can also change the directory on the DOS partition for the server boot files (typically C:\NWSERVER) from this screen. Select the Continue option when you are finished.

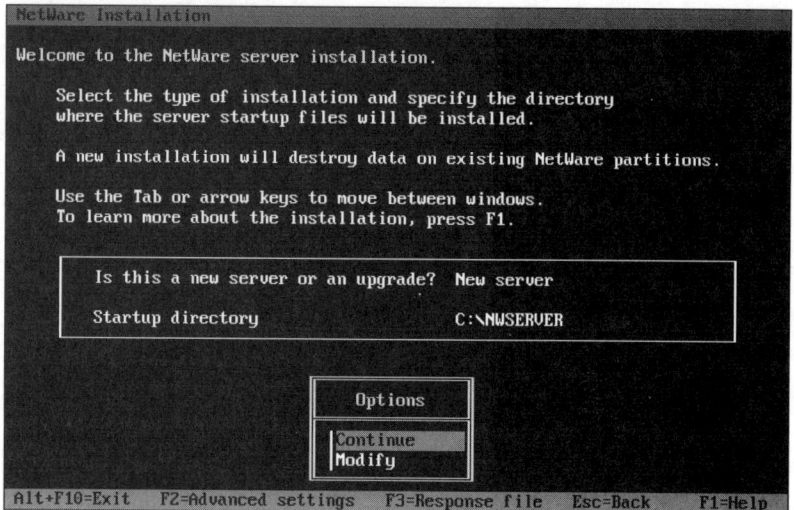

4. Next, you are prompted for international settings for the keyboard, code page for text, and country. The US options are selected by default. If you are not in the United States, select the appropriate options.

5. You are prompted to choose the type of mouse (PS2, COM1 serial, or COM2 serial). The mouse should already be attached. Specify VGA or Super VGA for the monitor. You can change these settings later, if desired.

6. You are prompted to specify Platform and HotPlug support modules, a new type of hardware support. Also specify HAM (hardware adapter module) drivers for each interface card in the computer. In most cases, they are detected automatically.

PROCEDURE 2.2 (CONTINUED)

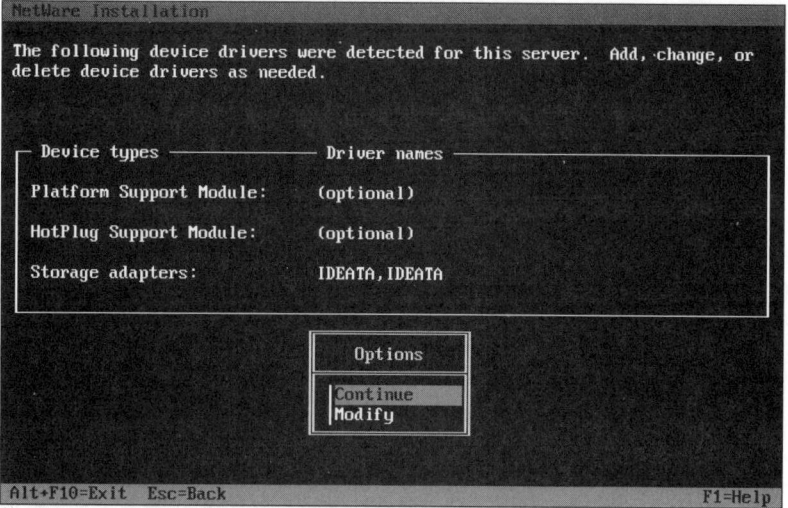

7. Next, select CDM (custom device module) drivers for each disk or CD-ROM drive. These are usually detected automatically.

8. In the same screen, specify one or more network card (LAN) drivers. NetWare 5 attempts to detect the card. If the driver is not listed, select the Modify option, then click Insert to display a list of drivers. You can also specify optional NLMs to be loaded from this screen.

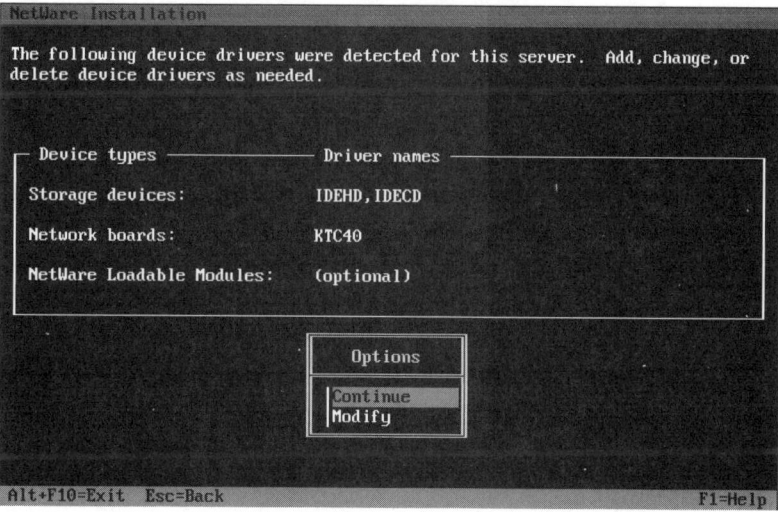

PROCEDURE 2.2 (CONTINUED)

9. The final text-based screen prompts you to create a NetWare partition and the SYS volume. You can specify the size of each. If you want to create additional volumes, including NSS volumes, you can use the GUI console to do so after you complete the installation.

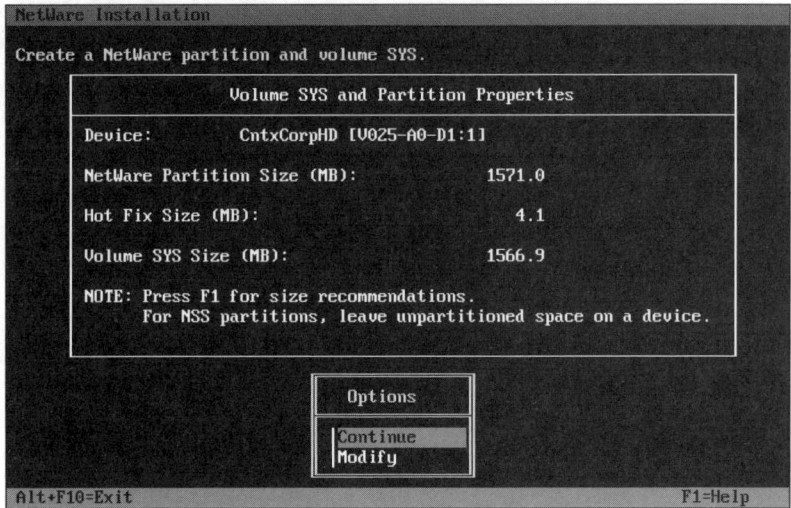

```
NetWare Installation

Create a NetWare partition and volume SYS.

        ┌──────────────────────────────────────────────────────────┐
        │          Volume SYS and Partition Properties             │
        │                                                          │
        │  Device:        CntxCorpHD [V025-A0-D1:1]                │
        │                                                          │
        │  NetWare Partition Size (MB):            1571.0          │
        │                                                          │
        │  Hot Fix Size (MB):                         4.1          │
        │                                                          │
        │  Volume SYS Size (MB):                   1566.9          │
        │                                                          │
        │  NOTE: Press F1 for size recommendations.                │
        │        For NSS partitions, leave unpartitioned space on a device. │
        │                                                          │
        └──────────────────────────────────────────────────────────┘
                              ┌──────────────────┐
                              │     Options      │
                              │ ┌──────────────┐ │
                              │ │Continue      │ │
                              │ │Modify        │ │
                              │ └──────────────┘ │
                              └──────────────────┘
Alt+F10=Exit                                                  F1=Help
```

10. A number of files (including the contents of the DOS partition) are now copied to the server from the CD-ROM.

After this portion of the installation completes, the NetWare 5 graphical user interface (which is based on X Windows) starts. The remaining steps of the installation are handled by the Installation Wizard, which prompts you for information with graphical dialogs. Follow the steps in Procedure 2.3 to complete the GUI portion of the installation.

PROCEDURE 2.3

Installing NetWare 5 on a New Machine (GUI Portion)

1. The Installation Wizard starts and displays a dialog prompting you for a name for the new server. Choose a name, enter it, and click the Next button.

PROCEDURE 2.3 (CONTINUED)

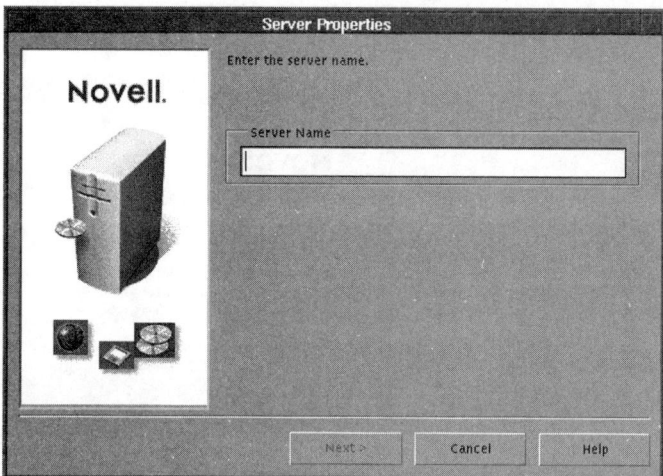

2. You must choose a protocol for each of the installed network cards. You can choose IP, IPX, or both; IP is accepted by default. For IP support, you must specify the IP address and subnet mask, and you can specify an optional router (gateway) address.

3. The Installation Wizard displays a list of time zones. Select the appropriate time zone for your area, and choose whether NetWare should automatically adjust for daylight saving time.

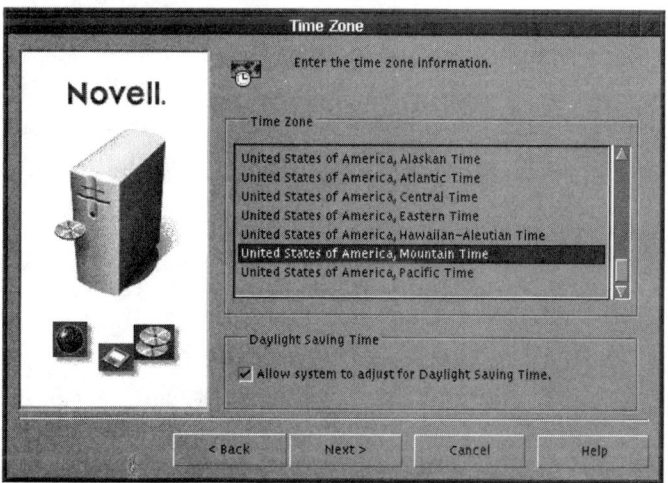

4. The next dialog prompts you for NDS options. Choose whether to install the server into an existing tree or a new tree.

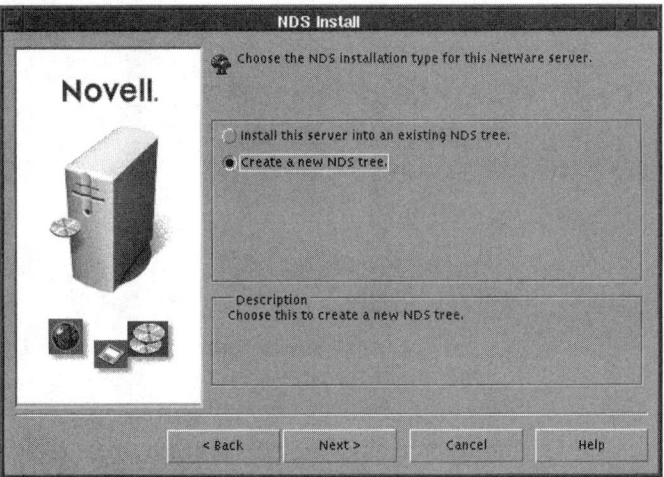

5. If you are creating a new NDS tree, enter the tree name and the context (organization or organizational unit) for the server object. This dialog also prompts you for the name, NDS context, and password for the Administrator account (by default, ADMIN in the server context).

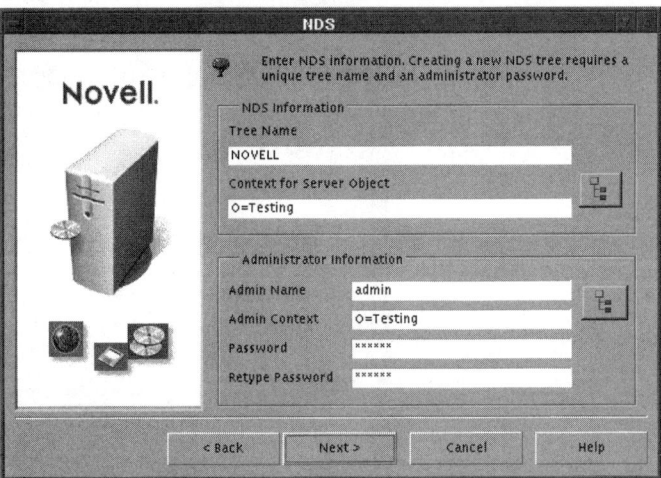

6. At this point, the installation program scans the network and attempts to connect to the desired NDS tree. For a new tree, it verifies that there are no trees with the same name in the network. If this process is successful, a summary of the NDS configuration is displayed; click Next to continue.

7. The next dialog prompts you to specify a license for the server. The NetWare 5 license is usually on a floppy disk included with the CD-ROM package. Insert the disk and specify the filename for the license file, or use the browse button to find the file. (You can also install NetWare 5 without a license and add one after the installation.)

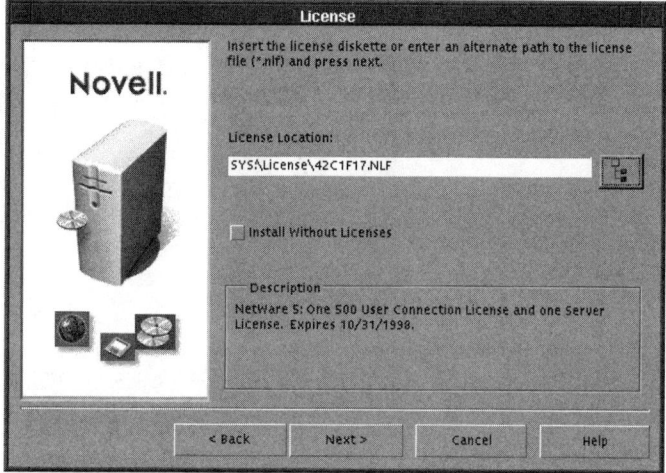

8. Select the NetWare 5 components to install. (You can modify this list after installation using the GUI-based Install utility, described in Chapter 5.)

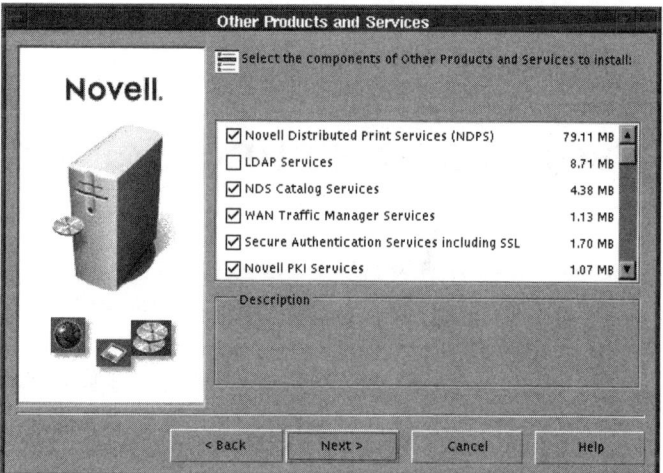

9. Depending on the components you chose to install, one or more additional configuration dialogs may be displayed.

PROCEDURE 2.3 (CONTINUED)

10. After you answer the questions in the last dialog, a summary screen is displayed, and you have one more chance to change the installation options. When you click the Finish button, the files are copied to the SYS volume.

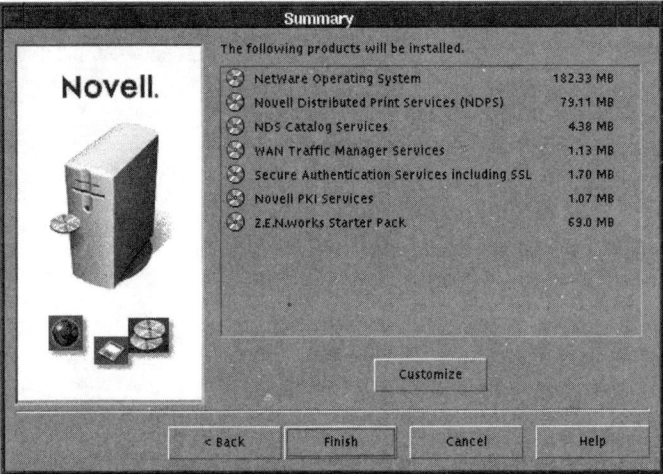

11. The file copy process may take several minutes. When it completes, you are prompted to reboot the server. After rebooting, the server is ready for use.

Upgrading an Existing Server

You may not have the luxury of purchasing an entirely new server to run NetWare 5. Luckily, the new version makes it easy to upgrade from NetWare 3.1x or 4.x. Because this process uses the installation program to convert the existing server to a NetWare 5 server, it's called an in-place upgrade.

In the following sections, you'll learn how to prepare your server and network for an in-place upgrade to NetWare 5. We will also look at the process of upgrading using the installation program.

Preparing for the Upgrade

The preparation process is a bit more complicated when you are upgrading an existing server. You'll have to be sure you don't lose any data during the upgrade and that the upgrade has as little negative impact on users as possible. The following sections describe the tasks you should perform to prepare for the upgrade to NetWare 5.

Backing Up the Server

The most important part of your preparation for the upgrade should be to make a backup of all the data on the server. Be sure the backup includes all of the files, along with the bindery or NDS data. Although the upgrade process rarely disturbs existing data, you should be prepared to restore it and revert to the previous version if NetWare 5 doesn't work properly.

To be completely safe, make at least two backups (one stored off-site) and test them to ensure that files can be restored. You'll never regret being too cautious; however, many administrators have regretted not making enough backups.

Documenting the Server

If you've been a reliable and efficient administrator with the current NetWare network (and haven't been overworked), you already have a binder full of detailed documentation about the network (including the various directories and what they're used for, the security access required by various departments and how it's implemented, and so on).

If you don't have documentation, now is the time to start documenting—before you upgrade to NetWare 5. Although most of the server's configuration details should be transferred in the upgrade, you will need to know how the system is supposed to work. This is especially helpful if you have a problem after the upgrade, because you can tell whether the problem is caused by NetWare 5 or not.

Make sure you have proper documentation for the following details:

- The organization of the file system and its directories (in particular, where user and common directories are stored and who should have access to them)

- The groups, organizational roles, other NDS objects, and the file system and NDS rights they have been granted

- The configuration (IRQ and memory addresses, network addresses, etc.) for each network adapter

- The server's current utilization and memory use, as reported by the MONITOR utility (to help you determine if NetWare 5 is slower and if you need to add memory after the upgrade to maintain performance)

Verifying Hardware Compatibility

Before you attempt to upgrade to NetWare 5, you should make sure that your machine meets the minimum requirements for NetWare 5 discussed earlier in this chapter. You should also verify that all of the devices installed in the server are compatible with NetWare 5.

In particular, disk adapters and drives may not work on NetWare 5 if the appropriate HAM and CDM drivers are not available. Check with the appropriate manufacturers if necessary, and be sure you have these drivers ready before you upgrade.

NetWare 5 uses the same format for LAN drivers that earlier versions used, but not all drivers written for NetWare 4.*x* or an earlier version will work with NetWare 5. You should verify that the network boards and drivers are compatible with NetWare 5 before you begin the upgrade.

Last but not least, you'll need to add a mouse to the server. You may also need a better video card and monitor to support the new management features of the GUI console.

If your server currently runs a bit sluggishly using NetWare 3.1*x* or 4.*x*, don't consider an upgrade to NetWare 5 without hardware upgrades. The new operating system is bigger and more sophisticated and, therefore, will run a bit slower on the same machine.

Verifying Software Compatibility

You should make sure that any software you are using is compatible with NetWare 5 or that an equivalent product is available for NetWare 5. This includes any third-party backup utilities, virus checkers, or application servers currently in use on the network.

Planning a Network-Wide Upgrade

If the server is part of a larger network, you should plan the upgrade process for the entire network before you upgrade any machines. If you have several NetWare 4.*x* servers with a partitioned directory structure, you will need to upgrade the server storing the replica of the root partition to NetWare 5 before any others. You should also upgrade NDS on all of the servers before upgrading any of them to NetWare 5, as described earlier in this chapter.

If you plan to upgrade all of the servers, you should also consider whether to switch from IPX (or NetWare 4's IP support) to NetWare 5's Pure IP format. Until you do so, you can use the NetWare 5 servers with the existing IPX network; however, NetWare 5 is actually less efficient with IPX than previous versions, so you should seriously consider moving to IP.

Choosing an Installation Time

As a final consideration, you should plan the upgrade to NetWare 5 so that the users of the current server are disturbed as little as possible. You will be taking the server down to perform the upgrade. If the upgrade is performed flawlessly, it may take as little as half an hour— but you should plan for the worst.

If possible, plan the upgrade on a day when users aren't logged in at all, such as on a weekend, and leave yourself ample time to test the server after the upgrade. You should also have time to restore the old version of NetWare and get the server running if NetWare 5 doesn't work properly.

The Upgrade Process

The process of upgrading to NetWare 5 is similar to a new installation. The difference is that the installation program detects the previous installation and prompts you with several choices during the upgrade process. Follow the steps in Procedure 2.4 to upgrade a machine to NetWare 5.

This procedure is similar whether you are upgrading a NetWare 3.1*x* or NetWare 4.*x* server. You cannot use the installation program to upgrade NetWare 2.*x* or earlier versions.

PROCEDURE 2.4

Upgrading to NetWare 5 with the Installation Program (Text Portion)

1. Be sure all users are logged off the existing server, and type **DOWN** and **EXIT** at the console prompt to return to the DOS prompt.

2. Insert the NetWare 5 Operating System CD-ROM, and type **INSTALL** to begin the installation.

3. The license agreement is displayed. Press F10 to accept the conditions of the license and continue.

4. You are prompted to choose whether to install a new server or upgrade an existing server. Choose the upgrade option for the appropriate operating system (NetWare 3.1*x* or 4.*x*.) You can also change the directory on the DOS partition for the server boot files (typically C:\NWSERVER) from this screen.

5. You are prompted for international settings for the keyboard, code page for text, and country. The US options are selected by default. If you are not in the United States, select the appropriate option.

6. You are prompted to choose the type of mouse (PS2, COM1 serial, or COM2 serial). The mouse should already be attached. Specify VGA or Super VGA for the monitor. You can change these settings later, if desired.

7. You are prompted to specify Platform and HotPlug support modules, a new type of hardware support. Also specify HAM (hardware adapter module) drivers for each interface card in the computer. In most cases, they are detected automatically; if you were using HAM drivers under NetWare 4.*x*, the same driver is selected.

8. Select CDM (custom device module) drivers for each disk or CD-ROM drive. These drivers are usually detected automatically. If your server used HAM and CDM drivers under NetWare 4.*x*, the same drivers are used.

9. In the same screen, specify one or more network card (LAN) drivers. NetWare 5 attempts to detect the card or use the configuration from the old server. If no driver is listed, select the Modify option, then click Insert to display a list of drivers. You can also specify optional NLMs to be loaded from this screen.

10. The final text-based screen asks you how to handle the existing SYS volume. You can either create a new volume or mount the existing volume. In most cases, you will want to mount the existing volume.

11. A number of files are now copied to the server from the CD-ROM, including the updated contents of the DOS partition.

After this portion of the upgrade completes, the NetWare GUI is loaded. The Installation Wizard then presents a series of configuration dialogs. You can specify the information requested in each dialog and use the Back and Next buttons to navigate between the dialogs. Follow the steps in Procedure 2.5 to complete the GUI portion of the upgrade process.

PROCEDURE 2.5

Upgrading to NetWare 5 with the Installation Program (GUI Portion)

1. You are prompted to mount any other volumes on the server. You can mount these volumes now or after the installation.

2. The Installation Wizard prompts you for the protocols for each installed network board. Select IP, IPX, or both, and specify the IP details.

3. You are prompted for the administrator name, context, and password for the existing NDS tree to which the server is attached (the same tree as before the upgrade).

4. You are prompted to insert a license disk or browse for a license file. (NetWare 4.x or earlier licenses do not work with NetWare 5.)

5. The Wizard displays a list of optional components. Select any components you want to add to the server. Where equivalent components are already installed on the server, they are selected automatically.

6. A summary of the installation details is displayed. Click Modify to change the installation options, or click Finish to continue.

7. The files are now copied to the SYS volume. This process may take several minutes. When it completes, you are prompted to reboot the server. After rebooting, the server is ready for use.

Migrating to a New Server

If you choose to migrate to a new server, NetWare 5 includes an improved migration utility that makes the process easy. Because data is copied over the network from the old server to the new server, this migration is referred to as an across-the-wire migration.

The following sections describe how to prepare the server and workstation for the across-the-wire migration and how to perform the migration process itself.

Preparing to Migrate

Migration requires less preparation than an upgrade, because you will not be modifying the existing server. Nevertheless, some preparation is necessary. You will need to back up and document the old server, install a new server, and set up the Upgrade Wizard on a workstation.

Backups and Documentation

As with an upgrade, you should first document the existing network before performing the migration. You should also make a backup of the data on the server—although the data on the old server should not be affected by the migration process, it's best to be safe.

Installing the New Server

Next, you'll need a new server to replace the old server. To select a machine and install NetWare 5 on it, follow the instructions given earlier in this chapter for a new installation.

You don't need to perform any special steps in the installation process. Because the old server and the new server will be on the network at the same time, you should choose a different name for the new server; you can change this name after the installation and migration are complete.

Installing the Upgrade Wizard

You'll need a workstation to perform the migration using the Upgrade Wizard. This should be a reasonably fast machine. The Upgrade

Wizard will run under Windows 95, Windows 98, or Windows NT 4.0 or later.

In order to run the Upgrade Wizard, the workstation must be logged into the NDS tree, and it must be running version 2.2 or later of the Novell client for Windows 95, or version 4.11 of the IntranetWare client for Windows NT.

The Upgrade Wizard is not installed to the SYS volume on the new server. Instead, you'll install it on the workstation from the NetWare 5 CD-ROM. Follow the steps in Procedure 2.6 to install the Upgrade Wizard at a workstation.

PROCEDURE 2.6

Installing the Upgrade Wizard

1. Insert the NetWare 5 Operating System CD-ROM, and run the UPGRDWZD.EXE program, which is located in the \PRODUCTS\ UPGRDWZD directory.

2. A Welcome screen for the installation program is displayed, as shown here. Click Next to continue.

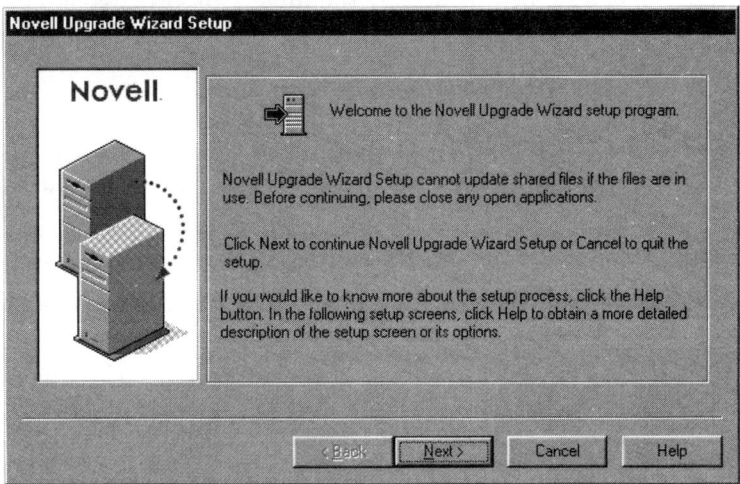

3. The license agreement for the Upgrade Wizard is now displayed. To accept the agreement and continue, click the Accept button.

PROCEDURE 2.6 (CONTINUED)

4. Choose the location on the workstation's disk where you want to install the Upgrade Wizard. This dialog is shown in the following graphic:

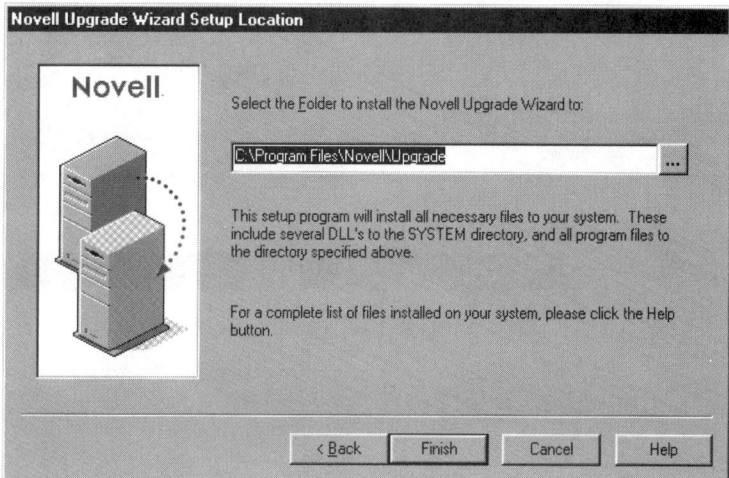

5. Click Finish to complete the installation process.

The Migration Process

Once you have successfully installed the Upgrade Wizard at the workstation, you can run it by selecting Programs ➤ Novell ➤ Novell Upgrade Wizard from the Start menu.

When you run the Upgrade Wizard, the dialog shown in Figure 2.1 is displayed. You will need to create an upgrade project, which stores settings for the migration. Select the Create a new Upgrade Wizard project option, then follow the steps in Procedure 2.7 to create the project.

FIGURE 2.1

The initial dialog of the Novell Upgrade Wizard

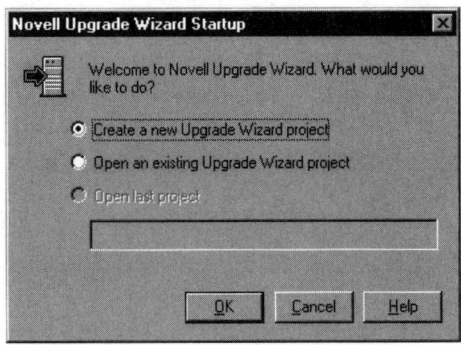

PROCEDURE 2.7

Creating an Upgrade Project

1. Choose a name for the project and a filename in which to save the project.

2. You are prompted for the source servers, destination servers, and a destination NDS tree for the directory data.

3. Click the Create button to create the project.

4. The Project window is displayed, showing the source server's resources on the left and the destination server's resources on the right. Drag-and-drop to indicate which resources (volumes, bindery, or NDS data) will be moved to which destination.

5. Use Save from the File menu (File ➣ Save) to save the project.

After you create the project, you can perform the migration. Follow the steps in Procedure 2.8 to perform the migration.

PROCEDURE 2.8

Performing Across-the-Wire Migration

1. Verify Project from the Project menu (Project ➣ Verify Project). The verification process checks for potential problems (such as a name conflict) with the migration.

2. Specify passwords for administrative accounts for the source and destination servers.

3. Select the items to verify (name conflicts, file conflicts, etc.).

4. If any errors are found during the verification process, the Wizard will prompt you to fix them.

5. If the verification was successful, upgrade from the Project menu (Project ➤ Upgrade) to perform the actual migration.

6. A summary screen is displayed, and the verification process double-checks for remaining problems. Click Next to continue.

7. Click the Upgrade button to begin the migration. The upgrade process may take anywhere from a few minutes to several hours, depending on the network bandwidth available and the speed of the servers and workstation.

Upgrading NetWare Clients

Although previous versions of NetWare client software can access NetWare 5 servers, you should eventually update the clients to the latest software to ensure full compatibility. There are two ways to upgrade NetWare clients to NetWare 5:

- Use the installation files on the NetWare Client CD-ROM, included with NetWare 5. To install the client, run the SETUP or INSTALL program for the appropriate client operating system.

- Use Automatic Client Upgrade (ACU) to upgrade clients automatically. This allows you to modify a login script to upgrade clients when they log in.

The ACU option is the easiest for large numbers of clients. To configure and use ACU, follow the instructions in the following sections.

Copying the Installation Files

To use ACU, you will need to copy the client software to the NetWare 5 server. To do this, create a directory under the SYS:PUBLIC directory called CLIENTS. Copy one or more of the following subdirectories from the PRODUCTS directory on the NetWare Client CD-ROM, depending on the client operating systems in use:

WINNT   Windows NT client

WIN95   Windows 95/98 client

DOSWIN32   DOS and Windows 3.1*x* clients

ADM32   Administration tools

Creating a Login Script

To run the client setup utility, modify a login script (container or profile) to run the appropriate setup utility. Assuming the installation files are stored under SYS:PUBLIC\CLIENT, here are the command lines for various operating systems:

- Windows 95/98: SYS:PUBLIC\CLIENT\WIN95\IBM_ENU\ SETUP.EXE /ACU

- Windows NT: SYS:PUBLIC\CLIENT\WINNT\I386\SETUPNW .EXE /ACU

- DOS and Windows 3.1*x*: SYS:PUBLIC\CLIENT\DOSWIN32\ NLS\ENGLISH\SETUP.EXE /ACU

If your network supports clients with multiple operating systems, you can use IF statements in the login script to run the client setup program for the appropriate operating system. For example, here is a script that supports Windows 95/98, Windows NT, and Windows 3.1*x* clients:

```
IF <OS> = "Windows_95" THEN BEGIN
#SYS:PUBLIC\CLIENT\WIN95\IBM_ENU\SETUP.EXE /ACU
END
```

```
IF <OS> = "Windows_NT" THEN BEGIN
#SYS:PUBLIC\CLIENT\WINNT\I386\SETUPNW.EXE /ACU
END
IF <OS> = "MSDOS" AND PLATFORM = "WIN" THEN BEGIN
@SYS:PUBLIC\CLIENT\DOSWIN32\NLS\ENGLISH\SETUP.EXE /ACU
END
```

Review

NetWare 5 includes an improved installation program and a Migration Wizard which simplifies the process of moving to a new server. In this chapter, you learned the hardware requirements for NetWare 5 and how to prepare for installation. The new server installation process is straightforward.

Planning an Installation

Before installing NetWare 5, you should plan the process of installing or upgrading. This includes the upgrade method to be used, the file system and other considerations, and checking hardware requirements. NetWare 5's hardware requirements include:

- A Pentium processor (100Mhz or faster recommended)

- 64MB of RAM (128MB recommended)

- 450MB of disk storage for the NetWare partition (1GB or more recommended)

- 35MB of disk storage for the DOS partition

- A network card for the appropriate network media

- A mouse (optional) and VGA or Super VGA monitor for GUI support

Upgrading to NetWare 5

To upgrade an existing server, you can use one of two methods:

- An *in-place upgrade* uses the installation program to install NetWare 5 on the same machine as the older system.

- An *across-the-wire migration* uses the Upgrade Wizard to migrate data from the old server to a new server, using a workstation to manage the migration process.

After the installation is complete, you will want to familiarize yourself with the NetWare 5 user interface, particularly the new GUI features. For more information about these features, refer to Chapter 5.

Upgrading Clients

NetWare 5 will work with NetWare 4.*x* or earlier client software, but you should upgrade the clients to the latest version for better NetWare 5 support. There are two ways to upgrade clients for NetWare 5:

- Using the installation program on the NetWare Client CD-ROM

- Using ACU (automatic client upgrade) from a login script

Installation Practice Questions

1. The size limit for a single file in the traditional NetWare file system is:

    A. 1MB

    B. 1GB

    C. 2GB

    D. 8TB

2. What is the minimum amount of RAM required for the installation of NetWare 5?

    A. 12MB

    B. 16MB

    C. 32MB

    D. 64MB

3. How much disk storage is required for the installation of NetWare 5, including the DOS partition?

    A. 1GB

    B. 230MB

    C. 485MB

    D. 2GB

4. If you upgrade a NetWare 4 machine to NetWare 5 without upgrading any hardware, it will run faster. (True or False.)

5. Which of the following hardware items are required for the installation of NetWare 5? (Select all that apply.)

    A. CD-ROM drive

    B. Network card

    C. Network connection

    D. Floppy drive

    E. Mouse

    F. Pentium-class processor

6. Which extensions are used for disk drivers in NetWare 5? (Select all that apply.)

   A. DSK

   B. DLL

   C. NLM

   D. HAM

   E. CDM

7. Which of the following are advantages of the NSS file system? (Select all that apply.)

   A. Less memory is required for large volumes.

   B. Larger file sizes are possible.

   C. It is compatible with older NetWare versions.

   D. It has faster access to files.

8. If you buy a new machine to run NetWare 5 and replace the old server, you need to use the _____ upgrade method to install NetWare 5.

9. Which program is used to migrate data to a new server?

   A. Migration Wizard

   B. MIGRATE.EXE

   C. MIGRATE.NLM

   D. Upgrade Wizard

10. Which versions of NetWare can you upgrade to NetWare 5 by using the installation program? (Select all that apply.)

   A. NetWare 4.*x* only

   B. NetWare 3.1*x* or 4.*x*

   C. NetWare 2.*x* through 4.*x*

   D. Previous versions of NetWare 5 only

CHAPTER

3

Novell Distributed
Print Services (NDPS)

Roadmap

This chapter covers the latest level in network printing, Novell Distributed Print Services (NDPS).

Topics Covered

- We'll learn the four main elements of Novell Distributed Print Services.

- We'll discuss their overall functionality.

- We'll distinguish NDPS from the queue-based printing services that NDPS replaces.

- We'll look at the functional differences and implementation processes for the two types of printers possible on a NetWare 5 network:
    - Public Access Printers
    - Controlled Access Printers

Skills You'll Learn

- Configuring workstations for printers with Public and Controlled Access

- Configuring the network for NDPS with NDPS objects in NDS

- Creating an NDPS Manager

- Configuring the Hewlett Packard Gateway

- Configuring the Xerox Gateway

- Configuring the Novell Gateway

- Creating a Public Access Printer

- Creating a Controlled Access Printer

- Configuring NDS to download print drivers

- Manually installing a printer on the workstation

- Configuring a printer

Printing has always been an important reason to have a network. Nonetheless, a network can be a major source of dissatisfaction when printing problems arise. Novell Distributed Print Services (NDPS) makes printing easier and more scalable. NDPS adds more administrative functionality (e.g., Plug and Print) to network printing and requires less red tape to administer. The NDPS goal is to automate printing as much as possible, without losing the functionality of feature-rich bidirectional communications, hierarchical control, and security.

Distributed Print Services versus Queue-Based Print Services

Some aspects of NDPS are simpler to use than previous queue-based print services. With NDPS, administrators create a Printer Agent, which takes the place of the print queue, the printer object, and the print server. The Printer Agent eliminates the need to use Capture statements to send print jobs to the queue. Instead, each printer has its own Printer Agent, and print jobs are sent directly to the printer by the software.

With queue-based printing services, Plug and Print was not an option on the network, as it is now with NDPS. As long as the printer does not need to have the security or reporting intricacies provided by a Controlled Access Printer, it can be installed as a Public Access Printer. A Printer Agent is then automatically created for it. The network automatically detects the new device, and all network users then instantly have access to the printer.

Common print drivers are stored by NDPS on NDS (Netware Directory Services) and automatically downloaded and installed on each workstation. As new printers and drivers become available, the drivers can be added to the pool. This eliminates the need to store the print drivers on the workstation and allows them to be centrally managed on NDS.

NDPS reduces network traffic because SAP (Service Advertising Protocol) is turned off, along with all of the traffic it produced. NDPS communicates directly with the printer and keeps track of printer parameters.

NDPS has full backward-compatibility with queue-based systems. Therefore, if different network segments are not upgraded to NetWare 5, you can still use queue-based printers from NDPS. It works the other way as well. Legacy clients can print through a queue to NDPS-aware printers.

Novell has added some partnering to the NetWare 5 Printing environment. Both Hewlett Packard and Xerox have incorporated Novell Printer Agents into their new-generation printers. Novell also provides compatibility between other manufacturers and the NetWare 5 server.

While Public Access Printers offer simplicity to the user, Controlled Access Printers add the flexibility and complexity required to meet today's printing demands in the enterprise.

The NDS Controlled Access Printer incorporates directory advantages (such as security control and single-point administration of printing resources) to the printing environment. With queue-based systems, only unidirectional communications from the printer take place. With NDPS, bidirectional feedback and printing control is configurable for users and administrators. Real-time information is available to anyone with security rights to interact with a printer regarding:

- Print job status. (Messages or notifications can be routed to whomever needs to know that toner is low, paper is out, etc.).

- Notification of job completion.

- Print job properties (such as scheduling order, number of copies, whether the printer is active or on hold, etc.).

- Other available printers and their status. (Reported details can become as complex as printer manufacturers' design capabilities.)

Different printing accessibility or functionality can be assigned to users. You can assign color printing access to some users and deny access to others. You can limit access times. You can apply multiple configurations to individual printers or to groups of printers in a department.

NDPS should cut down on time-consuming network printing problems, saving NetWare 5-equipped companies the costs associated with those printing problems. Installing and configuring Public Access Printers is simple; however, some companies require the more complex security, access, and communications that are possible with Controlled Access Printers.

Configuring and Installing NDPS

The minimum system requirements for an NDPS server are:

- 80MB of disk space in the SYS Volume

- 4MB of RAM more than the minimum amount of RAM needed to run NetWare 5

Make sure that you have Supervisor rights to the server object on the initial server that has NDPS installed. For all subsequent servers, make sure you have all rights *except* Supervisor for the container of the server on which you are installing NDPS.

NDPS is initially installed by default during NetWare 5 server installation. An NDPS Broker is also automatically created. The Three Hop Rule lets this NDPS Broker function for three hops in any direction on your network. This Three Hop Rule requires you to create a Broker for servers more than three hops away from the initial NDPS Broker.

To install NDPS on a server:

1. Make sure system requirements are met.

2. Install NDPS.

3. Create and load an NDPS Manager.

4. Create Printer Agents.

The Four NDPS Elements

To make sense of Novell Distributed Print Services, you must first understand the four constituent elements of NDPS and their assigned tasks. These four elements are:

- The NDPS Manager
- The Printer Agent
- The NDPS Broker
- The three gateways: the Hewlett Packard (HP) Gateway, the Xerox Gateway, and the Novell Gateway

The NDPS Manager

The NDPS Manager is the functional utility used to create and manage the Printer Agents. The NDPS Manager runs as a utility on the NetWare server. Only one NDPS Manager can be loaded on any one server. It must be loaded on any server that will have to control printers and their Printer Agents.

Printer Agents have a one-to-one relationship with the printers with which they work. A single NDPS Manager can control any conceivable number of Printer Agents. An NDPS Manager object must be created in the NDS tree before server-based Printing Agents can be created. If a server is to have any printers attached to it, those servers should have their own NDPS Managers loaded and the NDS objects created before the printers are attached.

The NDPS Manager can be loaded manually at the server console, or it will automatically load anytime you use NetWare Administrator to create a Printer Agent. To have an NDPS Manager object created on your network, perform the steps as listed in Procedure 3.1.

PROCEDURE 3.1

Creating an NDPS Manager

1. Go to NetWare Administrator, and click the container in which you want the printer object to reside.

2. Choose Object ≻ Create ≻ NDPS Manager, and click OK. The following dialog box will appear.

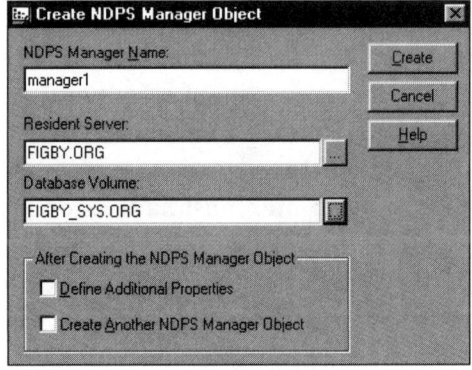

3. Type an NDPS Manager name.

4. Browse to the server on which you want the NDPS Manager to reside. (This server can be chosen from any server in the network that has NDPS installed and does not have an NDPS Manager installed.)

5. Browse to the volume on which you want the NDPS Manager database to be installed.

6. Click Create.

PROCEDURE 3.1 (CONTINUED)

7. You may load the NDPS Manager manually by typing the following command at the server console prompt:

NDPSM manager_name_and_context

Or you can have NDPS Manager load automatically by adding the previous command to the AUTOEXEC.NCF file.

Although some printing management and configuration tasks are performed through NDPS Manager, NetWare Administrator is the main tool for performing these tasks.

The Printer Agent

The Printer Agent combines the functionality of the printer object, print queue, spooler, and print server into one intelligent element. Each Printer Agent is assigned to a printer and, therefore, establishes the one-to-one ratio of printers to Printer Agents. Just remember that every printer must have its own separate agent, a printer can have only one agent, and an agent can have only one printer.

The Printer Agent can reside on the server, or (in the case of the new NetWare-aware printers) it can reside embedded in the printer itself. On the server, it can manage a printer that is attached to a workstation or the server. Therefore, the printer can be attached somewhere else on the network.

The Printer Agent software becomes the individual brain of a particular printer, managing that printer's functionality. As such, it communicates information regarding those printing functions to clients or administrators and reports progress on individual jobs or on that printer's abilities.

The Printer Agent reports printer problems to designated problem solvers. Job completion messages may go to the person printing, while paper and toner deficiency notices might go to the person who happens to sit next to the printer, etc.

You can think of the Printer Agent as a trainable, artificial printing intelligence that will interact with users or administrators with whatever degree of complexity is needed. The single-printer responsibility of the Printer Agent makes network printing flexible and scalable.

The Printer Agent can operate with either a Public Access Printer or a Controlled Access Printer. It can protect or portion out printer functionality when that is an issue. This capacity broadens the scalability of your printing choices and allows you to choose your printing freedom and limitations.

 If you try to create a Printer Agent without loading NDPS Manager, NetWare will ask you if you want to load it.

The NDPS Broker

The NDPS Broker is analogous to the central brain or governing agency that organizes and manages information for all the Printer Agents in the network.

When NDPS is installed, the NDPS Broker is loaded automatically on your network by the installation utility. A single NDPS Broker functions within a network for three hops. A server more than three hops away would need another NDPS Broker installed. If NDPS Broker is installed on a server, it will automatically check to make sure it is not in the three-hop domain of another NDPS Broker.

NDPS performs three transparent network support services. The NDPS Broker logs into the network and authenticates each of these services. These three important services and their functions are:

- Resource Management Services (RMS) contains the central pool of information, which includes print drivers and printer definition files and fonts that can be downloaded to administrators and the user workstations or printers that need to use them.

This is where new print drivers are stored when printers are added to the network.

- Service Registry Services (SRS) includes the information set with all of the printers' addresses, types, manufacturers, model numbers, and other information. This service allows Public Access Printers to advertise themselves from a central location so administrators and users can easily find them. The traffic generated still constitutes a large reduction from the traffic generated by the Service Advertising Protocol (SAP), which was formerly used by network printers to advertise their presence.

- Event Notification Services (ENS) allows printers to send customized messages regarding print jobs. Different delivery methods (including e-mail, NetWare pop-up screens, and log file messages) are supported.

The Three Gateways

Gateways are software entities that allow printers without embedded Printer Agents to function with NDPS. They access print systems that require jobs to be placed in a queue and send print jobs to non-NDPS printing systems, such as UNIX, QMS, mainframe, Macintosh, and similar systems.

The gateway ascertains the type of the printer it accesses and translates NDPS queries and commands to a printer-specific language, thereby controlling the printer.

In addition to providing NDPS-aware printers that have Printer Agents embedded in their software, Hewlett Packard and Xerox have designed specific gateways to communicate with their printers that are not NDPS aware.

The Hewlett Packard (HP) Gateway and the Xerox Gateway represent the first step in enlisting the participation of hardware (printer) manufacturers to develop network operability within the Novell NetWare 5 environment. Novell designed the catchall Novell Gateway to communicate with the remaining types of printers.

The Hewlett Packard Gateway

When you choose a Hewlett Packard (HP) Gateway, the screen shown in Figure 3.1 will appear. Procedure 3.2 will walk you through the steps necessary to configure the Hewlett Packard Gateway. This process will turn an HP printer into a Public Access Printer. Your control over that printer will be limited. Remember that no NDS object is created for a Public Access Printer.

FIGURE 3.1

Configuring the
Hewlett Packard
Gateway

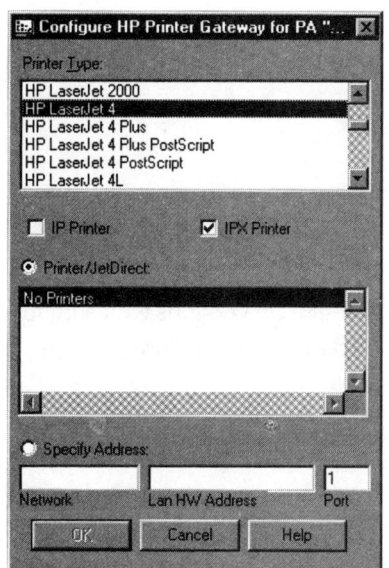

PROCEDURE 3.2

Configuring the Hewlett Packard Gateway

1. Go to NetWare Administrator, and double-click NDPS Manager.

2. On the Identification page, click Printer Agent List.

3. Click New, and choose a name for this Printer Agent.

4. Choose the HP Gateway under Gateway Types, and click OK.

PROCEDURE 3.2 (CONTINUED)

5. In the Configure HP Gateway dialog box, choose the printer type.

6. Choose IP or IPX protocol.

7. Indicate the IP address, or choose the printer from the advertised Jet-Direct card list.

8. Click OK. (The Printer Agent and gateway will load automatically.)

9. Select a printer driver for Windows 3.1, Windows 95, or Windows NT. Click the chosen driver.

10. Click Continue. Read the information screen, and click OK twice.

 JetDirect cards that support NDS (X.03.06 or greater) have full bidirectional functionality when they are used with the HP Gateway. You can upgrade older NDS versions with a utility available at Hewlett Packard's Web site at http://www.hp.com/go/support.

The Xerox Gateway

When you choose a Xerox Gateway, the Xerox Setup Wizard shown in Figure 3.2 will appear. Using the Wizard, as indicated in Procedure 3.3, is relatively simple.

PROCEDURE 3.3

Configuring the Xerox Gateway

1. Repeat Steps 1–3 in Procedure 3.2. At Step 4, choose the Xerox Gateway in Gateway Types, and click OK.

2. The Wizard will ask you a series of system-specific questions. To configure this gateway, you simply answer the Wizard's prompts by clicking the correct responses.

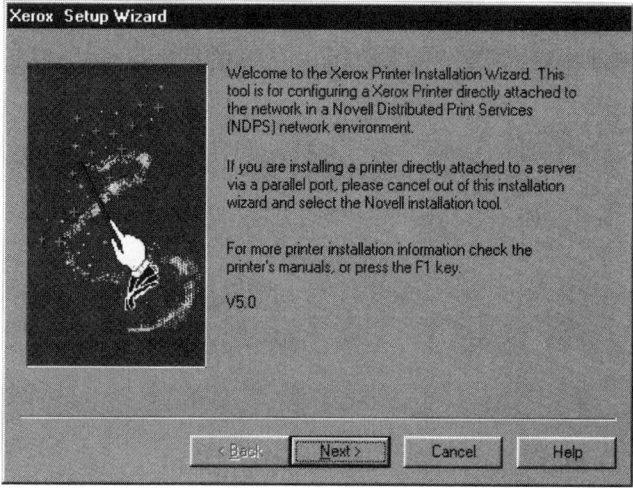

FIGURE 3.2

Configuring the Xerox Gateway

The Novell Gateway

This gateway consists of an NLM that loads when:

- A Printer Agent is created, and the printer is not connected directly to the network.

OR

- The printer isn't running in PSERVER mode, and the printer is not a new HP or Xerox with an embedded Printer Agent.

This NLM can query the printer directly in its native language (PostScript or PCL).

When you choose a Novell Gateway, the screen shown in Figure 3.3 will appear. To configure the Novell Gateway, you must follow the directions in Procedure 3.4.

PROCEDURE 3.4

Configuring the Novell Gateway

1. Repeat Steps 1–3 of Procedure 3.2. At Step 4, choose Novell Printer Gateway, and click OK. From the Configure Novell Printer Gateway dialog box, choose the printer type.

PROCEDURE 3.4 (CONTINUED)

2. Select the Novell Port Handler.

3. Click OK.

4. Mark the connection type.

5. Mark the port type.

6. Click Next.

7. Additional screens will appear depending on the type of connection you have chosen. Complete these screens by filling in the correct information.

FIGURE 3.3

Configuring the Novell Gateway

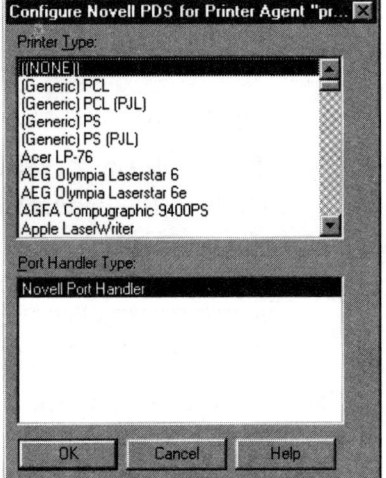

The Port Handler ensures that the NLM can communicate with the printer regardless of the type of interface used. These interfaces may include parallel ports, serial ports, QMS protocols, or a remote network protocol.

NDPS Printer Types

We have already introduced the two types of NDPS printers:

- Public Access Printers
- Controlled Access Printers

Public Access Printers allow easy installation and free usage across the network without restriction. On the other hand, Controlled Access Printers have an associated NDS printer object representing them on NDS that allows administrative control, tuning, and communication with the printer.

Public Access Printers

A Public Access Printer has the following qualities:

- It allows plug-and-print freedom.
- It does not have an NDS object in the NDS tree.
- Communications are not configurable. The status of a printer and jobs cannot be directed.
- Security and hierarchical usage plans cannot be configured.
- It is managed through the Tools menu on NetWare Administrator.

To create a Public Access Printer, follow the steps in Procedure 3.5.

PROCEDURE 3.5

Creating a Public Access Printer

1. From NetWare Administrator, double-click the NDPS Manager you want to manage this printer.

2. In the Identification page, click Printer Agent List.

PROCEDURE 3.5 (CONTINUED)

3. Click New, and the following dialog box will appear:

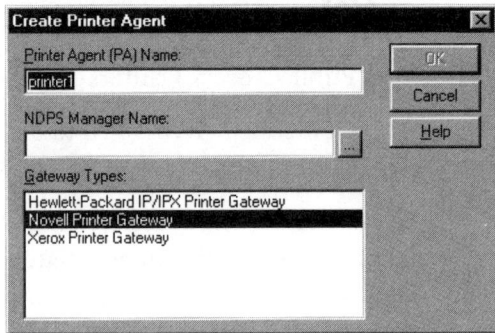

4. Choose a name for this Printer Agent.

5. Choose and configure the gateway type. Answer all the prompts that appear throughout the process.

Controlled Access Printers

A Controlled Access Printer has the NDS printer object. This extends the NDS, giving a Controlled Access Printer the following qualities:

- It can employ a full range of NetWare security options.

- It can communicate specifically about a full range of printing-process events and their status.

- It can facilitate simple or automatic client installation.

- It is managed through NetWare Administrator, which can schedule access, adjust printer values, and configure event notification. Access is automatically extended to all users in the same container that the printer object is in, while additional access must be granted.

To create a Controlled Access Printer, perform the steps in Procedure 3.6.

PROCEDURE 3.6

Creating a Controlled Access Printer

1. Go to NetWare Administrator, and click the container in which you want the printer object to reside.

2. Choose Object ➤ Create ➤ NDPS Printer. Click OK. The following dialog box will appear:

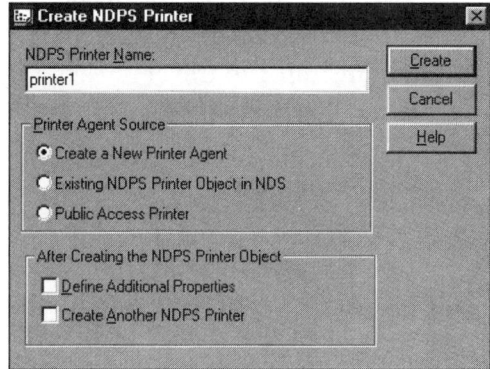

3. Choose a printer name. This name can include information related to its location or its container.

4. Choose either Create a New Printer Agent or Existing NDS Printer Object in NDS. (You could choose to make the printer a Public Access Printer by selecting the last circle, but we're creating a Controlled Access Printer in this Procedure.)

5. If you are creating a New Printer Agent, select an NDPS Manager and the gateway type (see Procedure 3.5). If you are choosing an Existing NDS Printer Object, go to Step 6.

6. Choose the printer drivers for each client's operating system.

7. Assign users, groups, or containers to the printer's Access Control list.

Workstation Configuration to Print to NDPS Printers

NDPS can automatically download print drivers from its large print driver database. This database resides centrally in NDPS and can be added to whenever necessary. This download function is available as long as client workstations are running Windows 3.1, Windows 95, or Windows NT.

NDPS will automatically designate a default printer for each workstation and each user, effectively eliminating the costly need for an administrator to travel to each physical location and perform a manual configuration.

There are two ways to configure the workstation to print to an NDPS printer:

- You can manually configure the workstation by using Novell Printer Manager.

- You can automatically download the drivers and configure the workstation's printing by configuring NDS.

To have a printer and its respective driver downloaded to your workstation, follow the steps in Procedure 3.7.

PROCEDURE 3.7

Configuring NDS to Download Print Drivers

1. Go to the details of the container where the users of the printer are located.

2. Go to the NDPS Remote Printer Management page.

3. Click the Add button under the Printers to Install to Workstations field.

4. Browse to the Printer Agent. Click the Printer Agent.

5. Click Update Driver.

6. Choose Set as Default (if desired).

Manually Configuring Workstations

Novell Printer Manager, shown in Figure 3.4, allows users to manage all of their printing needs from their workstations.

FIGURE 3.4

When you install the client software, a list of installed printers appears in the Novell Printer Manager window.

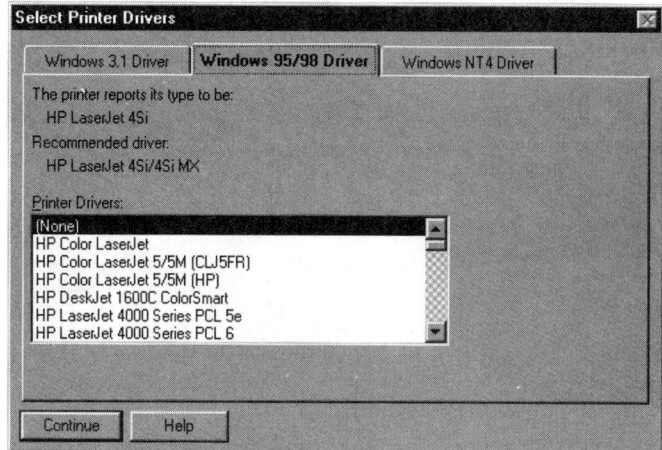

Novell Printer Manager allows you to:

- Access and upgrade the printer list
- Add printers to the list
- View a list of all print jobs
- Access the real-time status of those jobs
- Change the order of those jobs (security willing)
- Pause, delete, or resume printing jobs
- Submit jobs with a hold
- Configure the spooling of print jobs

To manually install a printer on a workstation, follow the steps in Procedure 3.8.

PROCEDURE 3.8

Manually Installing a Printer on the Workstation

1. Go to the PUBLIC/WIN32 directory, and type **NWPMW32**.

2. In the Printer menu, click New. The Novell Printers dialog box appears with a list of printers, as shown here.

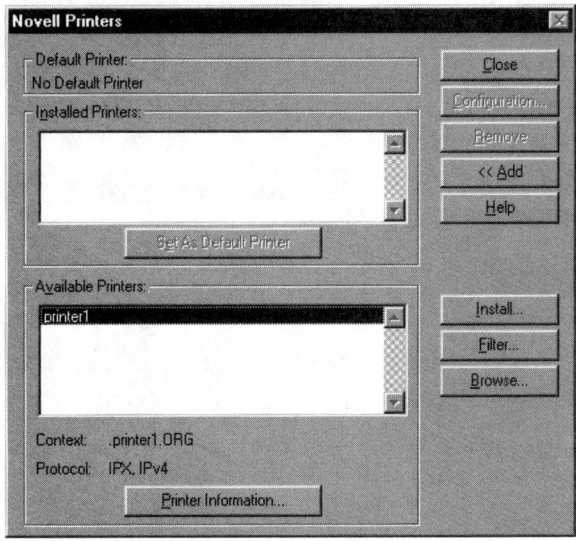

3. Click Add. A list of available printers will appear.

4. Click the desired printer, and then click Install.

5. Download the printer driver. Click OK.

6. Click Close.

After you have installed your printer, you can use the Filters dialog box, shown in Figure 3.5, to specify the printer's settings.

To then configure the printer, follow the directions in Procedure 3.9.

F I G U R E 3.5

The Novell Printers
Filter dialog box

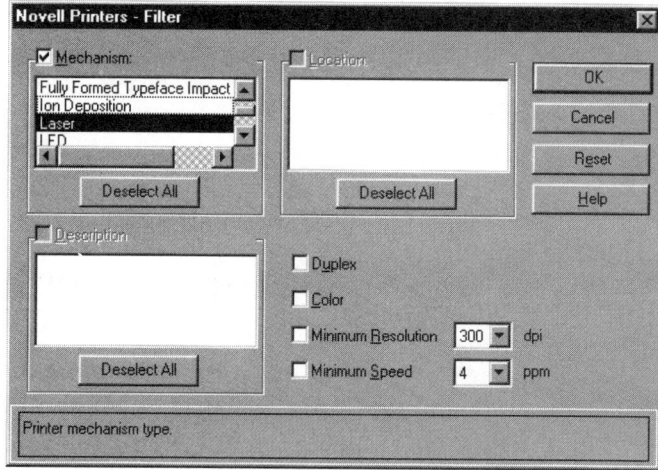

PROCEDURE 3.9

Configuring a Printer

1. Click New in the Printer menu.

2. Click Add.

3. Click Filter. The Filter dialog box will appear.

4. Choose the features you want for the printer. Click OK, which will bring up a list of the printers with the features you selected.

5. Choose the printer you desire. Click Install, which will place the printer in the Printer Manager window (indicating that it is ready to print).

Review

In this chapter, we took a hands-on tour through Novell's NDPS. We observed some of the new improvements over previous queue-based print services. We saw how much easier Public Access Printers are to use and install. We also saw how Controlled Access Printers allow greater flexibility when using bidirectional control and communications.

NDPS Elements

We learned that Novell Distributed Print Services contains the following four constituent elements:

- The NDPS Manager that was shown to manage the Printer Agents.

- The Printer Agent that combines the functionality of the printer object, print queue, spooler, and print server in one intelligent software entity.

- The NDPS Broker is the intelligent entity that manages the information for the Printer Agents. It includes three important support services:

  - Resource Management Services (RMS)

  - Service Registry Services (SRS)

  - Event Notification Services (ENS)

- The three gateways create an interface between HP, Xerox, and the remaining brands of printers and the NetWare 5 network.

NDPS Printing

We reviewed how Novell Printer Manager enables you to install and manage printing on client workstations.

So this is the New World of NetWare printing. This New World can make an administrator's job a lot easier. For complicated, multifunctional high-demand printers and competitive enterprise environments, NDPS just might bring order to a potentially chaotic office environment.

NDPS Practice Questions

1. A plug-and-print printer on Novell Distributed Print Services is also called a _____Printer.

2. A printer capable of bidirectional communication on Novell Distributed Print Services is also called a _____ Printer.

3. The new intelligent element that becomes the individual brain of each network Printer is called:

A. A print queue

B. A print server

C. The Printer Agent

D. A print object

4. For how long does a single NDPS Broker function in the network?

A. As long as the capture statement is functional

B. As long as there are Controlled Access Printers on the network

C. For three hops

D. For all servers within two hops

5. Which of the three gateways uses a Setup Wizard?

A. The Novell Gateway

B. The Hewlett Packard Gateway

C. The Epson Gateway

D. The Xerox Gateway

6. Which of the following statements regarding a Public Access Printer is not true?

    A. It allows plug-and-print freedom.

    B. You cannot configure it for hierarchical usage.

    C. It is managed through its NDS object.

    D. Its print job status can't be directed.

7. Regarding a Controlled Access Printer, which of the following is true?

    A. A full range of NetWare security options is denied.

    B. Bidirectional communications are not allowed.

    C. Access to users in a container must be individually granted on NDS.

    D. It is managed through NetWare Administrator.

8. Novell Printer Manager allows you to do which of the following? (Choose all that apply.)

    A. View a list of all print jobs

    B. Submit a job with a hold

    C. Access the real-time status of those jobs

    D. Pause, delete, or remove print jobs

    E. Change the printer gateway

    F. Access and upgrade the printer list

    G. Configure the spooling of print jobs

    H. Add printers to the list

    I. Check toner level

9. List the four elements that make up NDPS.

A. _____

B. _____

C. _____

D. _____

10. The minimum system requirements for an NDPS Server are 80MB of disk space and at least 8MB of RAM more than the minimum needed to run NetWare 5. (True or False.)

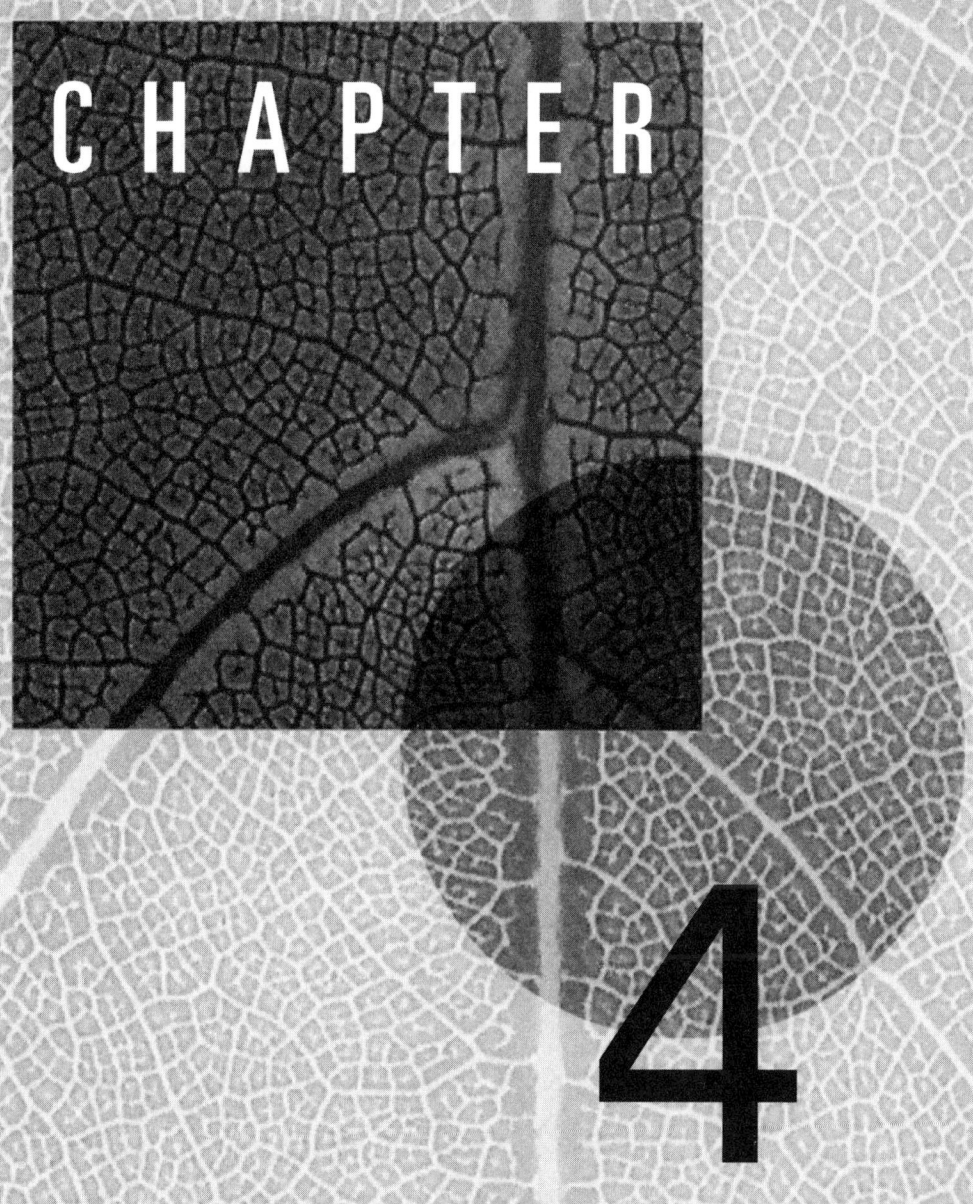

CHAPTER

4

Using TCP/IP with NetWare 5

Roadmap

This chapter covers the TCP/IP protocol suite and describes NetWare 5's TCP/IP support.

Topics Covered

- TCP/IP versus IPX/SPX

- TCP/IP protocols

- IP Addressing

- Host and domain naming

- NetWare 5's TCP/IP support modes

Skills You'll Learn

- Understand the TCP/IP protocols and the DOD model

- Choose an addressing scheme for an IP network

- Divide an IP network into subnets

- Understand IP host naming

- Install IP support on NetWare 5 servers and clients

Transmission Control Protocol/Internet Protocol (TCP/IP) is the suite of network protocols used with UNIX workstations and servers, and it is the basis of the Internet. These protocols range from basic communication protocols to specific protocols for messaging, file transfer, and other applications.

One of the most important new features of NetWare 5 is its support for TCP/IP. Although previous versions supported TCP/IP, they used a system that encapsulated packets using Novell's IPX and SPX protocols, which was not as efficient as true TCP/IP communication.

NetWare 5 supports TCP/IP directly as its primary protocol. It also includes an option, *Compatibility Mode*, that supports the traditional IPX/SPX system by encapsulating IPX packets within IP packets.

In this chapter, we'll first explore the basics of TCP/IP, which you may not be familiar with if you've worked exclusively with NetWare in the past. You'll also learn how to work with IP addressing. Finally, we'll look at NetWare 5's new TCP/IP support and how to implement it at clients and servers.

Understanding TCP/IP Basics

Transmission Control Protocol (TCP) and Internet Protocol (IP) are two communication protocols that an application can use to package its information for sending across a network or networks. For those acquainted with the traditional NetWare protocols, TCP is roughly equivalent to Sequenced Packet Exchange (SPX), and IP is roughly equivalent to Internetwork Packet Exchange (IPX).

The acronym TCP/IP also refers to an entire collection of protocols, or a *protocol suite*, based on TCP and IP. This protocol suite includes application protocols for functions such as e-mail, file transfers, and terminal emulation. It also has protocols that take application data and package it for transportation (for example, TCP and IP). There are also protocols for the physical transmission of data, such as Ethernet and Token Ring. All of these protocols are considered part of the TCP/IP protocol suite.

An example of an application protocol is the e-mail Simple Mail Transport Protocol (SMTP). E-mail programs running on personal computers, minicomputers, UNIX workstations, and even mainframes can use SMTP to exchange e-mail between applications. Most Internet mail clients use this protocol to send mail.

TCP/IP versus IPX/SPX

As a NetWare administrator, you are probably familiar with Novell's IPX and SPX protocols. They are the default protocols installed with NetWare 4.11 and earlier versions, and they are sufficient for basic networking. The TCP/IP protocols are intended for large-scale networks, such as the Internet; however, they are ideally suited to local intranets. With the release of NetWare 5, TCP/IP is the default protocol.

Before we cover the details of TCP/IP, you should be aware of the following basic differences between TCP/IP networks and IPX/SPX networks:

Hosts In IPX networks, there is usually a dedicated server—most likely a NetWare server—that offers services to the network. A TCP/IP network, however, can have any number of hosts. They may be dedicated servers or workstations. Any machine that offers a service to the network is referred to as a host.

Addressing You've learned the system of internal and external IPX network numbers used for IPX networks. Most of the time, you can assign these numbers yourself, with the only restriction being that there are no duplicates. TCP/IP addresses, as you'll learn later in this chapter, use strict rules. This is what allows TCP/IP to work on the Internet, despite the large number of machines.

Locating Hosts On an IPX network, your workstation locates the nearest server with the SAP protocol. Once you're logged in, the other servers you need to reach are catalogued by NDS. In a TCP/IP network, hosts are referred to by their addresses or names. A special type of server (DNS) exists to translate between names and addresses.

Security A typical Novell network is secure because workstations must log in and authenticate with NDS before using network resources. In a TCP/IP network, many services typically allow access to any user on the network without authentication. A hardware or software *firewall* is often used to add security to TCP/IP networks by refusing access to sites that are not trustworthy.

A Brief History of TCP/IP

In terms of computer networking, the 1950s and 1960s could be called "Before Internetworking." Almost all computer systems operated autonomously. They were not designed to connect to other computer systems. The hardware, operating systems, file formats, program interfaces, and other components were all designed to work with a particular type of computer system—and only that type.

In the late 1960s, the United States Department of Defense (DOD) became interested in some academic research concerning a packet-switched wide area network (WAN). The basic idea was to connect networks in multiple locations and allow data, in the form of packets, to be exchanged over the WAN.

The DOD's main interest in this technology was, not surprisingly, for national defense. They planned to create a fault-tolerant WAN that could carry command and control information in the event of a nuclear war. Because a network of this type would have sites in many locations, and data would be sent in a packet-switched manner, there would be no single point of failure in the system.

The research arm of the DOD was an agency called the Advanced Research Projects Agency (ARPA). This group's mission was to fund basic research that could possibly contribute to the defense effort. This agency funded and managed the project to create a packet-switched WAN. (ARPA was later disbanded and replaced by the Defense Advanced Research Projects Agency, or DARPA.)

This research lead to a standard set of application protocols that would be independent of the computer platforms and would create application-to-application communication. For instance, if a mainframe-based e-mail program and a PC-based e-mail program were both using the same standard protocol, they could exchange e-mail. This would be possible despite the use of two totally different systems. The same principle was used to create standard protocols for file transfers, terminal emulation, printing, network management, and many other areas.

In September 1969, the Advanced Research Projects Agency Network (ARPANET) connected four universities using 50Kbps voice lines and these protocols. Although the original purpose of this network was military in nature, it was soon used primarily for other purposes. Researchers at the different sites used the ARPANET to communicate with each other by sending files and electronic mail and by logging in to distant sites.

Because ARPANET was a government project and its details were available to the public, other universities, research organizations, and commercial organizations soon began to use this technology to create their own networks. Some of these networks were then connected to the ARPANET.

Over time, more and more networks were created with the TCP/IP protocols. Mainframes, minicomputers, and microcomputers became hardware platforms for these protocols. Likewise, software environments from Digital Equipment Corporation (DEC), International Business Machines (IBM), Novell, and many, many others developed products that supported TCP/IP.

Also, more and more of these networks began to connect to each other. There was originally one network, the ARPANET. After a time, there were many separate networks connected together. Eventually, all of the individual TCP/IP networks were interconnected to form the largest network on Earth— the *Internet*.

The TCP/IP Protocol Suite

The TCP/IP protocol suite can be viewed from a conceptual model called the *DOD networking model*. This model is similar in concept to the OSI reference model commonly used with NetWare protocols. Before we see how the DOD model compares with the OSI model, let's review the general concept of a reference model.

Understanding Reference Models

A *reference model* is a conceptual blueprint of how communications should take place. It addresses all the processes that are required for effective communication. These processes are divided into logical groupings, called *layers*.

Software developers can use a reference model to understand the communication process and to see what types of functions need to be accomplished at any one layer. If they are developing a protocol for a layer, all they need to concern themselves with is that layer's functions, not those of any other layer. The other functions will be handled by some other layer and protocol. The technical term for this concept is *binding*. The communication processes that are related to each other are *bound*, or grouped together, at a particular layer.

Advantages of Reference Models

The advantages of using a model are many. Because developers can focus on just one layer's functions, knowing that the other functions will be handled by a different layer, specialization is promoted. Likewise, if changes are made to one layer, those changes don't necessarily affect the other layers.

Another advantage is compatibility. If software developers adhere to the specifications outlined in the reference model, all protocols written to conform to that reference model should work together. This creates the potential for a large number of protocols to be written and used.

Physical and Logical Data Movement

Two additional concepts need to be addressed in a reference model:

- The physical movement of data

- The logical movement of data

As illustrated in Figure 4.1, the physical movement of data begins by going "down" the model.

For example, an application creates some information, which is passed down to a communication protocol for packaging and is then passed down to a transmission protocol for the actual physical

F I G U R E   4.1

Physical data flow
through a reference
model

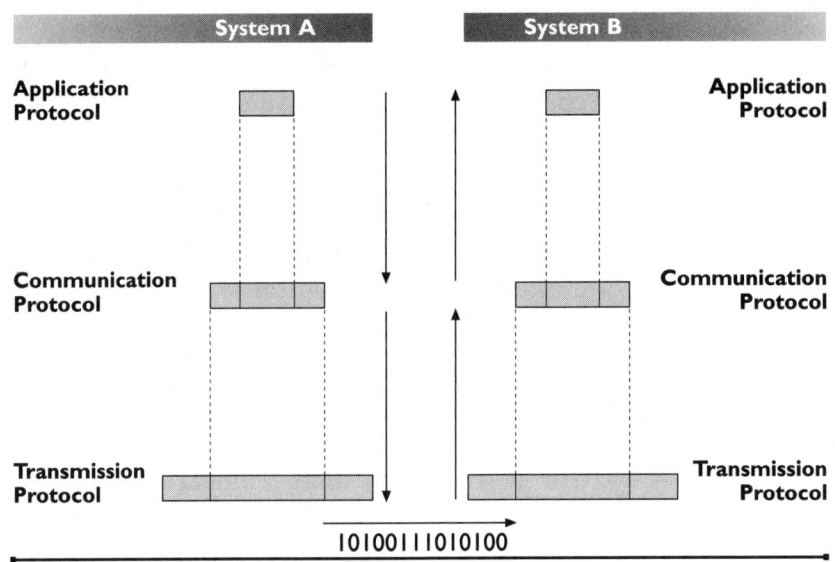

transmission. The data moves across the model, signifying movement across some type of physical channel (such as cable or radio frequency).

When the data reaches the destination computer, it then moves "up" the model. Each layer at the destination sees and acts only on the data that was packaged by its counterpart on the sending side. This is similar to the way you send a letter: post office employees see the addressing information you wrote on the envelope, but only the letter's recipient can read the letter itself.

The logical movement of data is another concept addressed in a reference model. From a logical perspective, each layer is only communicating with its counterpart on the other side, as illustrated in Figure 4.2. To continue our analogy, executives communicate with executives, secretaries communicate with secretaries, shipping personnel communicate with shipping personnel, and so on. This type of logical communication is called *peer-to-peer communication*.

FIGURE 4.2

Logical data flow
between OSI model
layers

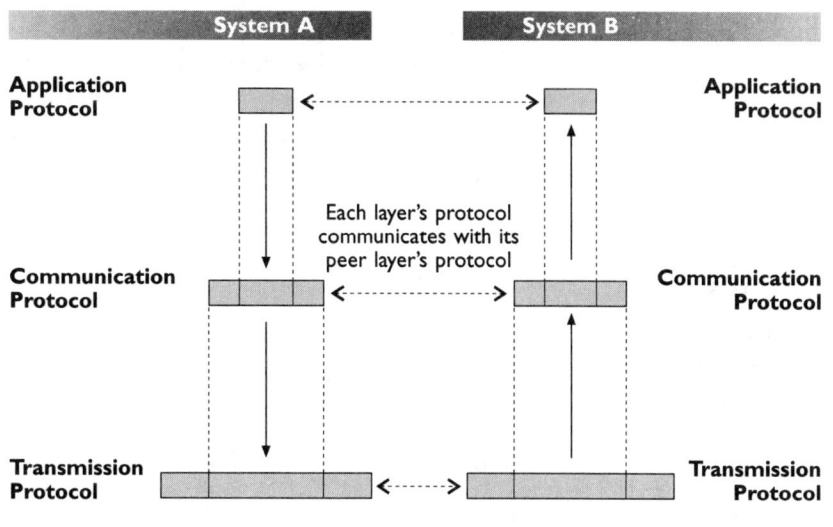

The OSI and DOD Reference Models

The open systems interconnect (OSI) reference model is a seven-layer communication model. It includes the following layers:

- Application
- Presentation
- Session
- Transport
- Network
- Data link
- Physical

The best way to understand this model is to organize the seven layers into larger pieces, which are illustrated in Figure 4.3. The top three layers (Application, Presentation, and Session) deal with functions that assist an application in its communication with another application. These layers deal with functions such as filename formats, code sets, user interfaces, compression, encryption, and other functions that relate to how one application will communicate with another application. They aren't concerned with transmission issues.

FIGURE 4.3

The layers of the OSI reference model can be grouped into larger layers.

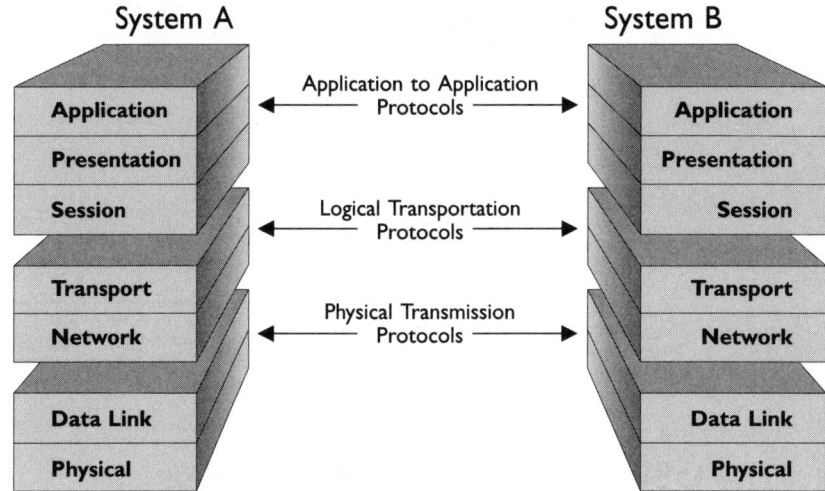

The next two layers (Transport and Network) deal with the logical issues of transmission. These layers shield the upper layers from the concerns of transmission by handling matters such as the size of the packets sent and received from each application, the degree of readability of packets reaching their destination, the logical addressing for each machine, and the routing of packets.

Finally, the bottom layers (Data Link and Physical) handle the physical transmission of data. These layers take what is passed down to them and put it into a format that can be sent over a physical transmission channel (like a cable).

The DOD model has fewer layers than the OSI model. Its four layers are:

Process/Application   Defines protocols for host-to-host application communication. It also controls user interface specifications.

Host-to-Host   Defines protocols for setting up the level of transmission service for the application. It can address the following issues:

Maintaining data integrity

Setting up reliable end-to-end communication

Ensuring error-free delivery of data

Sequencing of packets

Controlling the flow between the two applications

Internet   Defines protocols relating to the logical transmission of packets over the entire network. It can address the following issues:

Addressing of hosts, which is used to address packets

Routing of packets among multiple networks

Network Access   Defines protocols for the physical transmission of data.

Figure 4.4 shows a comparison of the four-layer DOD model and the seven-layer OSI reference model. As you can see, the two are similar in concept but have a different number of layers with different names.

The DOD Protocols

Although the DOD model and the OSI model are similar in design (similar types of functions happen at similar layers), the specifications for implementing their functions are different. This difference leads to a different suite of protocols for the DOD model than for the OSI model. Figure 4.5 summarizes how the protocols relate to the DOD model layers. We'll examine the layers and protocols in detail in the following sections.

FIGURE 4.4
Comparing the DOD
model and the OSI
model

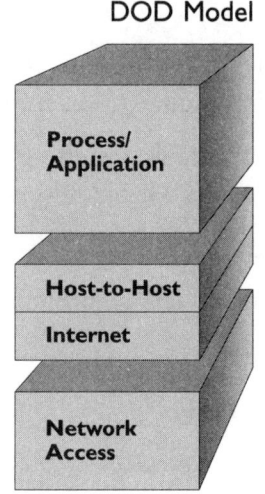 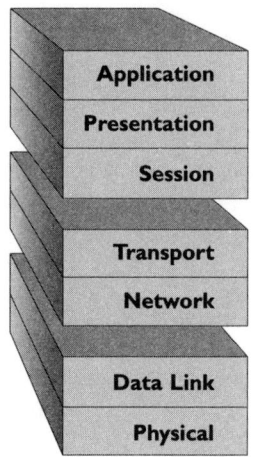

FIGURE 4.5
The protocols and
layers of the TCP/IP
protocol suite

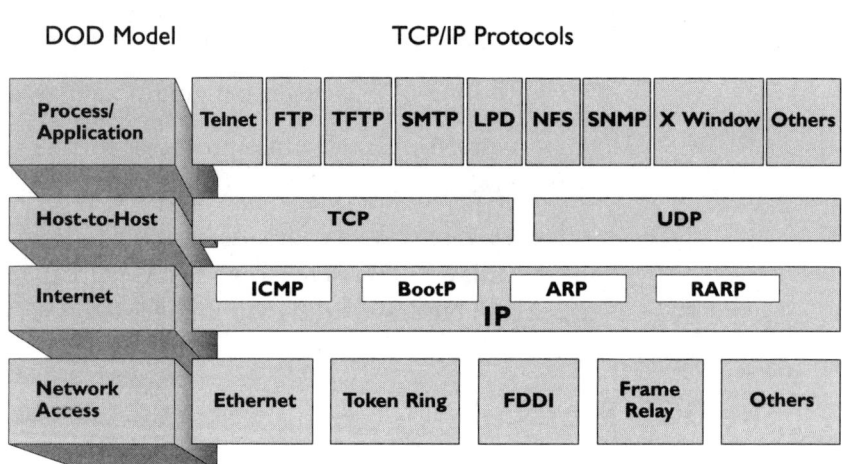

Process/Application Layer Protocols

As stated earlier, one of the design goals of the original creators of the
Internet was to enable applications running on different computer platforms to communicate. To accomplish this goal, the protocols of the

Process/Application layer were developed. They address the ability of one application to communicate with another application, regardless of the hardware platform, operating system platform, and other features of the two hosts.

Most of the applications written with TCP/IP protocols can be characterized as *client/server* applications. This means that there are two major parts to the software carrying out separate sets of tasks and probably running on two different machines.

The server software usually runs on the machine where the data resides. This machine tends to be powerful because much of the data processing, as well as storage, is performed on it. The client software sends requests to the server software for it to carry out. This can involve a search for information, printing, calculations, file transfers, and many other tasks. The server software is sometimes called a *daemon program*. Most daemon programs are usually running in what could be called *sleep* or *background* mode, which means that they are loaded but not actively doing anything. However, when certain events take place, such as a request from a client program, the daemon "wakes up" and carries out its assigned task.

Another function of the client software, in addition to sending requests to the server, is to provide an interface to the user. It can also allow the user to manipulate data that has been received from the server.

The following sections give a brief description of some of the protocols at the Process/Application layer of the DOD model.

Telnet (Terminal Emulation)   This protocol allows a user on a client machine, called the *telnet client*, to access the resources of another machine, called the *telnet server*, as if the client machine were a terminal directly attached to the telnet server.

FTP (File Transfer Protocol)   This protocol allows you to transfer files between any two machines that are using this protocol. It also allows you to access directories and files, and to perform certain types of directory operations (such as moving to a different directory). FTP transparently logs you into the FTP server (it uses telnet for this task) and then provides for the transfer of files.

TFTP (Trivial File Transfer Protocol)   TFTP is a stripped-down version of FTP. It doesn't do all of the functions of FTP, and it sends a much smaller amount of data than FTP. It also only allows you to access files to which any user would have rights.

HTTP (HyperText Transfer Protocol)   HTTP is the protocol used by the World Wide Web (WWW). This is a simple protocol that sends data in the form of HyperText Markup Language (HTML) documents to clients, called *Web browsers*.

NFS (Network File System)   The NFS protocol is designed for file sharing. NFS allows two different types of file systems to interoperate. For example, suppose that the NFS server software is running on a NetWare server, and the NFS client software is running on a UNIX host. This will allow a volume on the NetWare server to transparently store UNIX files and also be used by UNIX users. Even though the NetWare file system and the UNIX file system are different (they have different case-sensitivity, filename lengths, security, and so on), the UNIX users will be able to handle a file in their normal way, and the NetWare users can access the same file with their normal file system.

SMTP (Simple Mail Transport Protocol)   This protocol is designed to handle e-mail. SMTP uses a *spooled* (queued) method of mail delivery. Once a message has been sent to a destination, the message is spooled to some type of device, usually a disk. The server software at the destination periodically checks the spool for any messages and then delivers them to the recipient.

LPD (Line Printer Daemon)   This protocol is designed for printer sharing. LPD allows print jobs to be spooled and sent to network printers. Although created for use with UNIX machines, this specification is now supported by NetWare and Windows NT.

SNMP (Simple Network Management Protocol)   This protocol is for network management. SNMP provides for the collection and manipulation of network communication statistics and other information.

The official documentation on the Internet is referred to as Requests for Comments (RFCs). Each protocol has its own RFC, identified by a unique number. RFCs are also used by individuals, companies, and organizations to propose a new protocol or an improvement to an existing protocol, or to simply make comments on the state of the Internet. Anyone can receive electronic copies of these RFCs by using an anonymous FTP login at ds .internic.net or at any number of other hosts on the Internet.

Host-to-Host Layer Protocols

The goal of the host-to-host layer is to shield the upper-layer applications from the complexities of the network. This layer says to the upper layer, "Just give me your data, with any instructions, and I will begin the process of getting the information ready to send." The following sections describe the two main protocols at this layer.

TCP (Transmission Control Protocol)   TCP takes large blocks of information from an application and breaks them down into *segments*. It numbers and sequences each segment so that the destination's TCP protocol can put the segments back into the order the application intended.

Before it starts to send segments down the model, the sender's TCP protocol contacts the destination's TCP protocol in order to establish a connection. What is created is known as a *virtual circuit*. This type of communication is called *connection-oriented*. During this initial handshake, the two TCP layers also agree on the amount of information to be sent before the recipient TCP sends back an acknowledgment. This establishes reliable communication for the upper-layer application. TCP is also known as a *reliable* protocol, because the receiving end sends acknowledgments to the sender to indicate that packets were received correctly.

UDP (User Datagram Protocol)   UDP is a connectionless protocol and does not use a virtual circuit. This protocol can be used instead of TCP (but not at the same time). UDP is considered to be a *thin protocol* because it does not do all the things TCP does. It is an *unreliable* protocol, meaning acknowledgments are not sent for received packets. UDP receives upper-layer blocks of information and breaks them into segments. Each segment is given a number for reassembly into the intended block at the destination. This protocol does *not* create a virtual circuit. It does *not* contact the destination before beginning delivery. Therefore, it is considered a *connectionless* protocol.

UDP doesn't allow for the acknowledgment of received segments. It is, therefore, termed an *unreliable* protocol. This doesn't mean that UDP is ineffective—only that this particular protocol doesn't handle issues of reliability. UDP also doesn't sequence the segments. Each segment does have a number for reassembly purposes, but UDP doesn't care in what order the segments arrive at the destination.

Because UDP doesn't do everything that TCP does, UDP is a smaller protocol and takes up less overhead on each machine.

Key Concepts of Host-to-Host Protocols Here are some of the attributes you should remember concerning TCP and UDP:

TCP has the following characteristics:

- Connection-oriented

- Sequenced

- Reliable (acknowledged)

UDP has these characteristics:

- Connectionless

- Unsequenced

- Unreliable (no acknowledgements)

- Low overhead

A telephone analogy may help you understand how TCP works. For you to talk to someone using the telephone, you must first establish a connection by dialing the other person's number. This is like the TCP protocol's virtual circuit. Periodically during the conversation, you might say, "Did you get that?" This is like a TCP acknowledgment.

You might also periodically ask, "Are you still there?" and end the conversation with "Goodbye." TCP performs these types of functions.

By contrast, UDP is similar to sending a postcard. To send a postcard, you don't need to contact the other party first. You simply write your message, address it, and mail it. This is analogous to UDP's connectionless orientation. Because the information on the postcard is probably not a matter of life or death, the recipient does not need to send you an acknowledgment of its receipt. Similarly, UDP doesn't send acknowledgments.

The term *unreliable* doesn't necessarily mean that a protocol can't be counted on—it simply means that it does not guarantee reliability by sending acknowledgments for packets.

Internet Layer Protocols

The Internet layer has two main purposes:

- Routing

- Providing a single network interface to the upper layers

None of the upper-layer protocols have any functions related to routing. Likewise, the protocols below the Internet layer do not have anything to do with routing. The Internet layer's job is to carry out routing-related functions. The main protocol of this layer, the Internet Protocol (IP), could be said to "see" all the interconnected networks. It can do this because all the machines on the network have a software address called an IP address. (IP addressing will be covered in detail later in this chapter.)

The IP protocol looks at each packet's IP address. Then, using a routing protocol, it decides where this packet is to be sent next. The Network Access layer protocols (at the bottom of the model) don't see the entire network; they deal with only point-to-point physical links. It's up to IP to handle the routing issue.

The second main reason for the Internet layer is to provide a single interface to the upper-layer protocols. Without this layer, the application programmers would need to write the "hooks" for each different Network Access protocol into their applications. This would lead to different versions of each application: one for Ethernet, one for Token Ring, and so on. To prevent this situation, the Internet layer provides one single network interface for the upper-layer protocols. IP is the protocol that accomplishes this. It's then the job of IP and the various Network Access protocols to work together.

All of the other protocols at this layer, as well as all of the upper-layer protocols, use IP. All paths through the model go through IP. The following sections describe the protocols at the Internet layer.

IP (Internet Protocol)   This protocol takes segments from the Host-to-Host layer and fragments them into *datagrams* (packets). IP also reassembles datagrams into segments on the receiving side. Each datagram is assigned the IP address of the sender and the IP address of the recipient. Each IP machine that receives a datagram makes routing decisions based on the datagram's destination IP address.

ARP (Address Resolution Protocol)   When the IP protocol has a datagram to send, it has already been informed by upper-layer protocols of the destination's IP address. But IP must also inform the Network Access layer protocol (such as Ethernet) of the destination's hardware address. If IP doesn't know the hardware address, it uses the ARP protocol to find this information. ARP interrogates the network by sending a broadcast asking the machine with the specified IP address to reply with its hardware address.

ARP is, therefore, able to translate a software address (the IP address) into a hardware address (for example, the destination machine's Ethernet board address). This hardware address is technically referred to as the *media access control (MAC) address*.

RARP (Reverse Address Resolution Protocol)   When an IP machine happens to be a diskless machine, it has no way of initially knowing its IP address. However, it does know its MAC address. The RARP protocol sends out a packet that includes its MAC address along with a request to be told which IP address it has been assigned. A designated machine, called a *RARP server*, responds with the answer. RARP, therefore, uses its MAC address to learn its IP address.

BootP and DHCP   BootP is another protocol used by diskless workstations. Using this protocol, a diskless machine can learn its IP address, the IP address of a server machine, and the name of a file that is to be loaded into memory and executed at boot up. DHCP (Dynamic Host Configuration Protocol) is an enhanced version of BootP that is used to dynamically assign IP addresses to network clients. NetWare 5 includes a DHCP server.

ICMP (Internet Control Message Protocol)   ICMP is a *management protocol* for IP. The following are some of the events and messages that ICMP relates:

Destination unreachable   If a router can't send an IP datagram any further, it uses ICMP to send this message back to the sender.

Buffer full   If a router's memory buffer for receiving incoming datagrams is full, it will use ICMP to send out this message.

Time-to-live expired   Each IP datagram is allotted a certain number of routers, or *hops*, it may go through before giving up. If it reaches its hop limit before it arrives at its destination, the last router to receive that datagram throws it away and uses ICMP to inform the sending machine of this occurrence.

Network Access Layer Protocols

The protocols at the Network Access layer are responsible for many functions, all related to the physical transmission of data. Here are this layer's main functions:

- Receiving an IP datagram and framing it into a stream of bits (ones and zeros) for physical transmission. The information at this layer is called a frame.

- Specifying the MAC address. Even though the Internet layer determines the destination MAC address, the Network

Access layer protocols actually place that MAC address in the frame.

- Ensuring that the stream of bits making up the frame have been accurately received.

- Specifying the access methods to the physical network, such as contention-based for Ethernet and token-passing for Token Ring.

- Specifying the physical media, the connectors, electrical signaling, and so on.

Some of the technologies that implement this layer are:

- LAN-oriented protocols:

  - Ethernet (thick coaxial cable, thin coaxial cable, twisted-pair cable)

  - Token Ring

  - ARCnet

  - FDDI (Fiber Distributed Data Interface)

- WAN-oriented protocols:

  - Point-to-Point Protocol (PPP)

  - X.25

  - Frame Relay

Identifying Machines with IP Addressing

One of the most important topics in any discussion of TCP/IP is *IP addressing*. An IP address is a numeric identifier assigned to a machine on an IP network. The IP address designates where a machine resides. This address is a software address and is not hard-coded in the machine or network interface card.

How IP Addressing Works

An IP address is made up of 32 bits of information. These 32 bits are divided into four bytes (octets). There are two methods of depicting an IP address:

- Dotted-decimal, as in 130.57.30.56

- Binary, as in 10000010.00111001.00011110.00111000

Both of these examples represent the same IP address.

The 32-bit IP address could have been used in a flat, or nonhierarchical, manner. A social security number is an example of a flat addressing scheme. There's no structure or partition to the number. If this method had been used to identify Internet addresses, every machine on the Internet would need a totally unique address.

A benefit of a flat-addressing scheme is that it could handle a large number of addresses, namely 4.2 billion. However, this scheme would make routing difficult. Because every address is totally unique, every router on the Internet would need to store the addresses of every machine on the Internet. If even a fraction of the possible addresses were used, routing would be impossible.

The solution to this dilemma was to use a two-level hierarchical addressing scheme. An example of a hierarchical addressing scheme is a telephone number, which includes an area code, a local calling area, and a customer number.

Rather than treating the entire 32 bits of an Internet address as a unique identifier, part of the address is designated as a network address and the rest of the address is treated as a node address:

- The *network address* is unique to each network. Every machine on the same network shares that network address as part of its IP address. In the IP address 130.57.30.56, the **130.57** is the network address.

- The *node address* is a unique number assigned to each machine on a network. This number must be different from the number assigned to any other machine on that particular network. It identifies a particular machine rather than the specific network.

This number can also be referred to as a *host address*. In the sample IP address 130.57.30.56, the **30.56** is the node address.

How the IP address is subdivided into a network address and a node address is determined by the *class* designation of your network. The designers of the Internet decided to create classes of networks, based on network size. For the small number of networks that have a very large number of nodes, they created the class A designation. At the other extreme is the class C network, for the large number of networks with a small number of nodes. Medium-sized networks are called class B networks. Table 4.1 provides a summary of the three classes of networks, which are described in more detail in the following sections.

T A B L E 4.1:   The Three Classes of IP Addresses

Class	Format	Leading Bit Pattern	Decimal Range of First Byte of Network Address	Maximum Nodes per Network
A	Net.Node.Node.Node	0	1-127	16,777,216
B	Net.Net.Node.Node	10	128-191	65,534
C	Net.Net.Net.Node	110	192-223	254

In the interest of efficient routing, the Internet designers defined a mandate for the leading bits of each network class. For example, because a router knows that a class A network address always starts with a zero, it might be able to route a packet after reading only the first bit of its address. Figure 4.6 illustrates how the leading bits of a network address are defined.

Some IP addresses are reserved for special purposes. Table 4.2 lists these reserved addresses. These addresses shouldn't be assigned to nodes by network administrators.

FIGURE 4.6

Leading bits of a
network address

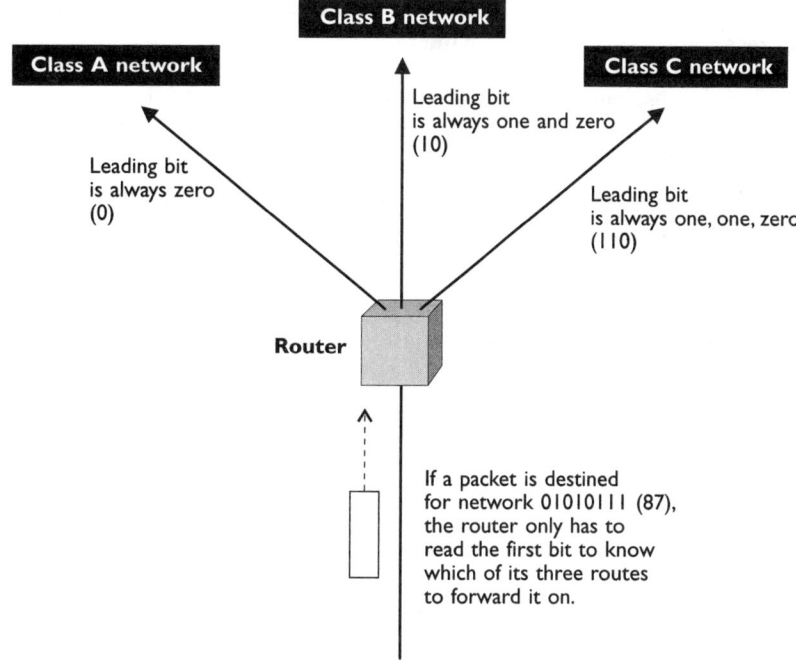

TABLE 4.2: Reserved IP Addresses

Address	Function
Network address of all 0s	Interpreted to mean "this network."
Network address of all 1s	Interpreted to mean "all networks."
Network address 127	Reserved for loopback tests. Designates the local node and allows that node to send a test packet to itself without generating network traffic.
Node address of all 0s	Interpreted to mean "this node."
Node address of all 1s	Interpreted to mean "all nodes" on the specified network. For example, 128.2.255.255 means all nodes on class B network 128.2.

T A B L E 4.2: Reserved IP Addresses *(Continued)*

Address	Function
Entire IP address set to all 0s	Used by the Router Information Protocol (RIP) to designate the default route.
Entire IP address set to all 1s (same as `255.255.255.255`)	Broadcasts to all nodes on the current network.

Class A Networks

In a class A network, the first byte is assigned to the network address, and the remaining three bytes are used for the node address. The format is:

`Network.Node.Node.Node`

For example, in the IP address `49.22.102.70`, **49** is the network address, and **22.102.70** is the node address. Every machine on this particular network has the network address of **49**.

Because class A network addresses have a length of one byte and the first bit of that byte is set to zero to indicate a class A address, seven bits remain for manipulation. This means that the maximum number of class A networks that could be created is 2^7, or 128. But an address of all zeros is also reserved, so the actual number of usable class A network addresses is 2^7 minus 1, or 127.

Each class A network has three bytes (24 bit positions) for the node address of a machine. This means there are 2^{24} or 16,777,216 unique combinations and, therefore, that many unique node addresses for each class A network.

Because addresses with the two patterns of all zeros and all ones are reserved, the actual maximum number of nodes per class A network is 2^{24} minus 2, or 16,777,214.

Class B Networks

In a class B network, the first two bytes are assigned to the network address, and the remaining two bytes are used for node addresses. The format is:

Network.Network.Node.Node

For example, in the IP address 130.57.30.56, the network address is **130.57**, and the node address is **30.56**.

Because the network address has two bytes, there would be 2^{16} unique combinations. However, the Internet designers decided that class B networks should start with the bits 1 and 0. This leaves 14 bit positions to manipulate and, therefore, 2^{14} or 16,384 unique class B networks.

Setting the first two bits to 1 and 0 means that class B networks have first bytes ranging from 128 to 191. Therefore, even though there are 16,384 different class B networks, you can always easily distinguish a class B network by looking at its first byte. If it's in the range of decimal 128 to 191, it's a class B network.

A class B network has two bytes to use for node addresses. This is 2^{16}, minus the two patterns that are reserved (all zeros and all ones), for a total of 65,534 possible node addresses for each class B network.

Class C Networks

The first three bytes of a class C network address are dedicated to the network portion of the address, with only one byte remaining for the node address. The format is:

Network.Network.Network.Node

For example, in the IP address 198.21.74.102, the network address is **198.21.74**, and the node address is **102**.

In a class C network, the first three bit positions are always binary 110. The network address is three bytes or 24 bits, minus the three reserved bits. This leaves 21 bit positions. There are, therefore, 2^{21} or 2,097,152 possible class C networks.

The first byte of class C networks ranges from 192 to 223. Although there are a total of 2,097,152 possible class C networks, you can always identify a network with a first byte in this range as class C.

Each class C network has one byte to use for node addresses. This means that there are 2^8 or 256, minus the two reserved patterns of all zeros and all ones, for a total of 254 node addresses for each class C network.

Other Classes of Networks

An additional class of networks is class D. This range of addresses is used for *multicast* packets. These addresses range from 224.0.0.0 to 239.255.255.255.

A multicast transmission is used when a host wants to transmit the same data to multiple destinations. For example, it's used when a host is attempting to learn the addresses of all routers on the network. The host uses the ICMP protocol to send out a *router discovery packet*. This packet is addressed to 224.0.0.2, identifying it as a multicast packet that will be sent to all routers on the network.

There is also a class E range of addresses running from 240.0.0.0 to 255.255.255.255. These addresses are reserved for future use. Because these addresses are reserved for special functions, you shouldn't assign class D or E addresses to any node on your network.

Another special range of addresses is the Class C range 192.168.0.0 to 192.168.0.255. These are reserved as nonroutable addresses, and cannot be used on the Internet.

Understanding Subnet Masking

Class C network addresses for the Internet are still available but are running out. The implementation of a new version of IP, IPv6, will solve this problem, but in the meantime there is a solution that works in most cases. *Subnet masking* is a technique for using part of the network address portion of the IP address to subdivide the network into smaller networks. Although subnet masking doesn't allow more than 254 machines in a class C network to be used on the Internet, it does allow a greater number to be used within a network.

This technique involves assigning a subnet address, or mask, to each machine on the network. This mask extracts the machine address from the IP address. This basically allows you to divide the network address and node address in the middle of a byte, providing a wider variety of options than are available with strict class A, B, and C addresses.

The subnet mask is a 32-bit binary number, similar to an IP address. The left portion of the mask consists of set (1) bits that indicate that the corresponding portion of the IP address should be treated as a network address, and the right portion consists of unset (0) bits that indicate that this portion of the IP address is treated as a node address. When you use subnet masking, you are basically borrowing bits from the node address (thus reducing the number of available nodes per network) and using them as a subnet address.

If a network is not divided into subnets, you should set the subnet mask for clients and servers to the default mask for the IP address class: 255.0.0.0 for class A, 255.255.0.0 for class B, or 255.255.255.0 for class C.

Using Host and Domain Names

You may have noticed that dealing with IP addresses is not particularly convenient for humans. To make IP addresses easier for humans to deal with, the Internet also uses a system of more accessible names for sites. These names are referred to as host names and domain names:

- A *host name* is the name of a machine on the Internet; this corresponds to the node portion of an IP address.

- Companies and organizations on the Internet are assigned *subdomain names* which can be used with several different hosts.

- A *domain name* specifies the type of organization or country. These include: com for company names, org for nonprofit organizations, net for network providers, mil for the U.S. military, gov for the U.S. government, and edu for educational institutions. International domains specify a standard two-letter country code. International domains are sometimes divided into subdomains based on their functions.

Table 4.3 lists a few examples of host and domain names with descriptions, ranging from simple to complex.

T A B L E 4.3:   Host and Domain Names

Subdomain	Refers To
sybex.com	The main machine in the subdomain named sybex in the com (company) domain
ftp.novell.com	A machine named ftp in the novell subdomain and the com (company) domain
www.starlingtech.com	A machine called www in the starlingtech subdomain and the com (company) domain

Address Resolution

Each host name corresponds with an IP address. Because the IP address is required to make a connection, the host name must be *resolved,* or converted, to an IP address. This is a service performed by *name servers.* These servers use a system called DNS (Domain Name System) to return information about a host name. Name servers exist for each domain and subdomain.

In a local TCP/IP network, DNS is unnecessary. You can simply use a *host table* to define IP addresses for hosts. The host table for a NetWare server is located at SYS:ETC\HOSTS by default.

Registering IP Addresses and Domain Names

IP addresses for the Internet are maintained by the InterNIC, a nonprofit organization assigned the task by the U.S. government, which originally funded it. It is now independently operated and funded through domain registration fees. For further information contact:

> Network Solutions
> InterNIC Registration Services
> 505 Huntmar Park Drive
> Herndon, VA 22070

You can also contact the InterNIC online at these addresses:

- E-mail: `hostmaster@internic.net`

- World Wide Web: `http://rs.internic.net/`

Of course, if your network isn't connected to the Internet, you can assign IP addresses in any manner you please—but you'll be in for a headache if you ever decide to add Internet connectivity.

NetWare 5 and TCP/IP

NetWare 4.*x* and earlier versions supported TCP/IP. However, they did this by encapsulating TCP/IP packets within IPX packets. Although this allowed NetWare to interoperate with other network operating systems, UNIX, and the Internet, it is not the most efficient way to handle TCP/IP.

With NetWare 5, the Pure IP feature was introduced. This means NetWare 5 supports TCP/IP directly, without encapsulation. You can configure a NetWare 5 server with no protocols except TCP/IP— in fact, this is the default choice during the installation.

NetWare 5 still supports IPX. You can choose to support IPX directly, support both IP and IPX, or support Pure IP. In the Pure IP configuration, IPX is still supported, but in the same way that older versions supported TCP/IP. It encapsulates IPX packets within TCP/IP packets. Although this will allow your NetWare 5 server to communicate with older NetWare servers, it isn't as efficient as a native IPX system.

To take advantage of NetWare 5's TCP/IP support, you should use Pure IP whenever possible, and upgrade all of the NetWare servers in the network if possible to avoid using IPX. However, because IPX support is available, you can implement this change gradually.

If you're using NetWare 5 in a network that also includes Windows NT servers, Pure IP is a good choice. As of NT 4, TCP/IP is the default protocol for Windows NT.

Supporting TCP/IP with NetWare 5

The NetWare 5 installation program allows you to choose whether to enable IP support, IPX support, or both on the server. If you install TCP/IP support, you'll need to specify an appropriate IP address and subnet mask. This process is explained in detail in Chapter 2.

The NetWare 5 client also supports Pure IP. When installing the client, you can choose IP, IPX, or both, as shown in Figure 4.7. The client is part of the Z.E.N.works suite, which is described in detail in Chapters 6 and 7. As with the server, the client can support IP, IPX, or both. The IPX option allows a client to connect to older servers as well as NetWare 5 servers running IPX.

To switch entirely to IP, you will need to upgrade all of the workstations on the network to handle TCP/IP. You can do this by installing the latest version of the client software, as described in Procedure 4.1. These instructions are for Windows 95/98; other client operating systems use a similar procedure.

FIGURE 4.7

The NetWare 5 client
allows you to support
IP, IPX, or both.

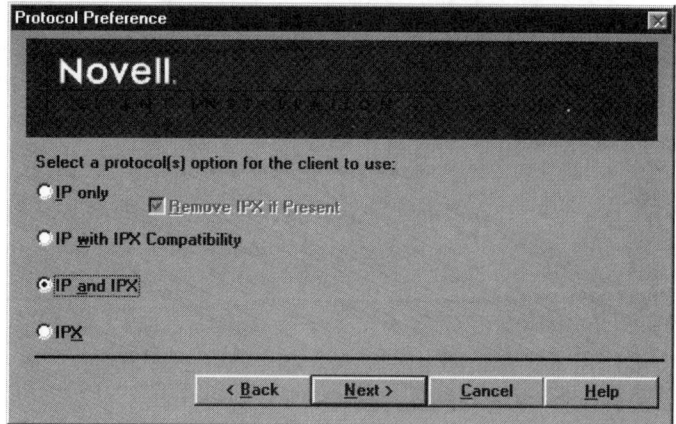

FIGURE 4.7

The NetWare 5 client
allows you to support
IP, IPX, or both.

PROCEDURE 4.1

Installing the New NetWare 5 Client Software for IP Support

1. Insert the NetWare 5 Client CD-ROM on the workstation. The installation program will load automatically.

2. A list of supported languages is displayed. Click English (or your choice of language).

3. Next, a menu of installation options is displayed. Click the Windows 95/98 Client option.

4. A list of client products is displayed. Choose Install Novell Client.

5. The client license agreement is displayed. Click Yes to accept the terms of the agreement and continue.

6. You are asked to choose between Typical and Custom installation options. Choose Custom, and click Next to continue.

7. Four protocol choices are displayed: IP Only, IP with IPX Compatibility, IP and IPX, and IPX only. Choose one of the first three choices, as described in the next section, then click Next.

8. You are prompted to choose either NDS (NetWare 4/5) or Bindery (NetWare 3) connections. Choose NDS and click Next.

9. A list of optional client components is displayed. Check the ones you wish to install, and click Install to begin the installation.

10. The client files are now copied. After the installation is complete, you must reboot the computer to log on to the network.

TCP/IP Support Options

Depending on how you configure them, NetWare 5 clients and servers will run in one of three modes:

- Pure IP mode, which handles IP and does not support IPX

- IPX mode, the traditional protocol

- IP Compatibility Mode, which uses Pure IP, but can support IPX by encapsulating IPX packets within IP packets

Because NetWare 5 is most efficient with the TCP/IP protocols, Compatibility Mode is mainly intended as a tool to be used during migration of an IPX network. After all of the clients and servers support IP, Compatibility Mode can be turned off to make the network more efficient.

NetWare 5 TCP/IP Services

Along with its integrated support for Pure IP, NetWare 5 includes a number of TCP/IP-related services that can be used on the server. These include the following:

- DNS (Domain Name Service) is a protocol that translates host names (such as novell.com) to IP addresses. NetWare 5 includes a DNS server.

- DHCP (Dynamic Host Configuration Protocol) allows you to dynamically allocate IP addresses from a pool of available addresses. NetWare 5 also includes a DHCP server.

- LDAP (Lightweight Directory Access Protocol) is a distributed protocol for directory services (information about users and other objects). NetWare 5 includes an LDAP server component that makes the information in the NDS directory available to clients using this protocol.

- Netscape FastTrack Web Server was developed jointly by Novell and Netscape. It allows the NetWare server to operate as a full-featured Web (HTTP) server. This feature is covered in Chapter 8.

Migrating Networks to TCP/IP

Although using Pure IP in a network provides a number of advantages, the process of migrating to TCP/IP can be complicated. NetWare 5 includes a number of components that can assist in the migration process. Although there is no dedicated migration utility, NetWare 5 features, such as IPX Compatibility Mode, are designed to allow both small and large NetWare networks to be migrated gradually to Pure IP support.

IP Migration Components

Migrating to TCP/IP can have an impact on every component of your network. Several components of NetWare 5 have features that are designed to make IP migration easier. These features are described in the following sections.

The Migration Agent

The *Migration Agent*, also known as the *Migration Gateway*, is a component that runs on a NetWare 5 server and provides connectivity between IP and IPX sections of the network. If this component is used on a server with both IPX and IP support and connected to both the IP and IPX portions of the network, it can act as a router between the two protocols.

Depending on the migration strategy you choose and the complexity of your network, the IP migration process may require a single Migration Agent or several. Networks with only a few servers can be upgraded without the use of a Migration Agent.

NetWare Clients and Servers

One of the most important features of NetWare 5 is that the core server and client software are protocol-independent. Although previous versions of the NetWare server were heavily dependent on the IPX protocol and could not support any other protocol with full efficiency, NetWare 5 is built to be protocol-independent. This allows the server to support IPX, IP, or both in a more efficient manner.

When you configure a NetWare 5 server or client with IP only, drivers to support IPX Compatibility Mode are installed. These drivers encapsulate IPX packets into IP packets and communicate with IPX-only machines by supporting a virtual IPX network. Because of this encapsulation, IPX connectivity is not as fast as in a Pure IP or IPX network. If you do not plan to upgrade to IP, configuring servers with IPX support rather than Compatibility Mode will increase efficiency.

NDS (Novell Directory Services)

Another important component of the IP migration process is NDS. The version of NDS supported in NetWare 5 is designed to work with IP-only, IPX-only, and mixed networks without causing synchronization problems. This allows you to migrate a large network gradually to full IP support without losing the integrity of the NDS database.

SLP (Service Location Protocol)

SLP is an Internet-standard protocol that allows clients to *discover*, or locate, network services. Because SLP eliminates some of the configuration tasks normally necessary when configuring a TCP/IP network, using it can streamline the IP migration process. SLP is described in Chapter 11.

DNS and DHCP

NetWare 5 also includes support for two Internet-standard protocols that can make the process of configuring an IP network easier:

- DNS (Domain Name Service) converts user-friendly host names to numeric IP addresses.

- DHCP (Dynamic Host Configuration Protocol) dynamically allocates IP addresses to clients from a pool of available addresses.

DNS and DHCP are fully explained in Chapters 9 and 10, respectively.

Choosing a Migration Strategy

The difficulty of the IP migration process depends on the size and complexity of your network. As an extreme example, a multinational network with hundreds of servers may take a year or longer to completely migrate to Pure IP. Conversely, a small company with a single server can migrate to IP almost instantly as part of the NetWare 5 installation process.

You should plan a strategy for IP migration based on these factors, and on your needs and priorities. The following sections describe some typical migration strategies.

Running IP and IPX Concurrently

In some cases, you might be happy with the current performance of your network, but want to add IP support to enable communication with the Internet or another IP network. In this scenario, the simplest approach is to upgrade the server or servers to NetWare 5 using the IP and IPX option.

In this configuration, the servers support both protocols. Because the existing clients are configured to use IPX, the network will not gain efficiency through the use of IP communications. However, the servers will support both protocols and can, therefore, be used as gateways to the Internet or other IP networks. This strategy does not require the use of a Migration Agent.

Migrating the Backbone

If you do choose to migrate the network to Pure IP, you can do this quickly or slowly, and you can migrate the various clients and servers on the network in any order. One strategy is to begin by upgrading the network *backbone* (the portion of the network that carries the highest traffic and is used to connect other segments together). Migrating the backbone can often provide immediate benefits, because IP routers and other components are efficient and inexpensive.

For this strategy, you will need one or more Migration Agents in each of the network segments. These will act as gateways between the IPX and IP portions of the network. The Migration Agent will communicate by using IPX with other machines in the same segment and by using IP with other Migration Agents across the backbone.

After all of the segments have been connected to the IP backbone with Migration Agents, you can upgrade the client workstations and gradually eliminate the use of IPX Compatibility Mode.

Migrating Network Segments

You can also migrate individual network segments one at a time. To accomplish this, you first upgrade one or more servers in the segment to NetWare 5 and configure them to act as Migration Agents. You can then gradually upgrade the remaining clients and servers, configuring them for IP support only. After all components within the segment are migrated, the Migration Agent can maintain connectivity with any other segments that have not yet been upgraded for IP support.

Configuring Compatibility Mode

NetWare 5 includes a NetWare Loadable Module, SCMD.NLM, that handles the server component of IPX Compatibility Mode. This component can also provide the Migration Agent service. When you install a new NetWare 5 server and choose IP only for the protocol, this NLM is automatically configured to load and support Compatibility Mode. For an upgraded server, you can load the NLM manually. Procedure 4.2 describes the process of configuring Compatibility Mode on a Net-Ware 5 server.

PROCEDURE 4.2

Configuring an Upgraded Server for IPX Compatibility Mode

1. First, you must unbind IPX from the server's network card. You can do this using the INETCFG utility. Type **INETCFG** at the server console. Choose the Protocols option, then remove IPX from the list of protocols.

2. After removing IPX support, take down and restart the server.

3. Next, start the INETCFG utility again. Select Protocols, then enable the TCP/IP option.

4. You are prompted for the IP address, subnet mask, and other IP information for the server. Specify this information, then press ESC to exit and save the settings.

5. After adding TCP/IP support, take down and restart the server.

6. Type **LOAD SCMD** at the server console to load the Compatibility Mode component.

Compatibility Mode Options

After you have installed Compatibility Mode, you can use the SET command at the server console to change options for the Compatibility Mode component. The following options are available:

SET CMD Network Number   Specify the IPX external network number that the Compatibility Mode system will use. This is a hexadecimal number. By default, this option is set to FFFFFFFD.

SET Preferred Migration Agents List   Specify a list of IP addresses for Migration Agents. These will be used to communicate with IPX-only portions of the network. If this option is not specified, the SLP protocol will be used to determine the Migration Agents to use.

SET CMD Preferred IP Address   If the server has more than one IP address, specify the address that the Compatibility Mode system will use for encapsulated IPX packets.

Configuring Migration Agents

NetWare 5 servers can also be configured to act as Migration Agents using the SCMD.NLM component. Procedure 4.3 explains how to configure a Migration Agent.

PROCEDURE 4.3

Configuring a Server to Act as a Migration Agent

1. Install Compatibility Mode on the server, as described earlier in this chapter.

2. Type **UNLOAD SCMD** at the server console to unload the Compatibility Mode component.

3. Using the INETCFG utility, add a binding for IPX to the server's network card.

4. Reload the SCMD component. This time, type **LOAD SCMD /g** to enable the Migration Agent (gateway) feature.

When you are using Migration Agents to communicate with an IP backbone, an additional option is needed in the LOAD command for the Compatibility Mode driver. Type **LOAD SCMD /g /bs** to enable backbone support.

NetWare IP Synchronization

As you should know, if you manage a NetWare network, NDS uses a system of partitions (portions of the Directory tree) and replicas (stored copies of a partition's database). To keep replicas synchronized between servers, NDS uses a process called *synchronization*. Synchronization normally requires that all of the servers with replicas of a partition be able to communicate with one another.

As you gradually migrate a network to IP, you will have both IPX and IP servers on the network. IPX servers and IP servers can not directly communicate, which prevents the normal NDS synchronization process from working. To compensate for this problem, NetWare 5 supports *transitive synchronization*.

Transitive synchronization allows an IP-only server and an IPX-only server to synchronize their replicas using an intermediate server to relay the synchronization instructions. The intermediate server runs both IPX and IP; a Migration Agent server can often be used for this purpose.

Using WAN Traffic Manager

NetWare 5 supports large and complex networks, and a network that is in the process of IP migration can be even more complicated than usual. The NDS synchronization process uses quite a bit of network bandwidth, and it may cause serious network traffic problems if it is not managed correctly. NetWare 5 includes a feature called WAN Traffic Manager, which allows you some control over the NDS synchronization process.

WAN Traffic Manager includes two main components: the server component, WTM.NLM, and a snap-in for NDS and NetWare Administrator that allows you to manage the traffic. The snap-in allows you to manage a new NDS object, the LAN area object, and adds properties to Server objects. You can create *policies* for each of these objects.

WAN Traffic Manager policies allow you to specify the type of synchronization that can be performed and the times that synchronization is allowed for both IP and IPX network segments. By tuning these settings, you can alleviate network traffic problems caused by synchronization.

Synchronizing Time

Time synchronization is an essential part of a large-scale NetWare network. In order to keep NDS synchronized, all servers that share the same Directory tree must have their clocks set to the same time. This prevents conflicts when the same object is modified from different servers. NetWare 4 accomplished this through the use of time synchronization. NetWare 5 supports the same synchronization features, and it adds support for NTP (network time protocol). NTP is a protocol, originally developed for use on UNIX networks, that allows IP nodes to obtain the current time from a server.

NetWare 5 uses two components for time synchronization: TIME-SYNC.NLM, which is loaded on all servers and manages normal time synchronization, and NTP.NLM, which adds support for NTP. To enable NTP support, type **LOAD SYS:ETC\NTP.NLM** at the server console. NTP uses a configuration file, NTP.CFG, located in the server's SYS:ETC directory. You can edit this file using a text editor and specify the host names or IP addresses of one or more NTP time servers.

The default NTP.CFG file uses a time server address of 127.127.1.0. This is an IP loopback address and, therefore, points to the local server.

Review

TCP/IP (Transport Control Protocol/Internet Protocol) is a suite of protocols that are widely used on UNIX machines, the Internet, and networks based on Windows NT and other operating systems. This suite includes protocols ranging from basic network transports to platform-independent applications.

TCP/IP Basics

The TCP/IP protocols can be mapped to the DOD reference model, which uses four layers of communication:

Process/Application   Supports applications, such as e-mail or file transfer

Host-to-Host   Ensures reliable communication between hosts

Internet   Handles IP addressing and routing between networks

Network Access   Handles the transport of data over the network media

IP Addressing

IP addresses represent a host with four bytes, also known as octets. Part of the address is used for a network address, and the rest is used for a node address. There are three main classes of IP address:

- Class A addresses begin with a bit set to 0, and use one byte for the network address. This allows 128 networks and 16,777,216 nodes per network.

- Class B addresses begin with bits set to 10, and use two bytes each for the network and host addresses. This allows 16,384 networks and 65,534 nodes per network.

- Class C addresses begin with bits set to 110, and use three bytes for the network address and one for the node address. This allows 2,097,152 networks and 254 nodes per network.

Subnet addressing is a technique that divides the available node addresses into node and subnet components, adding versatility to IP addressing.

NetWare 5's TCP/IP Support

One of the most important new features of NetWare 5 is its direct support for Pure IP, meaning that the TCP/IP packets are not encapsulated within IPX packets. This allows NetWare 5, using TCP/IP, to communicate faster than any previous version. NetWare 5 supports two IP modes:

- Pure IP uses IP only and is the most efficient.

- IP/IPX Compatibility Mode uses IP as the primary protocol, and supports IPX by encapsulating IPX packets within IP packets. This is primarily useful for upgrading networks to Pure IP gradually.

Migrating to TCP/IP

Several components are involved in the process of migrating from IPX to TCP/IP in a NetWare network:

- Migration Agents act as gateways between IPX and IP portions of the network.

- NetWare clients and servers are not protocol-specific in NetWare 5, and they can use Compatibility Mode to support IPX in an IP environment.

- NDS supports IPX, IP, and transitive synchronization.

- SLP (Service Location Protocol) allows Migration Agents and other services to be detected by clients.

- DNS (Domain Name Service) translates between numeric IP addresses and alphanumeric host names.

- DHCP (Dynamic Host Configuration Protocol) allocates IP addresses automatically, eliminating some of the administrative burden of an IP network.

IP Synchronization

NetWare 5 supports transitive synchronization, which allows IP and IPX servers to synchronize NDS replicas by communicating through an intermediate server with both IP and IPX support. An additional component, the WAN Traffic Manager, allows you to manage the NDS synchronization traffic on the network. WAN Traffic Manager extends the NDS schema with objects for traffic management, and it allows you to create policies that control the synchronization process.

NetWare 5 also supports the Internet-standard NTP (network time protocol) for time synchronization between IP and IPX networks. This protocol is supported by NTP.NLM, which you must load manually. The SYS:ETC\NTP.CFG file specifies one or more NTP servers for synchronization.

TCP/IP Practice Questions

1. The TCP and IP protocols are analogous to which NetWare protocols? (Select two choices.)

   A. IPX

   B. NFS

   C. LPD

   D. SPX

   E. NCP

2. Which of the following protocols are considered to be connection-oriented? (Select one or more choices.)

    A. TCP

    B. UDP

    C. SPX

    D. IPX

3. Which of the following statements is *not* true of IP?

    A. It is similar to IPX.

    B. It resides in the Process/Application layer.

    C. It performs routing functions.

    D. It has a 32-bit address space.

4. Which of the following protocols relates to electronic mail?

    A. SMTP

    B. SNMP

    C. TFTP

    D. ARP

5. The Token Ring protocol resides at the _____ layer of the DOD model.

6. Which of the following statements is *not* true of UDP?

    A. It is a connectionless protocol.

    B. It is rarely used.

    C. It doesn't require acknowledgments.

    D. It's more efficient than TCP.

7. An IP address is how many bits long?

   A. 42

   B. 30

   C. 32

   D. Depends on the class of network

8. In the IP address `164.33.103.4`, the node address is _____.

9. Which of the following is the correct format for class A network addresses?

   A. `Node.Net.Net.Net`

   B. `Node.Node.Net.Net`

   C. `Net.Net.Net.Node`

   D. `Net.Node.Node.Node`

10. What are the leading bits of a class B address?

   A. `110`

   B. `10`

   C. `1`

   D. `011`

11. Which of the following statements is true concerning NetWare 5?

   A. IPX packets can be encapsulated within TCP/IP.

   B. TCP/IP packets are encapsulated within IPX.

   C. IPX is not supported at all.

   D. TCP/IP requires IPX to work properly.

12. Which component allows you to set policies for NDS synchronization?

   A. NTP.NLM

   B. WAN Traffic Manager

   C. Migration Agent

   D. IPX Compatibility Mode

13. Which server component (NLM) handles IPX Compatibility Mode?

14. Which server component should be run on a Migration Agent server?

   A. SCMD.NLM

   B. WAN Traffic Manager

   C. MIGRATE.NLM

   D. Migration Gateway

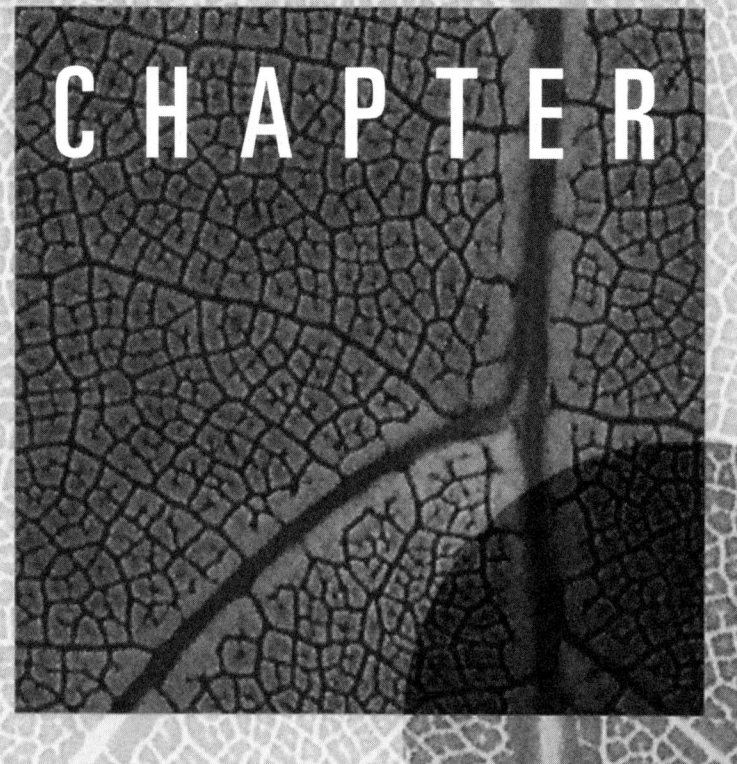

CHAPTER

5

Managing NetWare 5
with the Java Console

Roadmap

This chapter covers the GUI (Java) console of NetWare 5 and describes how to use it to manage the server.

Topics Covered

- Features of the Java console
- Setting up the console
- Using ConsoleOne
- Using RConsoleJ

Skills You'll Learn

- Setting up the Java console for maximum usefulness
- Understanding the difference between the text and GUI consoles
- Managing text-based consoles from within the GUI
- Using ConsoleOne to manage NDS and the file system
- Adding options to the GUI menu

Although it isn't the most important improvement for your network, certainly the most obvious new feature of NetWare 5 is the GUI-based console. This console is installed with NetWare 5, and it allows you to manage the server using a mouse and user-friendly utilities.

Although the console looks a lot different from the server console in previous versions, much of the change is cosmetic. The old console is still there, and you'll still need it for many administrative tasks. Fortunately, you can access the standard console screens from within the GUI. In fact, you can monitor several screens at once.

In this chapter, we'll explain how you can set up the console for the most efficient operation. You'll also learn about the ConsoleOne utility, which allows you to manage NDS, the file system, and other aspects of the server without leaving the GUI console, and the Install utility, which allows you to change installation options. Finally, you'll learn how to run your own Java applications using the console.

Introducing the Java Console

The NetWare 5 GUI is also known as the *ServerTop*, because it provides a graphical desktop for the server. The GUI console not only represents a new look for NetWare servers, it represents a new architecture for NetWare server management applications. The following sections describe the architecture and operation of the console and explain how to configure it for the best performance.

How the Console Works

If you've been following the computer industry for the past few years, you've probably heard something about Java. Java is a popular language for Web and Internet applications, and it is also showing up nearly everywhere else. NetWare 5 is no exception—the GUI console is based on Java, and it supports Java applications. Let's take a look at Java and how it is integrated with the NetWare 5 environment.

What Is Java?

Since its development by Sun Microsystems, Java has been taking the world by storm, primarily as a language for Web applications. Although the language itself isn't revolutionary (it's very similar to C++), the architecture it is based on is what makes Java different.

With most computer languages, programs are written, then compiled into the native language (machine language) of the computer platform on which they will run. If a program needs to run on two platforms—say, Windows 98 and a NetWare server—it has to be compiled separately for each platform and often rewritten entirely.

Java programs are also compiled, but they are compiled into a *bytecode*. This is a pseudo-machine code that is designed to run on a simulated machine: the Java Virtual Machine (JVM). The idea is that this virtual machine can be implemented on any number of computer platforms. Once a version of the JVM exists for a platform, it can run Java applications—even if they were written for a different platform.

NetWare 5 uses a version of the JVM licensed from JavaSoft, the Sun Microsystems subsidiary responsible for Java development. Any Java application written for this version of the JVM can now run on the NetWare server.

The X Windows Environment

The Java language specification also includes a specification for a standard windowing system for use by Java. This allows standard GUI operations, such as opening and closing windows and displaying dialogs, to work from a Java application no matter which platform it runs on.

The Java windowing system is called the Abstract Window Toolkit, or AWT. This is the standard windowing system for Java applications on the Internet and is widely supported.

When a version of the AWT is created for an operating system, it's usually a simple task. On the Windows platform, for example, it's a simple matter of receiving a Java program's instruction to perform an action, then calling the operating system's built-in routine to perform the action.

Of course, NetWare doesn't normally have a GUI operating system at all, so the developers of NetWare 5 needed a system to form the basis for the AWT. Their solution was to use a version of X Windows, the most popular window environment for UNIX systems.

Although the NetWare 5 server runs a version of X Windows, you can't run programs written for X Windows with it. This subsystem exists strictly to handle the AWT needs of Java programs, and only Java-based programs can run under the NetWare 5 GUI.

Java Administration Tools

What Java-based program would you want to run on a NetWare server? As it turns out, NetWare 5 includes several useful ones. The utilities included on the GUI console, such as Install and ConsoleOne, are all Java applications. You'll learn the specifics of using these applications later in this chapter.

You are not limited to the built-in Java programs. You can run your own Java applications on the server and even add them to the Novell menu. This is explained later in this chapter.

Hardware Requirements

The Java console is part of the standard NetWare 5 installation, but it does have hardware requirements beyond those for the standard console. Although most PCs available today will meet the requirements, you should be aware of the specifics. These are explained in the following sections.

Memory and Disk Storage

As with NetWare 5 itself, Novell recommends a minimum of 64MB to run the GUI console. However, you may find that the console is slow with less than 128MB. Changing virtual memory settings, as described in Chapter 2, may help to improve performance. The console does not require any more disk storage space than the minimum required by NetWare 5, but you may need extra space to use the virtual memory option.

Mouse

The GUI console is the only NetWare 5 feature that requires a mouse, unlike the standard console. NetWare 5 detects supported mice during the installation process. You can also install a mouse driver after installation, as described later in this chapter.

NetWare 5 supports most available mice. Specifically, it supports PS/2 or serial (COM1 or COM2) ports, and mice supporting the Microsoft driver standard. In most cases, a mouse that works with Windows without installing an extra driver will also work with NetWare 5.

The NetWare 5 GUI will also work with the numeric keypad, although you'll find it much easier to use with a mouse.

Video Card and Monitor

The video card was not a critical item for NetWare 4.*x* and earlier versions, but it is important for the NetWare 5 GUI. The GUI can use resolutions up to 1,024 × 768, which makes it very convenient to monitor multiple server features at the same time.

NetWare 5 supports 256-color graphics with any video card that supports the VESA 1.2 standard. It should also work with any VGA card, but it will be limited to a resolution of 640 × 480 with 16 colors.

Using the NetWare 5 GUI

The NetWare 5 GUI desktop is very simple. It includes a Novell button in the lower-left corner that displays a menu of options, similar to the Windows 95 Start menu. (You can also access this menu by clicking in a blank area of the desktop.) The default options in the Novell menu include the following:

Exit GUI   Prompts you for confirmation, then exits the GUI console.

Install   Allows you to modify installation options.

ConsoleOne   A server-based administration tool similar to NWADMIN on the client.

Tools   Allows you to configure keyboard and video properties and set a background pattern for the desktop, as explained in the next section.

It's important to understand that the GUI console is *not* a replacement for the standard NetWare console. It runs on top of the standard console, and when you exit the GUI console you are returned to the standard console. Most of the NetWare 5 server's features are still managed using NLMs from the text console.

By default, the GUI console starts automatically when you run NetWare 5, although you can prevent this by changing the AUTOEXEC .NCF file. To start the GUI console manually from the command line, type **STARTX** at the console prompt. This launches the STARTX.NCF file, which starts the GUI console.

Configuring the GUI

The NetWare 5 GUI is easy to install and configure. In fact, if you successfully installed NetWare 5 following the instructions in Chapter 2, the GUI is already installed. The second phase of the server installation process, the Installation Wizard, is actually a Java program.

Although the configuration is largely automatic, you will need to watch out for some issues. You can change some options to make the console look better and work better. These are explained in the following sections.

Mouse and Video Drivers

Both mouse and video drivers are installed automatically by NetWare 5 during installation. If you replace the mouse or video card with a different model, you will need to configure another driver. NetWare 5 includes an NCF (NetWare Command File) to redetect the hardware devices. To install new drivers, type this command at the NetWare console:

VESA_RSP

Setting Video Resolution

When you install NetWare 5, the GUI will be configured to use the base VGA resolution, 640×480. Although this resolution already produces a display that looks more pleasant than the text-based console of earlier versions, you can set a higher resolution and gain more screen space.

The number of colors in the display cannot be changed, and it depends on the video card. For older VGA cards, the resolution and colors are limited to 640×480 and 16 colors. For cards meeting the VESA 1.2 standard, 256 colors are supported in resolutions up to $1,024 \times 768$.

To change the display resolution for the NetWare 5 GUI, follow the steps in Procedure 5.1. The available resolutions usually include 640×480, 800×600, and $1,024 \times 768$, but they may vary depending on your video card and monitor.

PROCEDURE 5.1

Changing the Display Resolution

1. Select Tools ➢ Display Properties from the Novell menu.

2. A dialog is displayed that lists the available resolutions and indicates the current setting. Select a different setting if desired.

3. If you have changed the resolution, click the Test button. The video mode is switched, and a test pattern is displayed.

4. If the resolution switched successfully, click OK. If the screen has become blank or scrambled, wait 10 seconds; the old resolution will be restored automatically.

5. Click the OK button to exit the Display Properties dialog.

Setting the Keyboard Type

You can also configure the keyboard for the GUI console. Specifically, you can choose a language if you are using a non-U.S. English keyboard. To change the keyboard language for the NetWare 5 GUI, follow the steps in Procedure 5.2. (You'll need a version of NetWare 5 that supports the desired language.)

Changing the Keyboard Language

1. Select Tools ➤ Keyboard Properties from the Novell menu.

2. A dialog is displayed listing the available keyboard types and indicating the current choice. The Keyboard Properties dialog box appears.

3. Select a language from the list if desired.

4. Click the Apply button to commit the change, and verify that the keyboard works properly with the new setting.

Using a Graphic Background

Although it won't make your administration job easier, you can make your server's console more attractive by selecting a graphic image to use as a background for the desktop. To set the GUI background, select Tools ➤ Backgrounds from the Novell menu. Select a background image, then click OK to make the change.

Using the GUI for Administration

NetWare 5 includes two GUI utilities for managing the server from within the Java Console. They are ConsoleOne, which includes a variety of administration features, and Install, which allows you to install or remove NetWare 5 components and other software. These utilities are explained in the following sections.

Using ConsoleOne

ConsoleOne is the most important part of the NetWare 5 GUI. In fact, without this utility, there would be almost no reason to run the GUI at all. This utility allows you to access the text-based server console. Additionally, you can use it to manage the file system and NDS objects, similar to the client-based NWADMIN utility.

To start ConsoleOne from the GUI, select ConsoleOne from the Novell menu. If you are not currently running the GUI, you can start the GUI and launch ConsoleOne by typing this command at the console prompt:

C1START

The main ConsoleOne window is shown in Figure 5.1. Similar to NWADMIN, this window displays a hierarchical list of objects on the left, and the contents of the current object on the right. There are two main divisions in this hierarchy:

My Server   This object is a container for information about the local server. You can use the objects under this object to manage local and remote server consoles and to access the file system.

The Network   This object contains the NDS tree. After opening this object, you can browse the tree and create and manage objects.

The administration tasks you can perform using these objects are described in the following sections.

FIGURE 5.1

ConsoleOne allows
you to manage
the server and the
NDS tree.

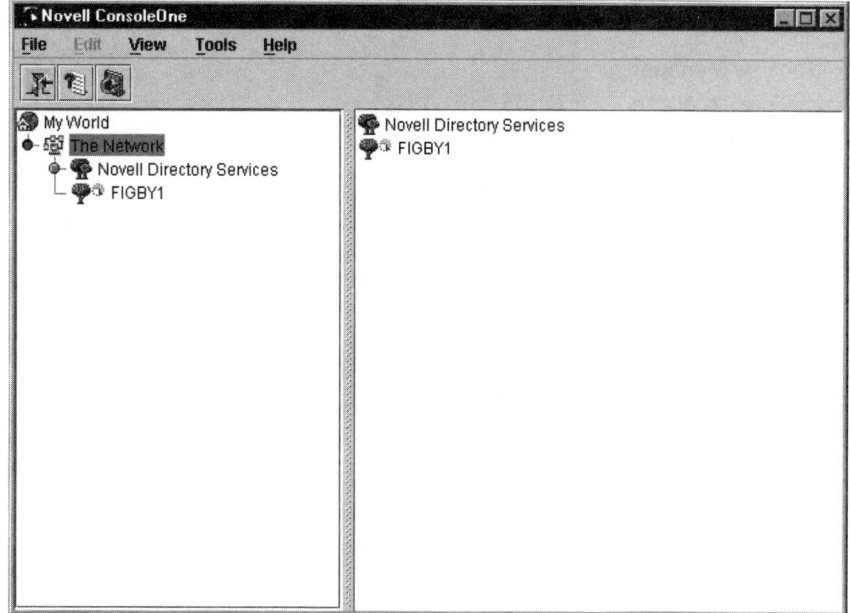

Managing the Local Server

One of ConsoleOne's most useful features is the ability to view and manage NetWare consoles (text-based screens). The main tool for doing this is Console Manager. To access this utility, open the Tools folder under the My Server object, then highlight Console Manager.

Before you can use Console Manager or RConsoleJ (described in the next section), the server must be running the remote console NLM. To load the NLM, type **LOAD RCONAG6** at the console prompt. You will be prompted for a password and TCP/IP and IPX ports for the console service.

When you start Console Manager, you are prompted for information to access the server. Enter the host name (usually **localhost**), port number (usually **2034**), and password, and select Connect to access the server console. The Console Manager window then displays icons for each of the current server console screens, as shown in Figure 5.2.

FIGURE 5.2

Console Manager
provides access to
NetWare console
screens.

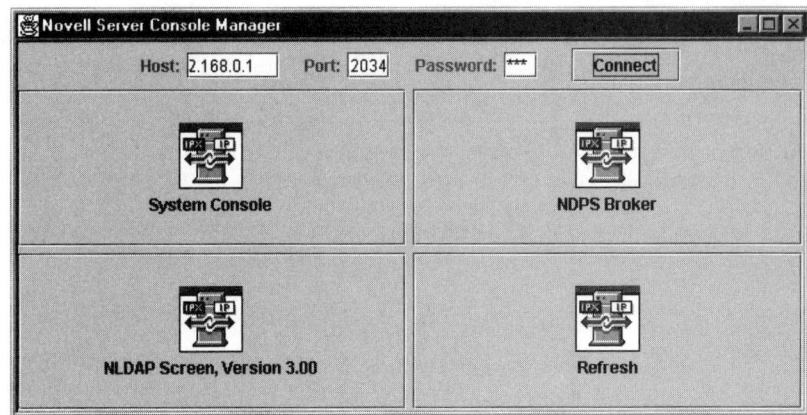

To open a console screen, click one of the icons. The screen is displayed as a window on the desktop, as shown in Figure 5.3. If you are using a high resolution for the GUI, you can display several screens at once.

FIGURE 5.3

Console Manager
displays a
NetWare console
screen within a
window.

```
System Console                                              _ □ ×
11-05-1998   2:57:44 am:      SERVER-5.0-3651  [nmID=50020]
    POLICY MANAGER - (5.00-27): Unable to get a Server Base license for Server
    FIGBY.   Error # 8000100C.

11-05-1998   2:57:44 am:      SERVER-5.0-3651  [nmID=50020]
    POLICY MANAGER - (5.00-27): Unable to get a Server Base license for Server
    FIGBY.   Error # 8000100C.

11-05-1998   2:58:24 am:      SERVER-5.0-3651  [nmID=50020]
    POLICY MANAGER - (5.00-27): Unable to get a Server Base license for Server
    FIGBY.   Error # 8000100C.

11-05-1998   2:58:24 am:      SERVER-5.0-3651  [nmID=50020]
    POLICY MANAGER - (5.00-27): Unable to get a Server Base license for Server
    FIGBY.   Error # 8000100C.

Thu Nov  5 03:02:29 1998
 RCONAG6 192.168.0.3:1036 Remote console connection granted
FIGBY:
```

Managing Remote Servers

ConsoleOne also includes a utility called RConsoleJ. This utility is primarily meant to access console screens on remote servers, although it can also be used with the local server. Any local or remote server must be running the RCONAG6 agent NLM, as described in the previous section.

To use RConsoleJ, open the Tools folder under the My Server object. Highlight RConsoleJ in the hierarchical list. The right portion of the ConsoleOne screen then prompts you for a server TCP/IP address and password.

After you specify the address and password, click the Connect button. The main RConsoleJ screen is displayed within one of the NetWare console screens, as shown in Figure 5.4. You can use the drop-down list at the top of the window to switch between the available screens.

Editing Configuration Files

ConsoleOne also provides a convenient way to edit the various text files used for the NetWare 5 server's configuration, such as AUTOEXEC.NCF and STARTUP.NCF. To access this feature, open the Configuration Files folder under the My Server object. Opening this object displays a list of available configuration files.

To edit a file, double-click it or select Edit from the File menu. A window-based text editor opens with the contents of the file, as shown in Figure 5.5. You can use the commands in the text editor's menus to save the file and exit when needed.

FIGURE 5.5

The graphical text editor allows you to modify configuration files.

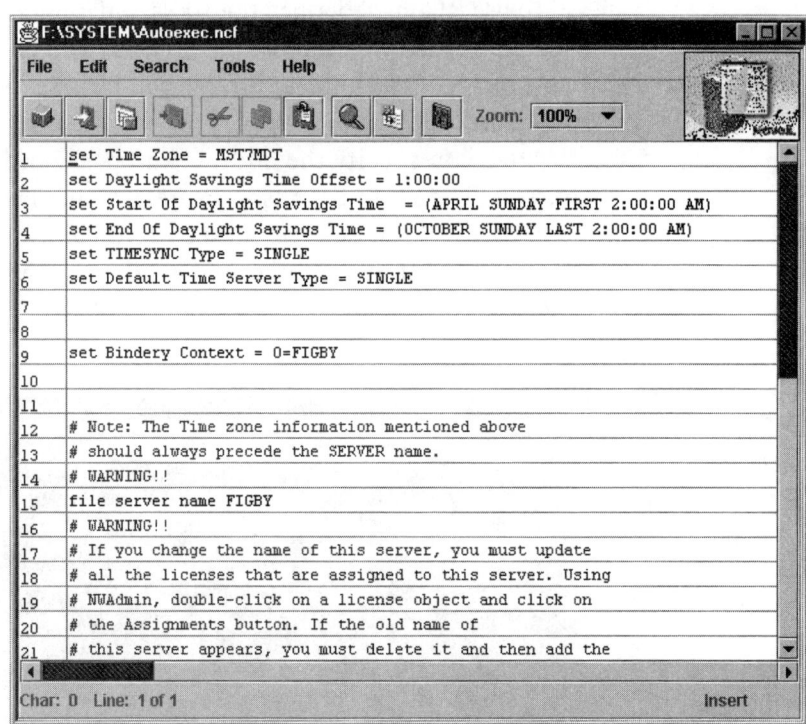

 You can also edit any other text file using this editor by browsing for the file from the file system, as described in the next section.

Managing the File System

You can also use ConsoleOne to browse and manage the server's file system. To open the file system, select the Volumes folder under the My Server object. You can then open a volume and browse its directory.

Once you browse the file system and find the file or directory you want to work with, you can use the commands in the File menu to rename, delete, copy, or edit a file.

Managing the NDS Tree

Last but not least, ConsoleOne provides access to NDS objects. While not as powerful as the NWADMIN utility, this provides a basic way to manage users, printers, and other NDS objects.

To browse the NDS tree from within ConsoleOne, select The Network object from the hierarchical display. Under this object is a list of available NDS trees. Double-click a tree name to open the tree.

When you first open an NDS tree, ConsoleOne prompts you for a username and password to access the tree, as shown in Figure 5.6. Use Admin or another account with administrative access to gain full access to the NDS tree.

FIGURE 5.6

ConsoleOne prompts you for a username and password for NDS access.

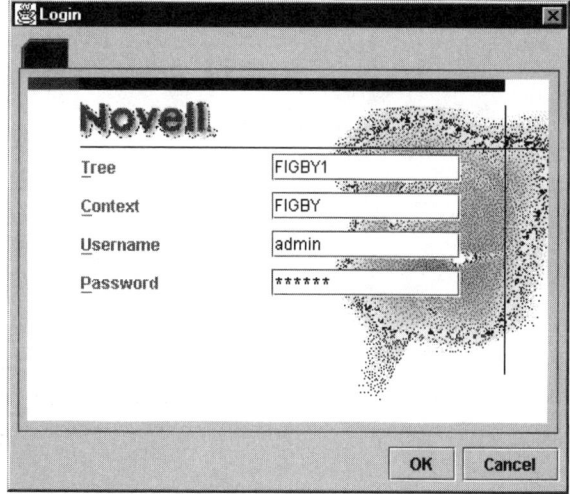

Once you're authenticated with an NDS tree, you can browse through its container objects. You can also perform some basic NDS management tasks:

- Creating Objects
- Managing Object Properties

Creating Objects   To create an NDS object, highlight the container object and select New from the File menu. ConsoleOne is limited to creating Organization, Organizational Unit, Group, and User objects.

Managing Object Properties   You can also edit the properties of NDS objects (including all objects, not just the ones you can create) from ConsoleOne. To view the Properties dialog for an object, highlight the object, right-click, and select Properties. The Properties dialog includes a number of tabbed sections depending on the type of object, as shown in Figure 5.7.

FIGURE 5.7

ConsoleOne displays the Properties dialog for a User object.

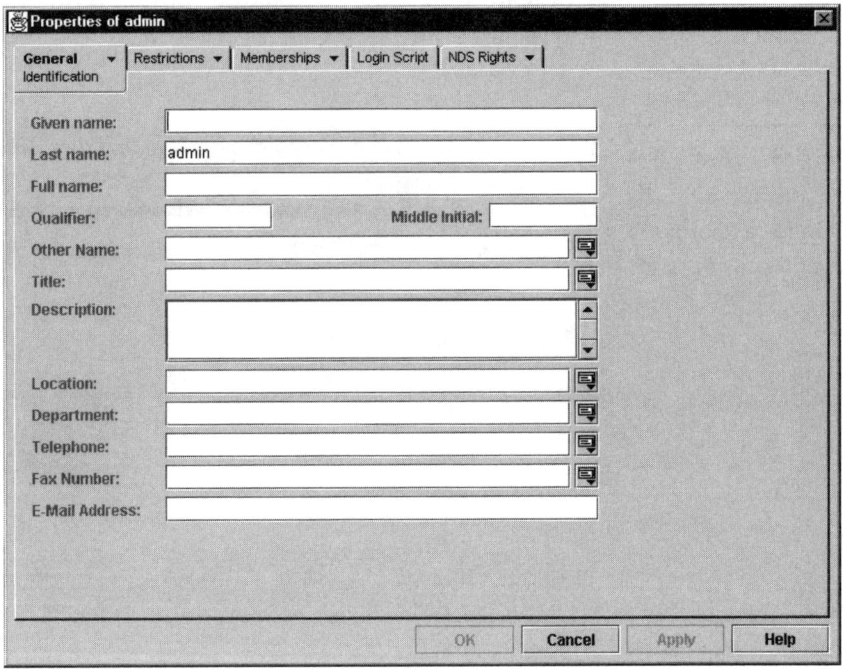

Using the Install Utility

The Java Console also includes an Install utility, which you can use to view the current list of components, add NetWare components, or add third-party components. To start this utility, select Install from the Novell menu in the server console.

The Install dialog displays a list of components currently installed and their version numbers. Click the New button to add a component, and you are prompted for a disk or server location for the installation files.

Running Java Programs

Along with the NetWare 5 utilities we've already described, the GUI console can run other Java programs. In fact, just about any Java program will run under the NetWare console, although most Java applications are not very useful on a server.

Applets versus Classes

The Java language was originally designed for stand-alone programs, but it has become a popular language for downloadable applications on Web pages. There are actually two types of Java programs:

- *Applications* are stand-alone programs, designed to be used with an implementation of the Java Virtual Machine.

- *Applets* are designed to run within a Web browser. The HTML <APPLET> tag is used in the document to insert the applet and supply parameters to it.

The NetWare 5 GUI supports both types of Java programs, although you will need to use different methods to start them. A module called JAVA.NLM supports the Java Virtual Machine under NetWare 5.

Running Java Programs

When a Java application is compiled, a *class file* is created. This is a file containing bytecodes for the Java Virtual Machine. Class files are typically stored with filenames ending with the extension .class. The following sections describe how to run Java applets and applications from the NetWare 5 server.

Loading a Java Class

For a stand-alone Java application, you can use the JAVA.NLM module to load and display the application. To start a Java application, type **JAVA** at the console prompt, followed by the class filename for the application. For example, this command starts the Java Virtual Machine and runs an application called test.class in the SYS :PUBLIC directory:

```
JAVA SYS:PUBLIC\test.class
```

Viewing an Applet

Applets are designed to work within HTML documents. To use a Java applet in NetWare 5, you must create an HTML document that includes the <APPLET> tag for the appropriate class file.

The NetWare 5 applet viewer isn't a true HTML viewer. It doesn't display HTML images, headings, or other elements. It only searches for an <APPLET> tag in the document, and it executes the Java applet in a window.

After you've created the HTML document, you can use the Java Virtual Machine to run it. First, type **JAVA** at the server console's prompt to start the Java interpreter. Next, type the APPLET command followed by the filename for the HTML document. For example, this command displays the applet contained in the SYS:PUBLIC\ TEST.HTML document:

```
APPLET SYS:PUBLIC\TEST.HTML
```

Adding Java Programs to the Menu

You can now run Java applets and applications from the console prompt. As you might have noticed, it's not too practical to start graphical applications from the command line. Fortunately, you can also add Java programs (both applets and applications) to the Novell menu in the GUI console.

The definition for the Novell menu is stored in a text file on the SYS: volume of the server. You can edit this file with any text editor, including the ConsoleOne editor described earlier in this chapter. The complete filename for the file is:

```
SYS:JAVA\NWGFX\FVWM2\FVWM2RC5XX
```

This file includes a section labeled MENUS, which you can edit to add an item to the menu. You can add an item in the same format as the ones that are already there. The basic format for menu items is as follows:

```
+ "Menu Name" Exec command
```

Replace Menu Name with the appropriate name for the application, which will be displayed on the menu. The command can be a JAVA command for an application or an APPLET command for an HTML file containing an applet, as described in the previous sections.

Any changes you make to the GUI menu affect only the current server. The changes will not take effect until the next time you start the GUI.

Review

The Java Console is one of the most useful new features of NetWare 5. It provides a graphical interface for server management. In this chapter, you learned about the architecture and hardware requirements of the Java console, and you learned to set up and use the console.

The Java Console

Java is an object-oriented language developed by Sun Microsystems. NetWare 5 includes an implementation of the Java Virtual Machine (JVM), which allows Java programs to be run. The NetWare 5 JVM runs under a customized version of X Windows.

The Java console can run on most machines that run NetWare 5. The console requires the following hardware:

- 64MB of memory minimum

- A mouse (PS/2 or serial)

- A video card (256 colors, VESA 1.2 preferred)

The GUI console includes a Novell button in the lower-left corner that launches a menu of administrative tools. These tools are not a substitute for the text-based NetWare console, but they do provide some useful functions.

Administrative Tools

NetWare 5 includes a number of Java-based administrative tools that can run on the GUI console. These include the following:

ConsoleOne   Allows you to edit configuration files, view text-based consoles on local and remote servers, and manage objects in NDS and the file system.

Install   Displays a list of currently installed NetWare 5 components and allows you to add components.

Java Programs

The NetWare 5 GUI supports the two available types of Java programs:

- *Applications* are stand-alone programs.

- *Applets* are designed to run within a Web browser.

You can use the JAVA and APPLET commands at the console to run Java applets. You can also edit a configuration file and add items to the GUI console menu.

Java Console Practice Questions

1. The graphical Java console in NetWare 5 replaces the text-based console used in previous versions. (True or False.)

2. Which two hardware devices are specifically required to run the GUI console in NetWare 5? (Select two.)

A. VGA or better video card

B. CGA or better video card

C. Mouse

D. 64MB of RAM

E. 200MB of disk storage

F. CD-ROM drive

3. _____ are Java programs that are designed to run within a Web page.

4. Which types of graphical applications can run under the NetWare 5 GUI console? (Choose one or more.)

   A. Java applets

   B. Java applications

   C. X Windows applications

   D. NetWare Loadable Modules (NLMs)

   E. Windows applications

5. Which of the following statements is true of the Java language?

   A. Java creates programs for Windows platforms only.

   B. Java is compiled into machine language.

   C. Java classes can work on multiple platforms.

   D. NetWare 5 supports only Windows-based Java applets.

   E. All programs require an HTML document to launch.

6. Which of these NetWare 5 tools allows you to view multiple server consoles, each in its own window in the server GUI?

   A. RConsoleJ

   B. Console Manager

   C. NWADMIN

   D. Install

7. If you install a new video card in the NetWare server, which of the following is the correct command to set up the driver for the new card?

   A. VESA

   B. VESA_RSP

   C. INSTALL

   D. CONFIG

8. Which of the following is *not* a function available in the ConsoleOne utility?

   A. View text-based consoles for the local server

   B. View text-based consoles for remote servers

   C. View graphic consoles for remote servers

   D. View properties of NDS objects

9. Which of these file system operations are available from the ConsoleOne utility? (Choose one or more.)

   A. Delete a file

   B. Rename a file

   C. Salvage a deleted file

   D. Edit a text file

10. You need to add a Java applet to the Novell menu in the server GUI. The applet is stored in the test.class file and referenced in the TEST.HTML document. Which of the following is the correct command to add to the menu configuration file?

   A. `+ "Test applet" Exec TEST.class`

   B. `+ "Test applet" Exec APPLET TEST.class`

   C. `+ "Test applet" Exec JAVA TEST.HTML`

   D. `+ "Test applet" Exec APPLET TEST.HTML`

CHAPTER

6

Z.E.N.works Part One

Roadmap

This chapter introduces the Z.E.N.works suite and looks at how to install and use these powerful tools.

Topics Covered

- The four components that make up Z.E.N.works
- The policy packages that store workstation rules
- The three phases of a Z.E.N.works implementation

Skills You'll Learn

- Understand Z.E.N.works' four components
- Understand policy packages and their functions
- Learn how to create and implement Z.E.N.works' policies
- Understand the three phases of a Z.E.N.works implementation
- Learn how to choose the best policy packages to implement on your network
- Learn to install Z.E.N.works with the Compact or Custom Installation
- Learn to install the Z.E.N.works Novell client locally and over the network
- Learn to perform the Automatic Client Upgrade
- Learn the three ways to set up the Workstation Agent to function automatically
- Learn how to verify your workstation registration
- Learn to import your workstation objects into your NDS tree

The Z.E.N.works utility suite facilitates workstation and application management by automating many network tasks, including software distribution, software maintenance, remote workstation management, and help desk notification. Because its desktop management tools will probably be in high demand, Novell is marketing Z.E.N.works in the scaled down Starter Pack with NetWare 5 and as an add-on product to Intranetware 4.11 networks.

Z.E.N.works stands for Zero Effort Networking—a worthy goal. Application maintenance is seamless, and desktop configurations (complete with their configured applications, assigned printers, etc.) follow users to wherever they log in. The Z.E.N. appellation recalls the Zen Buddhist sitting peacefully with a contented look on his or her face, a worthwhile aspiration for today's harried worker. Z.E.N.works may not reduce an administrator's workload to zero; however, it does reduce it to a new low by automating application installation, distribution, and maintenance and by enabling remote desktop management and maintenance.

The advantages of using a Z.E.N.works-equipped network include the ability to have applications installed, updated, repaired, and maintained automatically from the network. Help requests, pertinent information, and error messages are forwarded to the appropriate help desk personnel through Help Requester. Administrators can remotely configure and work on a user's workstation, facilitating a quicker response time. Desktop configurations, application rights, access rights, and printer rights follow users to any Windows workstation on the network.

With Z.E.N.works, many tasks that previously required a physical journey to a user's workstation can be accomplished automatically across the network. By adding the workstation, workstation group, and policy packages to NDS, administrators can benefit from their automated features. An information and control network path allows administrators to automate the installation of Z.E.N.works' components and applications and to make repairs and perform maintenance.

For more information regarding Z.E.N.works, visit the Novell Web site at: http://www.novell.com/products/nds/zenworks/index.html.

Figure 6.1 depicts the Z.E.N.works Welcome screen.

Z.E.N.works Components

Let's review the suite of applications and utilities included in Z.E.N.works (see Chapter 1). The four components are:

- Novell Workstation Manager
- NetWare Application Launcher
- Remote Control
- Help Requester

Novell Workstation Manager

This is the Z.E.N.works component that allows you to centrally configure and manage users' workstations through NDS. The policy packages in NDS give you the ability to:

- Manage workstation inventories in NDS with workstation objects and workstation group objects, without visiting the workstation

- Choose a standard user interface or specify interfaces for individual users

- Schedule functions on the workstation to occur during the evening or when users are logged off of the network

- Distribute and update clients, applications, and print drivers to the client workstations

NetWare Application Launcher

The Application Launcher allows you to make applications available from the network and manage them as NDS objects. Users are able to find or access applications from the Application Explorer or Application Launcher window.

Application functionality and upkeep is automated. The Application Launcher can recognize missing files and replace them when a user attempts to launch an application with missing files. This eliminates a lot of user frustration and downtime.

Administrators will benefit from the Application Launcher's ability to:

- Automate tasks that previously required a physical trip to a user's workstation

- Hierarchically situate application objects in the NDS tree through multilevel folders

- Take before and after "pictures" of a workstation's configuration after an application is installed with the snAppShot utility

- Grant file rights to users and assign access to them

- Allow registration with a secure Windows NT server through Windows NT Service Control Manager to make changes on the server or workstations

- Schedule times when application access will cease through an application suspension configuration.

Remote Control

Administrators can gain remote access to workstations that are configured to allow remote control access through their policies and rights parameters in the workstation objects in NDS. A signal or message informs the user that a remote session is imminent, and then an administrator can take control of the workstation.

Remote control duplicates the user's desktop environment on the administrator's desktop.

Help Requester

The Help Requester application facilitates communication by the user to the appropriate help desk personnel. Helpful information (e.g., error messages, the workstation's ID, and the user's context) is sent to the designated personnel.

Z.E.N.works Policy Packages

Policy packages are objects, created with NetWare Administrator and stored in NDS, that contain a set of policies or rules that govern users, workstations, workstation groups, or containers.

Seven different types of policy package objects exist. One type governs containers. Of the other six, three types govern users and three govern workstations.

These last six types are organized according to the Windows platform with which they work: Windows 3.1, Windows 95, or Windows NT.

These policy package objects can be configured and then associated with user and workstation objects or user group and workstation group objects.

This incorporation of policy packages in NDS extends the directory and eliminates the need to manually copy policies into the PUBLIC directories of the servers. NDS will replicate the policy packages throughout the network, guaranteeing fault tolerance by reproducing replicas. By having different types of policy packages, the types of objects they control are defined.

Through their NDS objects, workstations, users, and containers are associated with the policy packages that control them. This association allows easy access through NDS whenever you need to change policies. The policies can be changed, disabled, or enabled at any time.

Due to the increased functionality of the Registry, Windows 95 and Windows NT allow more Z.E.N.works policies than Windows 3.1 allows.

Container Policy Packages

The container policy package is the only one that is not specific to the desktop operating system. This policy package contains a single policy that enables you to search the container for the effective policies in that container as shown in Figure 6.2. You can change the search order of the policies in the container. The order is usually from user to workstation to container. You could change it, for example, to search from user to container, skipping the workstation object.

F I G U R E   6.2

The container policy package includes a single policy to search the container.

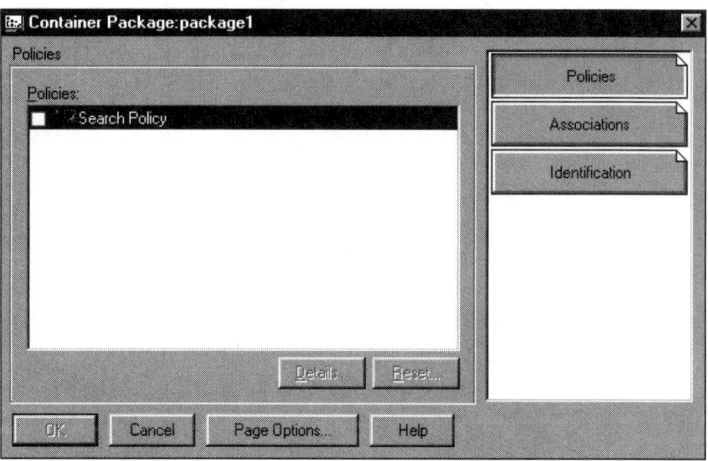

User Policy Packages

The user policy packages are objects in the NDS; they are associated with and, thereby, control specific user objects, user group objects, and containers. These policy package objects contain policies that control users when they log in to the network. In order to work, the Windows platform must be correctly associated with the policy package object. Figure 6.3 illustrates the types of policies present in the Windows NT User Package.

Users can log in from anywhere on the network. As long as the appropriate Windows platform policy package is associated correctly with its user objects, the policies will be functional. This association creates the "virtual persona" in NDS.

You can create multiple user policy packages for the same platform in the same container for the same users. If a conflict exists between associations, you will be warned. You might want to make policy packages that govern users on all Windows platforms on your network even if the users are in different departments. If a roving user then tries to log in from the other type of operating system, he or she will be successful!

Workstation Policy Packages

As with the user policy packages, the workstation policy packages are objects in the NDS that are associated with and, thereby, control specific workstation objects, workstation group objects, and containers. They control the workstation objects and must be matched with the workstation operating systems found at the desktop.

These workstation policy packages apply to the workstation regardless of the user who logs in. The workstation policy packages are specific to the workstation, and user policy packages are specific to the user. (See Figure 6.4.)

FIGURE 6.3

This dialog box shows the types of policies present in the Windows NT User Package.

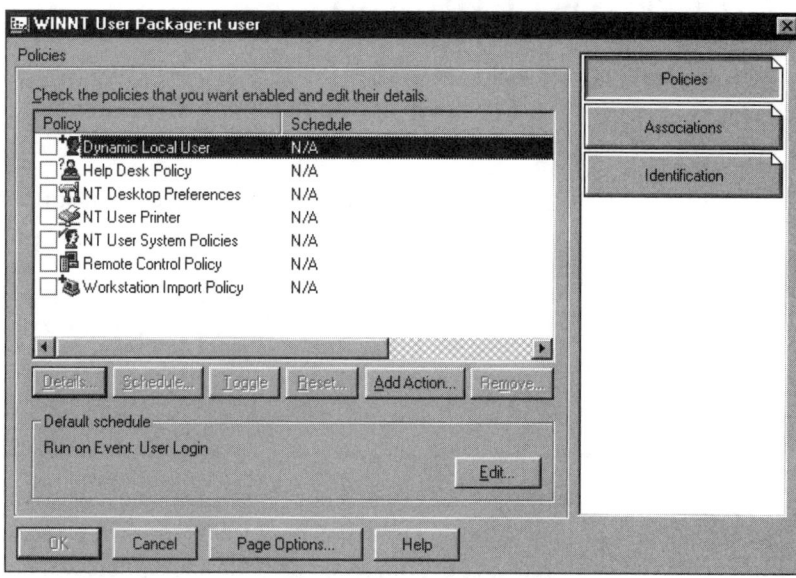

FIGURE 6.4

The Windows NT dialog box shows the policies found in the WINNT workstation policy package object.

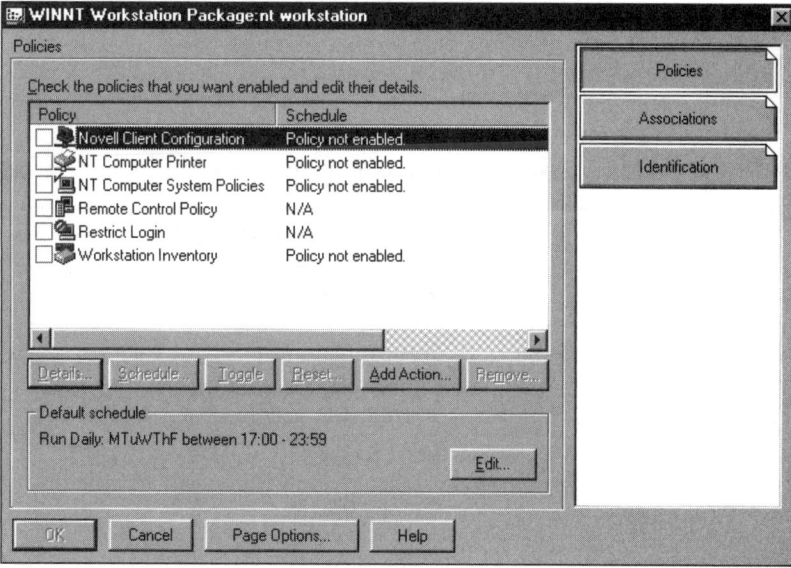

Z.E.N.works Policies

To create and implement Z.E.N.works' policies, you must perform the following steps:

1. Create a policy package object, configure the policies to the user or workstation, and choose the appropriate desktop platform.

2. Choose and enable the specific policy parameters.

3. Associate the policy package object with the chosen NDS objects (workstation or user, specific or group).

When you associate a policy package object with a container object, those policy package rules will apply to all users or workstations in the container. If you have previously created the appropriate workstation and user objects, the policies will go into effect when they are configured. The Novell client for Z.E.N.works must be installed on all workstations.

The policies that you configure in Z.E.N.works are illustrated in Table 6.1.

T A B L E 6.1: Z.E.N.works Policies and Functions

CONTAINER POLICY PACKAGES	
Z.E.N.works Policy	**Policy Function**
Search	This container-only policy package searches the container for policies associated with that container and can adjust their order.

WORKSTATION POLICY PACKAGES	
Z.E.N.works Policy	**Policy Function**
3x Computer System (Windows 3.1 workstation)	This policy allows you to download files from the network to the workstation. These files are limited to ASCII text (e.g., .INI, .CFG, or .BAT files) or binary files (e.g., .EXE, .DLL, or .EXE files). This policy function is more limited than the Windows 95 and Windows NT platforms that have the Registry. Windows 3.1 doesn't use Microsoft policies.

T A B L E   6.1:   Z.E.N.works Policies and Functions *(Continued)*

WORKSTATION POLICY PACKAGES

Z.E.N.works Policy	Policy Function
95 Computer System (Windows 95 workstation)	This policy is used to assign workstation-specific applications that are delivered to all Windows 95 workstations. This policy implements to any or all users.
95 RAS Configuration (Windows 95 workstation)	This policy will set dial-up networking settings.
95 Computer Printer (Windows 95 workstation)	This policy is also workstation-specific. It automatically downloads and installs print drivers and assigns printers to Windows 95 workstations.
NT Computer System (Windows NT workstation)	This policy is workstation-specific and assigns applications to all associated Windows NT workstations. This occurs with any and all users.
NT Computer Printer (Windows NT workstation)	This policy is also workstation-specific. It automatically downloads and installs print drivers and assigns printers to Windows NT workstations.
Workstation Inventory (Windows 95 workstation) (Windows NT workstation)	This policy is employed to view hardware configurations in the NDS tree. It includes an inventory of hardware assets found in the network's workstations.
Restrict Login (Windows 95 workstation) (Windows NT workstation)	This policy sets limits for associated workstations concerning login times and frequency.
Remote Control (Windows 95 workstation) (Windows NT workstation)	This policy configures remote session warning messages and specifies those associated workstations that can be accessed by remote control.
Novell Client Configuration (Windows 95 workstation) (Windows NT workstation)	This policy configures the Novell client, including the specific client used (Windows 95 or Windows NT), the login used, and the default capture settings. It specifies IP or IPX settings, and it configures the settings for Host Resources MIB, SNMP, IP Gateway, and Target Services Agent.

T A B L E 6.1: Z.E.N.works Policies and Functions *(Continued)*

USER POLICY PACKAGES	
Z.E.N.works Policy	**Policy Function**
95 User System Policies (Windows 95 users)	This policy is user-specific and defines application restrictions for associated users on Windows 95 desktops.
95 Desktop Preferences (Windows 95 users)	This policy will create a default desktop using Control Panel parameters for associated users on Windows 95 desktops.
NT User System Policies (Windows NT user)	This policy is user-specific and defines application restrictions for associated users on Windows NT desktops.
Dynamic Local User (Windows NT user)	This policy will manage user access to associated Windows NT workstations.
NT Desktop Preferences (Windows NT user)	This policy will create a default desktop using Control Panel parameters for associated users on Windows NT desktops.
NT User Printer (Windows NT user)	This policy is user-specific and automatically downloads and installs print drivers and assigns printers to Windows NT users.
Remote Control (Windows 3.1 users) (Windows 95 users) (Windows NT users)	This policy configures remote session warning messages and specifies those associated users that can be accessed by remote control.
Workstation Import (Windows 3.1 users) (Windows 95 users) (Windows NT users)	This policy sets standards for workstation naming and determines where workstation objects will appear in the NDS tree.

Designing and Implementing Z.E.N.works

Z.E.N.works is designed and implemented on a Novell network in three phases. The time required for each phase will vary, depending on the size of your network and the login habits of your users. The three implementation phases are:

Phase One: Designing the NDS Structure

Phase Two: Installation

Phase Three: Workstation Implementation

Z.E.N.works will add many new objects to your NDS tree, increasing your ability to manage users and workstations on your network. All the time and thought you put into the design and implementation of Z.E.N.works on the network will pay big dividends.

Phase One: Designing the NDS Structure

To begin the design phase of a Z.E.N.works implementation, you must compile an inventory of workstation hardware and user needs. You must develop a general strategy. Both user-specific and workstation-specific policy packages must be considered. Choose either or both to be implemented in individual containers.

You must choose containers to accommodate the new workstation and policy package objects in the NDS. You must quantify these new workstation objects and determine the desired results. You can configure a hierarchical implementation of policy packages with different users and workstations in the container.

You may want to redesign the NDS tree to facilitate the new objects. Network traffic is an important consideration. Administrators of larger networks must remember that each partition must contain fewer than 1,500 objects.

Because Z.E.N.works uses the policy packages and their associations to manage and configure the workstations for users, you must understand these policy packages and carefully choose them to reach your network goals.

First, you must identify the types of desktop platforms that will be present in a given container. Decide if conformity to a single user's mobile virtual persona is preferred or if a consistent desktop (workstation-specific) configuration would work best. Based on these decisions, you can choose the best policy packages to accomplish your goals.

After you determine the best policy packages and their required platform versions, you must choose the associations to make with the policy package objects and the objects they will govern. Finally, you must customize the policies to fit the needs of your users and management plans.

Let's take a closer look at these policy package design steps.

Choosing the Policy Packages

To choose the policy packages to create on your network, use the following criteria:

1. Determine the desktop platforms present in the container.

2. Consider the size of the network and the size of the container in which you are working.

3. Determine the need for multiple policy packages based on the needs of users and administrators. Consider the following points:

    A. Consider the benefits of workstation conformity when choosing workstation-specific configurations.

    B. Consider the benefits of user-specific configurations for mobile users.

    C. Create container packages at the highest NDS tree level without going beyond the location or site container.

    D. Create workstation packages in the same container that will have the workstations associated with them. You can create a workstation container with the single purpose of holding workstation policy packages and their associated workstation objects.

    E. It is best to create user packages in the same container as the associated users.

Choosing Policy Package Associations

When applying policy associations, consider the order in which the policies are applied. By default, policies are applied to leaf objects the same way NDS rights are applied.

Policies that are associated with a container will be applied after any user-specific or workstation-specific policies are applied. You can, therefore, give precedence to a policy by directly associating it with a user or workstation.

Another important consideration is the time it takes to create and manage the policies. It is much quicker and simpler to associate a policy with a container and all of the users or workstations in it than to do so on a user-by-user basis. Ease of management can conflict with flexibility of configuration for the users. These are the conflicting pressures you must weigh against each other.

Individual user needs on the network must be weighed against administrative ease and the benefits of a one-size-fits-all policy. Make sure you consider when your needs are likely to change. For example, if a new application platform will soon be added, you may want to wait a little while and then go with a workstation-specific policy.

Choosing Policy Configurations

When you are deciding on which policies to implement, you must think carefully and consider the ramifications of implementation. One of the biggest changes to impact a large network will be the addition of workstation and policy objects to its NDS tree. Many trees will grow to become twice their previous size or even larger.

As you know, the partition must not grow to contain more than 1,500 objects. When configuring the Workstation Import Policy, you must keep this in mind.

Network performance is affected by the placement of objects in the tree. You should keep associated workstations and users together in the same container. Access to workstation objects can be improved by placing those objects in close proximity to the NDS partition in the tree, rather than close to the associated user objects.

Creating a single-purpose container (such as one to hold workstation objects) has several disadvantages. This design can reduce access speed and negatively impact the scalability of the NDS tree. Increased partitioning can also reduce performance.

Phase Two: Installation

A full Z.E.N.works installation is completed from the Z.E.N.works CD. You can install the complete Z.E.N.works package or customize your installation by choosing only the Z.E.N.works components that you want to install.

Server Requirements

Z.E.N.works is installed on the server in SYS:PUBLIC. The Novell client must also be upgraded on the network workstations. Z.E.N.works will also install some files in the platform-specific client directories.

During the planning phase, make sure that you can meet the requirements for a Z.E.N.works installation:

- You must have either a NetWare 4.11 or NetWare 5 server.

- Your server must have 70MB of available memory and 205MB of disk space.

- The 32-bit version of NetWare Administrator (NWADMIN32 .EXE) must be installed in SYS:PUBLIC\WIN32.

The 32-bit version of NetWare Administrator functions more smoothly, allowing you to manage the new objects that Z.E.N.works adds to the NDS. This eliminates the need to update the Registry for the snap-in .DLL files that Z.E.N.works adds.

Client Requirements

All Windows clients are supported by Z.E.N.works. The DOS/Windows 3.1 client, however, can only use part of the Z.E.N.works features. Windows 95 and Windows NT are fully functional. The functionality of Windows 98 hasn't been determined yet.

All Windows clients must have the Z.E.N.works version of the Novell client that corresponds to the workstation's operating system installed. In the Z.E.N.works custom installation, you can install this on the server in the SYS:PUBLIC\CLIENT directory.

Users must connect through NDS in order for Z.E.N.works features to work correctly. Connections through the bindery will not work.

Rights Requirements

To install Z.E.N.works, you must have the necessary NDS and file system rights. To perform an installation, you must have Supervisor object rights to the [Root] of the NDS tree.

Read and Compare rights to All Property Rights are given by default to any user, group, or container object when it is associated with an application object. You don't need to manually assign these NDS access rights. Users can instantly access the application objects that are available in the Application Launcher.

Installing Z.E.N.works

Before you begin to install Z.E.N.works, confirm that you have Supervisor rights to the [Root] directory. Log in to each server on which you want to install Z.E.N.works. Make sure all applications are closed on the administrative workstation from which you are going to begin the installation. Procedure 6.1 lists the steps you must follow to install Z.E.N.works.

PROCEDURE 6.1

Installing Z.E.N.works

1. Mount the Z.E.N.works CD on the administrative workstation you are using.

2. The following dialog box appears.

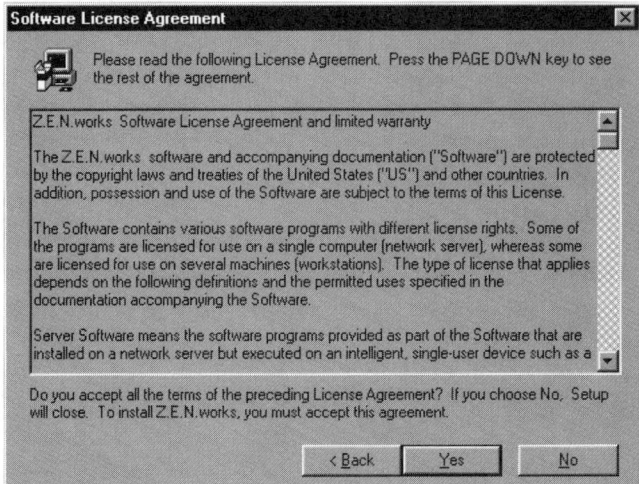

   Accept the License Agreement by clicking Yes.

3. Choose the Install Z.E.N.works option by clicking it. As shown in the
   following graphic, three Z.E.N.works installation options will appear.

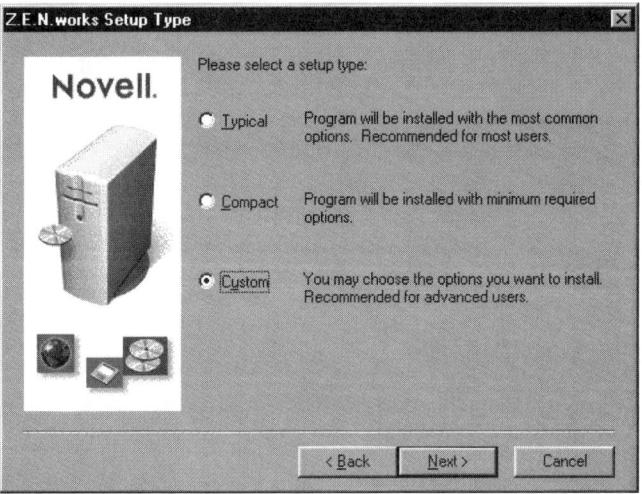

   Typical installs the most common options. Compact installs the least
   number of options. Custom lets you choose the components you want
   to install. Custom is the only choice that will copy the Novell client software to the server for later distribution.

4. Choose the type of installation you want to perform by clicking the appropriate option. If you select a Custom installation, you must choose the components that you choose to install.

5. The Select Components dialog box appears.

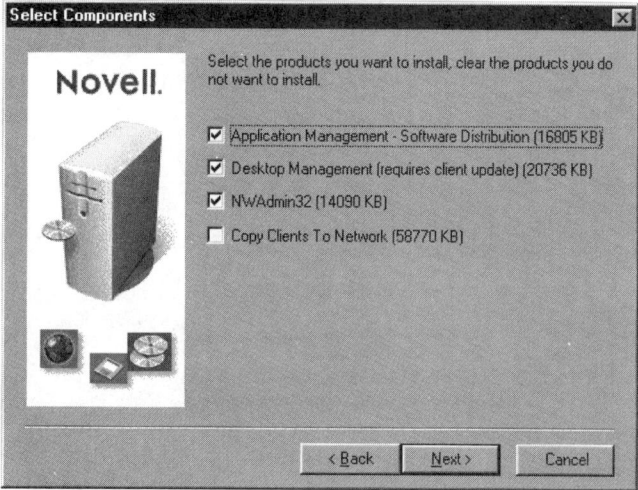

Choose the Z.E.N.works components you want to install, including the Novell clients, by clicking a checkmark into the boxes next to them.

6. A different Select Components dialog box appears.

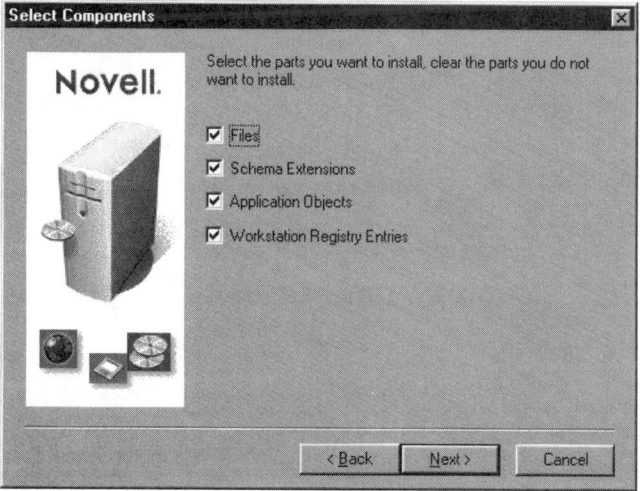

Select the items that you want to install.

7. The Z.E.N.works List of Tree/Servers dialog box will appear.

Click the NDS trees and servers on which you want to install Z.E.N.works. You must be logged in to and authenticated on any servers you want to appear in this box.

8. The Language Selection dialog box should indicate your choice of language.

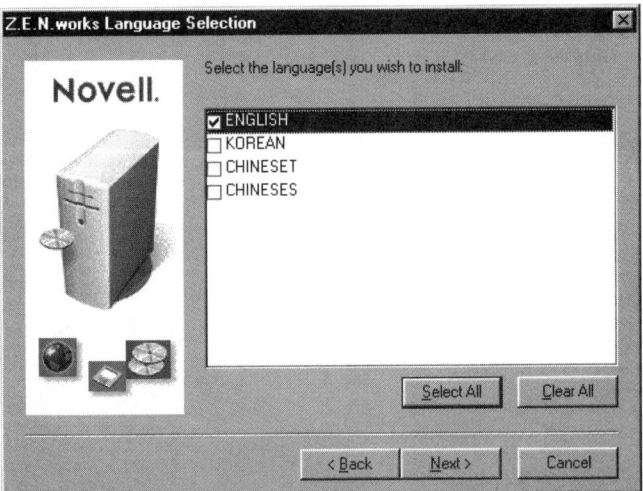

Confirm your language selection.

9. The Start Copying Files dialog box will appear.

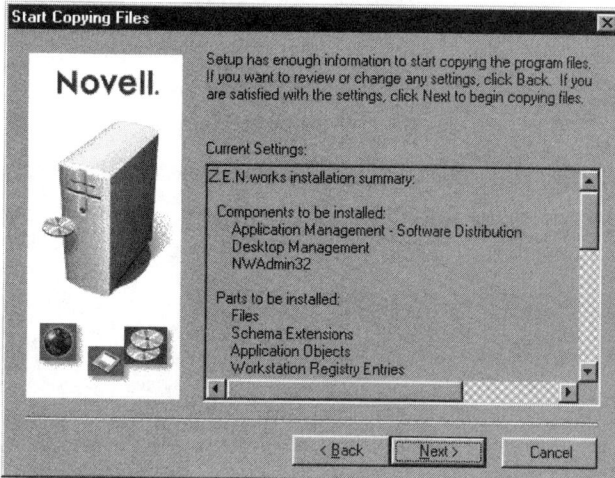

It will include a summary of the Z.E.N.works installation. Click to acknowledge the summary.

10. In the Z.E.N.works dialog boxes, choose and enter [Root] as the level of the NDS tree at which rights should be granted. As you can see in the dialog box, rights can be granted later using two different methods.

The second Select Components dialog box will appear. You can choose whether to install each of these components.

11. Choose the level of rights to be granted. Novell recommends that rights be granted at [Root] level. If part of the tree were denied rights, your ability to manage any workstations in that branch of the tree would be limited.

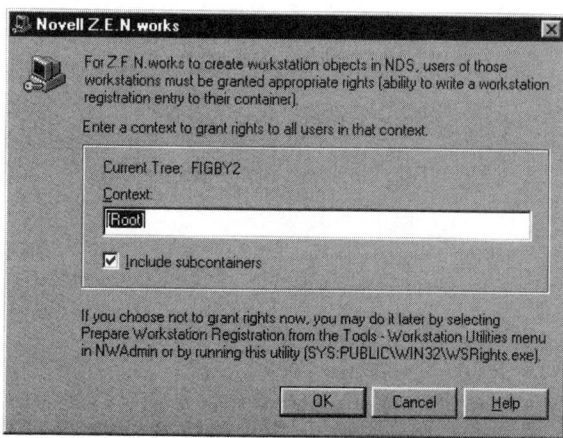

12. Follow the prompts to complete the installation. You may unmark the Read Me and Setup Log dialog boxes if you don't want to read them. Otherwise, use WordPad to display this information.

13. Your installation is now complete. The Setup Complete box celebrates the end of the Z.E.N.works installation.

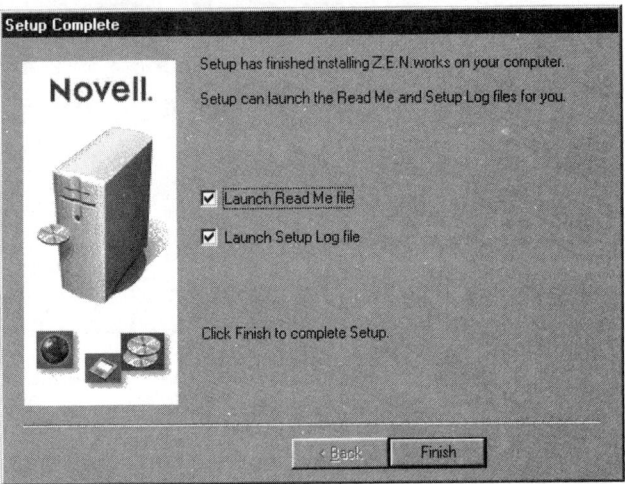

14. The Congratulations box appears.

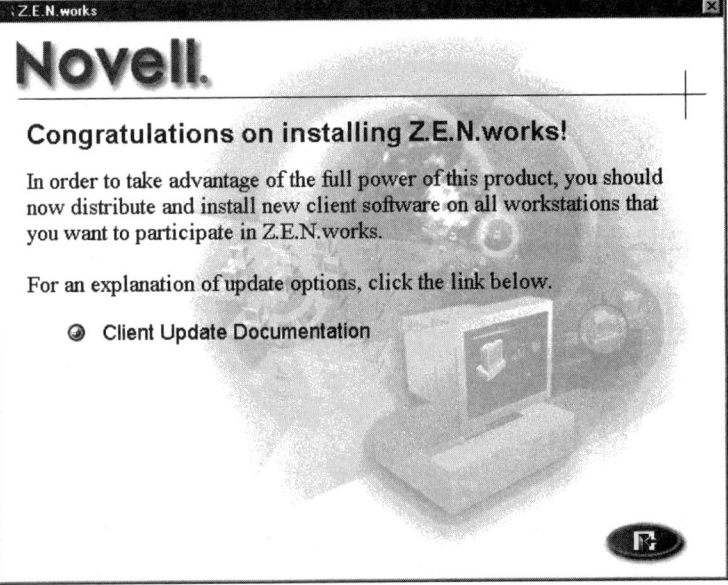

Installing the Z.E.N.works Novell Client

Each Windows clients on the network must have the Z.E.N.works Novell client corresponding to its operating system installed. Procedure 6.1 described the way the Custom Install option allows these client files to be copied to platform-specific directories in SYS:PUBLIC\ CLIENT.

The minimum system requirements necessary to run the Novell client are:

- Intel 486/33 processor or better

- 16MB of RAM for Windows 3.1 or Windows 95 Clients and 24MB of RAM for Windows NT Clients

- 24MB of hard disk space for a complete install

The client can be installed locally or from the network. The client can be installed on multiple workstations using either the Automatic Client Upgrade (ACU) or the unattended client install procedure. To install a Novell client over the network, you must perform the steps described in Procedure 6.2 from the workstation.

PROCEDURE 6.2

Installating a Novell Client over the Network

1. From the workstation, log in and authenticate to a NetWare server that has Z.E.N.works and the Client software installed.

2. Browse to the platform-specific installation program that corresponds to your workstation's platform. These installation files are listed in Table 6.2.

3. Double-click the appropriate workstation file.

4. For Windows 95 only, accept the license agreement by clicking Yes.

5. Select Custom Installation for Windows 95 or Custom Installation for Windows NT and click Next.

6. For Windows 95, select NDS and click Next.

PROCEDURE 6.2 (CONTINUED)

7. For Windows 95, you must choose your options by marking:

   - Novell Workstation Manager

   - Novell Distributed Print Services

   - Novell Remote Control Agent

8. For Windows NT, you must choose your options by marking:

   - Novell Workstation Manager

   - Z.E.N.works Application Launcher NT Service

   - Z.E.N.works Remote Control Agent

9. Choose Install for Windows 95 or Finish for Windows NT.

10. Reboot.

T A B L E 6.2: Network Installation Files and Locations

Client Platform	Location on Network	File Name
Windows 3.1	SYS:PUBLIC\CLIENT\DOSWIN32	INSTALL.EXE
Windows 95	SYS:PUBLIC\CLIENT\WIN95\IBM_ENU	SETUP.EXE
Windows NT	SYS:PUBLIC\CLIENT\WINNT\i386	SETUPNW.EXE

If a workstation is equipped with a CD-ROM, you can install the Novell client locally by following the steps in Procedure 6.3.

PROCEDURE 6.3

Installing a Novell Client Locally

1. Mount the CD on the workstation.

2. Select a language for the installation.

3. Choose and click the platform that corresponds to the workstation.

PROCEDURE 6.3 (CONTINUED)

4. Follow the installation prompts.

5. Reboot and log in.

Multiple Workstation Installation of Novell Clients

The two ways to install multiple workstations with Novell clients are the Automatic Client Upgrade (ACU) and the ACU with the unattended install process. With both of these methods, ACU checks to see if a client is current when that client logs in to the network. If the client is not current, ACU will upgrade the client.

This process can be interrupted and stopped by the user when only the ACU is running. If you add the unattended install parameter, it will force the upgrade. After the ACU and unattended install have run, a client can reboot and log in as a Z.E.N.works-enabled Novell client.

To perform an ACU, follow the steps in Procedure 6.4.

PROCEDURE 6.4

Automatic Client Upgrade

1. Enable the ACU by granting to users the Read and File Scan rights to the directories on the server that contain the installation files that will be read during client login. These are the same files and locations listed in Table 6.2.

2. Decide which workstations you want to automatically install the Novell client on. Modify the login scripts to launch ACU or ACU and unattended install. If you have many users, you will find it more efficient to change the profile or container login scripts.

When you have enabled the Automatic Client Upgrade (ACU) or the unattended installation process, it will automatically make the additions to the login scripts found in Table 6.3.

T A B L E 6.3: Login Script Changes for the Automatic Client Upgrade

Platform	To Add the ACU Process to the Login Script, Add the Following Instruction	To Add the Unattended Install Process to the Login Script, Add the Following Instruction
Windows 3.1 Workstations	#\\servername\volume\ ...INSTALL.EXE/ACU	#\\servername\volume\ ...SETUP.EXE/U
Windows 95 Workstations	#\\servername\volume\ ...SETUP.EXE/ACU	#\\servername\volume\ ...SETUP.EXE/U
Windows NT Workstations	#\\servername\volume\ ...SETUPNW.EXE/ACU	#\\servername\volume\ ...SETUPNW.EXE/U

WARNING For NT workstations, SETUPNW.EXE will work only for users logged in as members of the Power Users or Administrators groups.

The ACU will then check the configuration files on client workstations and determine which files are newer. If the unattended installation process doesn't force the install and the server's files are newer, the user can choose to continue or cancel the ACU process.

If the user declines the upgrade to the new client, the process will repeatedly offer to upgrade the workstation whenever a user logs in from a workstation with the old software.

If the user updates the client or if the unattended install forces the change, the upgrade will take place after a reboot and fresh login.

Phase Three: Workstation Implementation

For a workstation to be imported into the NDS tree and managed as a workstation object, it must be registered with NDS first. As you have seen, you must install the new Novell client on the workstation and then have the workstation with the new Novell client log in to the network.

Workstation Registration

When these conditions are met, the Z.E.N.works Workstation Registration Agent automatically registers workstations. It records their network addresses, login users, and the servers that authenticated the registrations.

A Workstation Registration Property in the user's container stores all of this information through a Workstation Registration Agent. As users log in after the new client has been installed, a list of these workstations is generated within this container property. After the workstations appear on the list, they can be imported into the NDS tree.

The Workstation Registration Agent will use one of the following files:

- WSREG16.EXE is used for workstations with 16-bit platforms with DOS and/or Windows 3.1 operating systems.

- WSREG32.EXE will work for 32-bit workstations using Windows 95 or Windows NT.

- WSREG32.DLL will work for all 32-bit Windows workstations using Desktop Management.

These files are specific to either the workstation platform or the workstations using Desktop Management.

In order to import workstation objects, your NDS design should include the preferred naming conventions and location on NDS. You will need to create workstation policy packages for each platform on your network as discussed previously.

A workstation import policy must be configured to create the workstation objects in the chosen locations on NDS and with the chosen naming conventions in NDS.

Registration Methods

Three methods can be used to set up automatic operation of the Workstation Registration Agent:

- Login Scripts

- Z.E.N.works Scheduler

- Z.E.N.works Application Launcher

Login Scripts   A container login script can run the Workstation Registration Agent's files when a user logs in. You can do this by adding the code lines found in Table 6.4 to the container login scripts.

T A B L E 6.4 Login Script Code Lines	**Platform**	**Line of Code**

	Windows 3.1	```IF "%PLATFORM"="WIN"THEN begin```
		```write "Register Windows 3.1 Workstation"```
		```#wsreg16.exe```
		```end```

	Windows 95	```IF "%PLATFORM"="W95"THEN begin```
		```write "Register 95 Workstation"```
		```#wsreg32.exe```
		```end```

	Windows NT	```IF "%PLATFORM"="WNT"THEN begin```
		```write "Register NT Workstation"```
		```#wsreg32.exe```
		```end```

Z.E.N.works Scheduler   The Z.E.N.works Scheduler will run the registration the first time a workstation logs in to the network. This utility only works with Windows 95 and Windows NT workstations.

The Z.E.N.works Novell Workstation is required to run the Scheduler. As users log in, the Workstation Registration .DLL file will register their workstations.

In addition, the Scheduler icon is displayed on each workstation's System Tray in the lower-right corner of the desktop. By double-clicking this icon, users can view the actions that the Scheduler is scheduled to perform.

The Z.E.N.works Scheduler dialog box, as shown in Figure 6.5, will appear when a user double-clicks the icon in the workstation's System Tray.

FIGURE 6.5

The Z.E.N.works
Scheduler dialog box
displays automated
processes that are
scheduled.

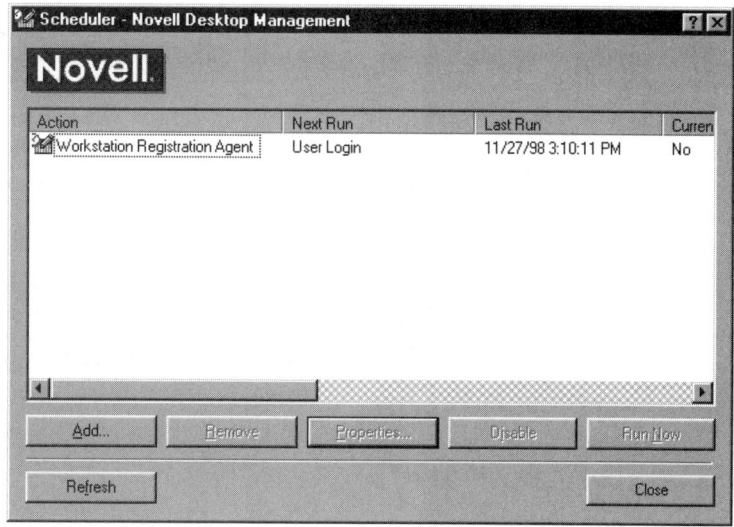

Z.E.N.works Application Launcher   To perform an upgrade with the Application Launcher, you must first create an application object for each platform's .EXE file. You must then associate the application object with each user, user group, or container object in the NDS tree.

The Workstation Registration Agent will then run automatically whenever a user logs in to the network. He or she will be listed with the appropriate workstation address in the NDS.

Registration Verification

When you have performed one or more of the workstation registration processes previously discussed, you can find a log file stating whether or not the registration was successful. The registrations are located in a log file at the root of the workstation's local hard disk.

For Windows 3.1 workstations, the registration is stored in WSREG16.LOG. In Windows 95 or Windows NT workstations, it is stored in WSREG32.LOG.

By accessing each container's details in NDS, you can view a list of the workstations that successfully registered in that container. The Registered Workstations page in the container details will show this list of workstations.

Importing the Workstations

After you have registered your workstations, you need to import them into the NDS tree. This is the step through which they become NDS objects. You can use either the Z.E.N.works Application Launcher or the Z.E.N.works Scheduler to perform the import.

Use the Application Launcher to associate an application object. Use the Scheduler to edit the schedule access through the Import Workstations utility.

This Import Workstations utility will extract the workstation's network address that is then stored in the Network Address page.

For smaller networks, you can import the workstations manually through NetWare Administrator. To do this, perform the steps in Procedure 6.5.

PROCEDURE 6.5

Manually Importing the Workstations

1. In NetWare Administrator, click the container in which you want to place the workstation objects.

2. Make a user policy package matching the workstation platform.

3. Enable and configure the Workstation Import policy. Enter configuration information into the Configuration Information fields on both the Workstation Location page and the Workstation Naming page.

4. Associate the policy package with the container object.

5. Save your policy package changes and return to NetWare Administrator.

6. Making sure your container is still highlighted. Go to Tools ➤ Import Workstations.

PROCEDURE 6.5 (CONTINUED)

7. Go to the Import From tab, as seen in the following dialog box.

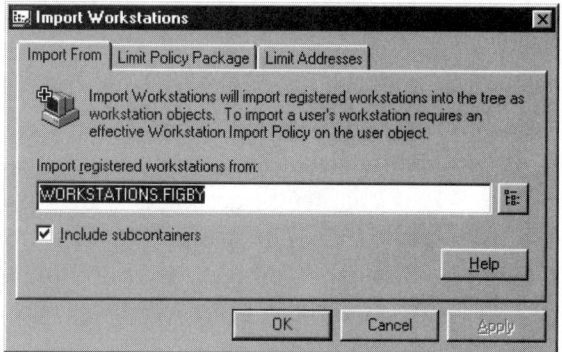

Enter the location where you would like to place the workstation objects or use the Browse button to find it.

8. After the workstation objects are created, a screen will indicate that the import is complete and report the number of workstation objects you have created, as shown in the following box.

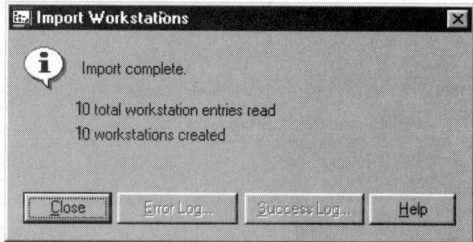

To further verify the success of your manual importation, view the Success Log on the notepad that lists the workstation objects created, or click and expand the tree from the container and scroll down to see the workstation objects you created. You may need to collapse the tree first and then expand the container object.

Another way to verify your successful importation of workstation objects is to double-click the container object and directly view the workstation objects on NDS.

Desktop Configuration

The workstation-specific and user-specific policies that you configure in your policy packages work in concert to create the desktop configurations your users will see. This means you can configure their desktops from a user perspective, a workstation perspective, or both.

From the workstation policy package, you can configure computer system policies. With these policies, you can associate applications that can then be accessed by the chosen workstations. An application will automatically launch if Run is checked on this page.

The NT Computer System Policies page, as shown in Figure 6.6, allows you to automatically associate and launch applications.

F I G U R E   6.6

This dialog box appears as the NT Computer System Policies page for Policy Schedules.

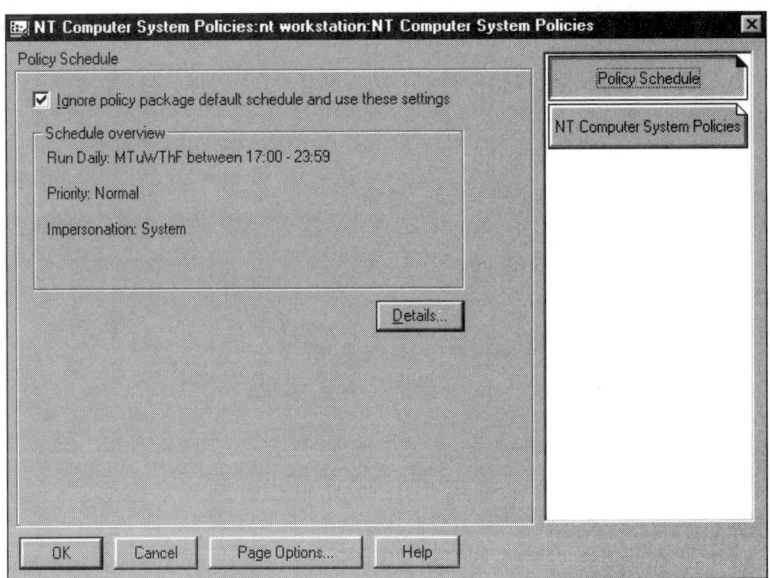

The next dialog box shown in Figure 6.7 is seen with the various types of computer system policies that can be enabled.

User system policies work in reverse from the previous policy packages. They designate the policies that a specific user will *not* be able to access. These applications are then hidden from the associated users.

FIGURE 6.7

FIGURE 6.7

This dialog box shows the various NT computer system policies.

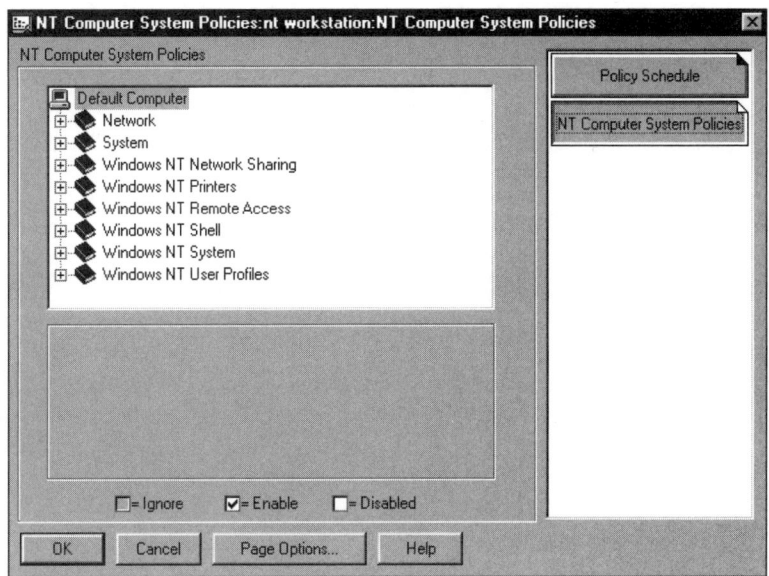

You can also add other restrictions with user system policies. (For example, you can remove the Run and Find commands from the Start menu.)

Desktop applications can be restricted using the user system policies. (See Figure 6.8.)

Remember that the policy packages you enable and associate with user and workstation objects go into effect only when they are associated with each other.

Configuring Printing Environments

Z.E.N.works allows you to configure the printing environment by associating users and workstations with printers and printer drivers through the policies in NetWare Administrator. Printing administration can be one of the most time-consuming tasks an administrator regularly faces.

FIGURE 6.8

The various NT
user system policies
are shown in this
dialog box.

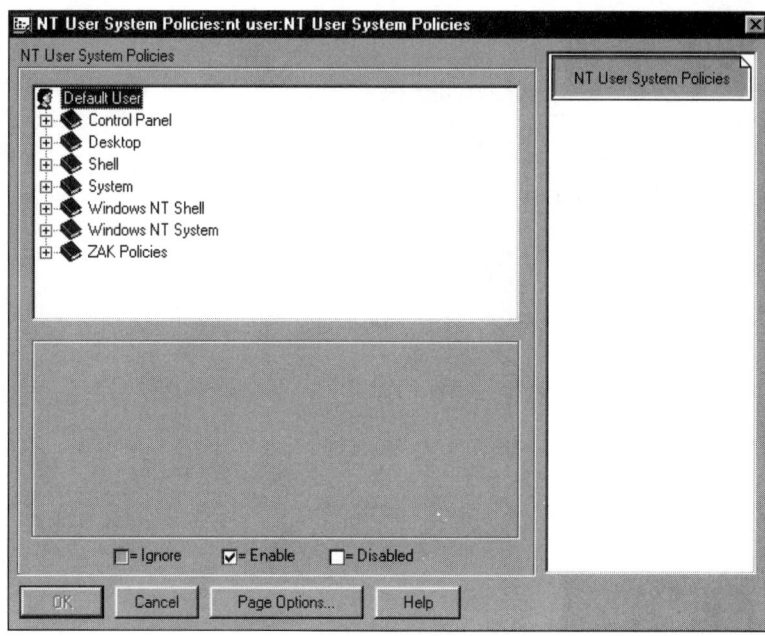

After a user or workstation has been associated with a printer and driver, users will then authenticate to the network. After login, they will find the printer objects and print drivers already installed on their desktops.

You can use the user policy package to associate a specific printer with a user. They will be able to use the printer from any workstation they use to log on to the network.

If your printers and workstations are segregated in discrete areas, you can associate the printer and its driver with a workstation group. Decide which method best fits the structure in your various departments.

Mandatory User Profiles

If conformity of appearance is important to your department or organization, you can use the Desktop Preferences policy in the user policy packages to configure all of the desktops to look alike. Most of the settings in the Control Panel (such as wallpaper, screen savers, and sounds) can be configured in a mandatory way. Every time users log in, they will see the same familiar desktop.

Review

Z.E.N.works is an important milestone in network development as it extends and maximizes the ability of administrators to include workstation objects and functional control components like policy package objects in the NDS. Its power and elegance can be really appreciated on large networks where the time and money it saves for companies will be readily apparent.

Z.E.N.works Components

In this chapter, you were introduced to the four Z.E.N.works components. The four components are:

- Novell Workstation Manager
- NetWare Application Launcher
- Remote Control
- Help Requester

Policy Packages

You learned a little bit about how Z.E.N.works will help reduce the Total Cost of Ownership (TCO) by allowing you to manage workstations in your network. You saw how the addition of workstation objects and policy package objects extends the NDS and permits the association of workstations and users with those policies.

You took a closer look at those three kinds of policies and at the three platform-specific policy packages.

- Container
- User
- Workstation

The three workstation platforms that determine the policy package you will choose are:

- Windows 3.1*x*
- Windows 95
- Windows NT

Z.E.N.works Design and Implementation

You saw the three phases of a successful Z.E.N.works design and implementation process. The three phases are:

Phase One: Designing the NDS Structure

Phase Two: Installation

Phase Three: Workstation Implementation

You learned about the important parameters you must use in order to design the NDS structure. Administrators with larger networks must remember that each partition must contain fewer than 1,500 objects.

You reviewed the procedures for installing Z.E.N.works and the Z.E.N.works client. In the Z.E.N.works installation you had to choose a compact or custom installation and the components you wanted to install with the custom installation.

You saw that the requirements for a Z.E.N.works installation include:

- NetWare 4.11 or NetWare 5 server

- 70MB of available server memory and 205MB of disk space

- The 32-bit version of NetWare Administrator (NWADMIN32 .EXE) must be installed in SYS:PUBLIC\WIN32

You studied how to register and import workstation objects into the NDS and how to configure desktops.

Z.E.N.works is a powerful new tool that allows desktop management without physically visiting users' workstations. In the next chapter, we will look more closely at the remaining Z.E.N.works components: Z.E.N.works Application Launcher, Remote Control, and Help Requester.

Z.E.N.works Practice Questions

1. Z.E.N.works stands for which of the following?

   A. Zinc Embedded Nexus

   B. Zero Entropy Networking

   C. Zero Effort Networking

   D. Zigzag Energy Network

2. Which of the following is not a Z.E.N.works component?

   A. Novell Workstation Manager

   B. NetWare Application Launcher

   C. Z.E.N.works Scheduler

   D. Help Requester

   E. Remote Control

3. Which of the following functions are not performed by Workstation Manager? (Choose two.)

   A. Manage workstation inventories in NDS with workstation objects and workstation group objects, without visiting the workstation

   B. Import network workstations into the NDS

   C. Distribute and update clients, applications, or print drivers to the client workstations

   D. Choose a standard user interface or designate specific interfaces for individual users

   E. Schedule functions on the workstation to occur during the evening or when users are logged off of the network

   F. Install and configure Z.E.N.works components on the server

4. The Z.E.N.works Application Launcher enables you to do all except which of the following? (Choose two.)

   A. Automate tasks that previously required a physical trip to a user's workstation

   B. Grant file rights to users and assign access to them

   C. Take "pictures" of a workstation's configuration before and after an application is installed with the snAppShot utility

   D. Hierarchically situate application objects in the NDS tree through multilevel folders

   E. Restrict application access through workstation-specific and user-specific policy packages

   F. Allow registration with a secure Windows NT server through Windows NT Service Control Manager to make changes on the server or workstations

G. Associate application objects with workstation objects in NDS

H. Use an application suspension configuration to schedule times for an application's access to cease

5. Choose three types of policy packages.

A. Container

B. [Root]

C. User Group

D. Workstation

E. Supervisor

F. Organization

6. The order in which policies are applied in policy associations is unimportant. (True or False.)

7. The number of objects must never exceed:

A. 750

B. 1,000

C. 1,500

D. 2,000

E. 2,500

8. The server in a Z.E.N.works installation requires how many megabytes of available memory?

9. When you are installing Z.E.N.works, the best context in which to grant rights is generally which of the following?

    A. Workstation Group

    B. User Group

    C. Container

    D. [Root]

10. For NT workstations, SETUPNW.EXE will work only for users in which two groups?

    A. Power Users Group

    B. Supervisor Group

    C. Administration Group

    D. Container Group

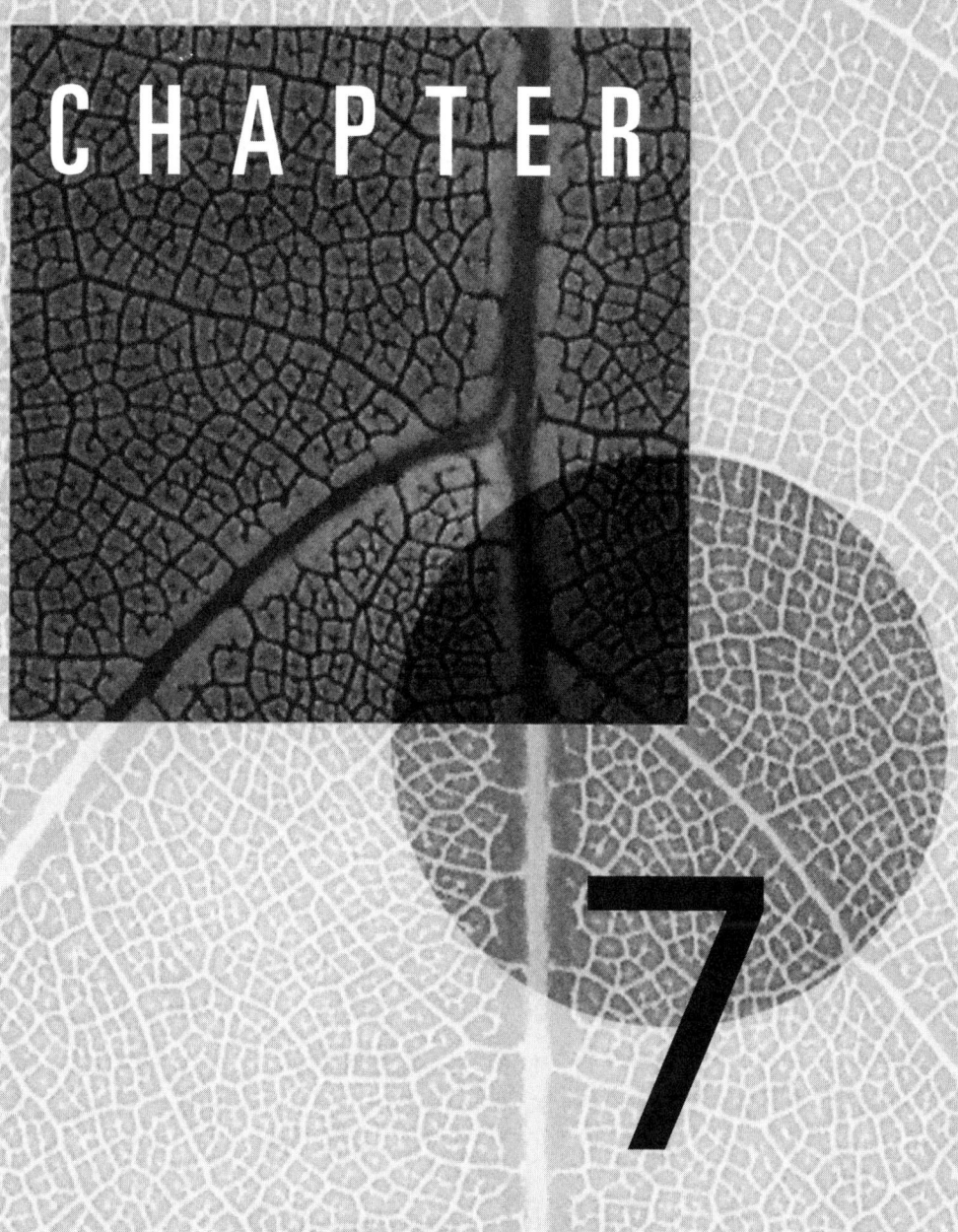

CHAPTER

7

Z.E.N.works Part Two

Roadmap

This chapter continues our look at the remaining components of the Z.E.N.works suite and at how to use these powerful tools.

Topics Covered

- The Application Launcher
- Remote Control
- Help Requester

Skills You'll Learn

- Understand Application Launcher's four components
- Learn to distribute applications with the Application Launcher
- Learn how to capture configurations with snAppShot
- Learn to make an application object from an Application Object Template (AOT) file
- Learn to distribute the Application Launcher
- Learn to use AOTs to create an application object
- Learn to distribute user agents
- Learn to use Remote Control to control a workstation
- Learn to use Application Launcher to distribute Help Requester
- Learn to use Help Requester

In the last chapter, we looked at Z.E.N.works, its four components, and the three phases of designing and implementing it. We focused on the policy packages associated with the workstation and the objects used to configure and control desktops through the Desktop

Manager. In this chapter, we will take a closer look at the remaining three components of Z.E.N.works:

- Application Launcher

- Remote Control

- Help Requester

These three components allow you to manage applications across the network, to manage workstations from a remote location, and to better communicate about workstation problems through the network. We will take an in-depth look at the functionality of these three components.

Application Launcher

The Z.E.N.works' Application Launcher allows installation, maintenance, control, and administration of applications on the network. When initially installing most applications (even server-based ones), you usually need to install desktop components. These desktop files are frequently corrupted or lost, requiring much management effort and time.

The Application Launcher automates these management tasks by facilitating automatic distribution and installation of desktop components and by "remembering" desktop application configurations and maintaining those files. The applications themselves are managed as objects on the NDS tree.

You can then manage these applications through their objects with NetWare Administrator. You can control applications without physically visiting the workstations. Users no longer need to be concerned about drives, application source directories, databases, or their own application configurations and upgrades.

Application Launcher Components

The Application Launcher has two components for users (see Figure 7.1) and two components for administrators (see Figure 7.2).

The two Application Launcher components for users are:

- Application Launcher window
- Application Explorer

FIGURE 7.1

The Application
Launcher window
is a familiar and
useful place for
users to launch
their applications.

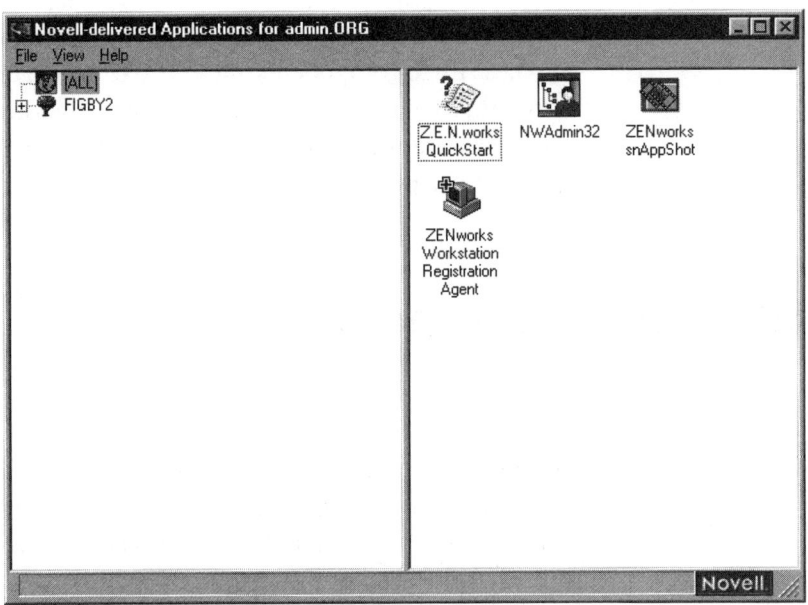

FIGURE 7.2

The Application
Explorer window
delivers applications
to your desktop and
elsewhere.

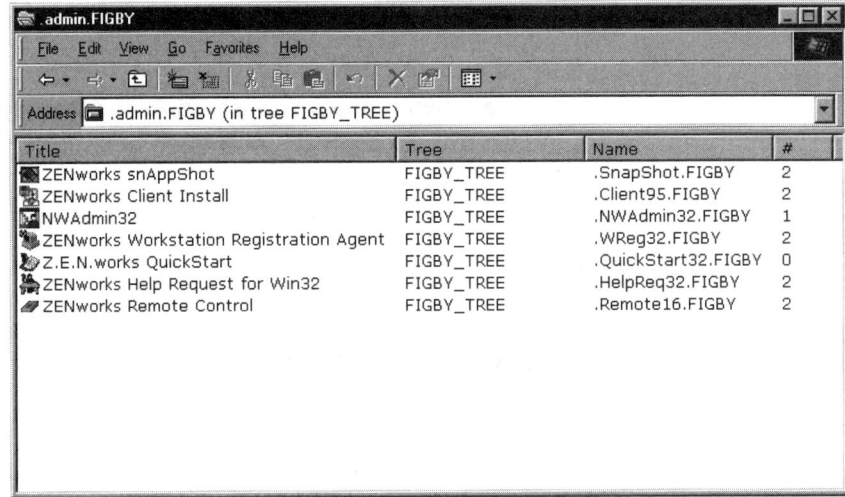

The two Application Launcher components for administrators are:

- NetWare Administrator Application Launcher Snap-In
- snAppShot

User Components

The Application Launcher window and the Application Explorer facilitate application access and execution for the user. Both of these components create pathways to applications. Both work on Windows NT and Windows 95 platforms. The Application Launcher window also works with Windows 3.1*x* platforms.

The Application Launcher window uses a *wrapper* technology with a wrapper executable file (NAL.EXE). The executable file for the Application Launcher window is SYS:PUBLIC\NAL.EXE.

NAL.EXE determines the correct executable file to launch the application, either NALW31.EXE for Windows 3.1 workstations or NALWIN32.EXE for workstations with a Windows NT or 95 operating system.

The NAL.EXE wrapper terminates itself once the correct executable file is executed. The wrapper will adjust to different platforms. For example, if a user moves to a new department and logs on from an NT workstation, rather than his or her personal Windows 95 desktop, the wrapper will adjust to the new desktop, even adding statements to a login script if necessary.

The Application Launcher wrapper will also update files on the workstation before it launches the application. These files are located in a client's WINDOWS\SYSTEM directory.

The Application Explorer can be used as an alternative to the Application Launcher window. The Application Explorer will deliver applications to:

- The Start menu
- The System Tray
- The Desktop
- The Application Explorer window
- The Windows Explorer

Administrative Components

The Application Launcher snap-in and snAppShot are the administrative components of Application Launcher. After successfully installing Z.E.N.works, you can use the Application Launcher to distribute applications to users by following the steps in Procedure 7.1.

PROCEDURE 7.1

Distributing Applications with Application Launcher

1. Use the snAppShot utility to capture the workstation's configuration.

2. Make the application object from the Template file created by snAppShot.

3. Associate the application object with the container, workstation group, workstation, user, or user group object.

4. Put the NAL.EXE wrapper in login scripts.

Application Launcher Snap-In   The Application Launcher snap-in is a Windows DLL file that gives you the ability to create and display application objects. Its filename is APPSNP32.DLL.

The Application Launcher snap-in provides a property page for the user, user group, or container objects. With it, you can set a property to associate an application with a particular user or with a group of users at the group or container level.

The Application Launcher snap-in adds the application object to the NDS tree at the level you choose. It will also add the following items (as shown in Figure 7.3) to the Tools menu in NetWare Administrator:

- Export Application Object
- Show All Inherited Applications
- Migrate Application Objects
- Search and Replace
- Sync Distribution GUIDs

- Generate New GUIDs

- AOT/AXT File Tools

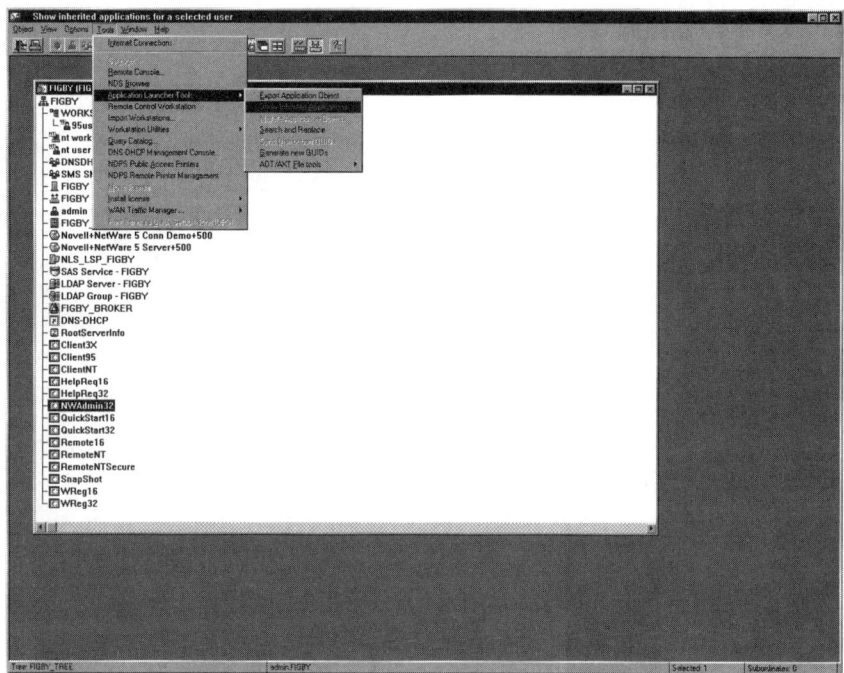

FIGURE 7.3

The Application snap-in adds these functions to the Tools menu.

SnAppShot SnAppShot takes "before" and "after" pictures of the configuration of the workstation on which it is run. After you take the "before" picture, you will be prompted to install an application. SnAppShot will then take an "after" picture. The first screen you see in snAppShot is shown in Figure 7.4. These pictures can be used to deduce the changes made to the workstation's configuration by the application.

These deduced changes form an Application Object Template (or AOT) that lists the changes made to the workstation. You can read and edit the AOT from NetWare Administrator.

All of the application's changes to the workstation combined with your changes become part of the application object used to distribute

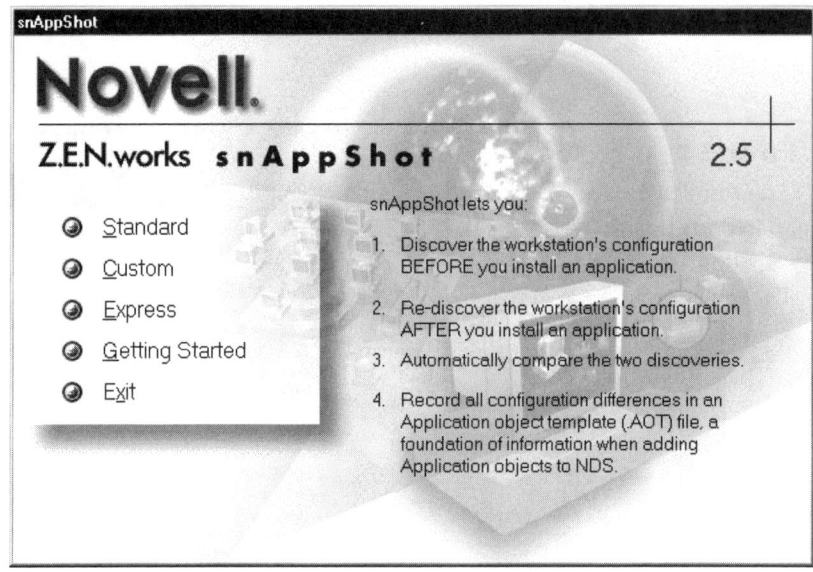

the application to users. These changes include changes to the Registry, INI files, text files, application files, DLLs, and Windows Shortcuts. Let's take a look at the actual steps involved in capturing a workstation's configuration with snAppShot in Procedure 7.2 and at how to make an application object from an AOT file in Procedure 7.3.

PROCEDURE 7.2

Capturing Configurations with snAppShot

1. At a workstation, run SNAPSHOT.EXE.

2. Choose the standard process for snAppShot.

3. Choose the application name that is represented as the application object in NDS.

4. Choose a short description of the application that will appear as a caption with the icon in the Application Launcher window or Application Explorer window.

PROCEDURE 7.2 (CONTINUED)

5. Choose a directory to store the application files in, and note its path. SnAppShot will make a copy of all application files that the application's setup file installs on the workstation. The extensions on these files are changed to .FIL. SnAppShot also creates a list of these files that will become a file in part of the AOT. This file is called FILEDEF.TXT.

6. Choose a directory and filename for the AOT. If you create this file on a network drive, other users can access it unless it is hidden.

7. Choose the drives containing applications to enter into Scan These Drives. By default, snAppShot will automatically scan the C: drive; however, any drives that hold applications must be entered.

8. SnAppShot will take the "before" picture of the workstation's configuration (including the Registry, INI files, text files, application files, Windows shortcuts, and DLLs).

9. Run the application installation or setup program by clicking Run the Application Install.

10. In the Application's Install Directory field, enter the pathname of the software that was just installed.

11. SnAppShot will take the "after" picture and store the information in the AOT file.

PROCEDURE 7.3

Making an Application Object from an AOT File

1. Open NetWare Administrator, and click the container in which you want the application object to reside.

2. Choose Object ➢ Create to make the application object.

3. Choose Using the AOT File to make the application object.

4. Browse to the directory with the AOT, and select the AOT you want.

PROCEDURE 7.3 (CONTINUED)

5. Confirm or enter the source and target directories as you follow the prompts. NetWare Administrator will give you the source and target paths. Verify that the source path is for the installation files for the application with which you are working. Make sure that the target path is for the directory in which you want to install the application.

6. Follow the prompts to complete the installation and close the application object's Details window.

Making Applications Available to Users

The most individual method of assigning an application to a user is to exclusively associate the user's user object with an application object. You can insert either a UNC or a drive mapping in the Path to Executable File field on the Associations page of the application object.

If you use a drive mapping, make sure that the drive is available to all of the users associated with the application so the application will work!

For most containers, user group objects or container objects can be associated with the application object giving users access to the application. This will also work with new users who are automatically added to the container or group.

File system rights are also granted when an application object is associated with users, groups, or workstations. To configure additional rights, choose specific directories for users, go to the File Rights page in the application object, and follow the steps in Procedure 7.4.

PROCEDURE 7.4

Associating Objects with the Application Objects

1. Go to and click Details of the application object and then go to and click the Associations page.

2. At the Associations property page, click Add.

3. Browse to and double-click an object (container, group, or user).

4. Click OK.

Using the Application Launcher

To make the Application Launcher available to users, place NAL.EXE in their login scripts. You can place NAL.EXE on the network where all users will have access to it (e.g., SYS:PUBLIC). Add one of the following statements to the container login script:

```
#\\servername\SYS\PUBLIC\NAL.EXE
```
or
```
@\\servername\SYS\PUBLIC\NAL.EXE
```

The @ command will let the login script continue while this NAL.EXE command is being processed. The # command requires the instruction to place NAL.EXE in the login script to be completed before the login script can continue.

The next time a user logs in, the Application Launcher will launch automatically, and all associated applications will appear in the Launcher window. When the user double-clicks the application icon, the Launcher will make all the necessary setup changes and install all the client files on the workstation.

The next time the application is ordered through a double-click, the Launcher will detect that it has already been installed. It will check the files and configuration on the workstation to make sure there are no missing files or changes that have occurred since the last use. If there are changes, the Launcher will reinstall the missing component before launching the application. Let's take a look at how to distribute the Application Launcher in Procedure 7.5 and at how we can create an application object with an AOT file in Procedure 7.6.

PROCEDURE 7.5

Application Launcher Distribution

1. Log in as Admin from a network workstation.

2. Create an application object or go to an existing one.

   A. To create the object, open NetWare Administrator and click the application object.

   B. In the Object menu, click Create.

   C. In the Object list, double-click Application.

   D. Choose Create Simple Application Object, and click Next.

   E. Type a name in the Application Object Name box.

   F. Browse to the application executable file.

   G. Mark the Define Additional Properties box, and click Finish.

3. Associate your application object with the container object.

4. Right-click your container object.

5. Choose Details.

6. Click Login Script.

7. Add the following lines to the bottom of the container login script:

   ```
   @\\servername\SYS\PUBLIC.NAL.EXE
   @\\servername\SYS\PUBLIC\NALEXPLD.EXE
   ```

8. To add application launcher icons, click Applications and mark the System Tray, Desktop, or Start menu boxes. Click OK.

PROCEDURE 7.5 (CONTINUED)

9. Log in to the network as a user from the container in which you are working.

10. From the icon you created, launch the application that you associated with the container by clicking the icon.

11. Close the application.

12. Launch the application from the Application Explorer by double-clicking the executable.

PROCEDURE 7.6

Using AOT to Create an Application Object

1. Log in as Admin from an administrative workstation.

2. Open NetWare Administrator.

3. Choose a container and click it.

4. In the Object menu, click Create.

5. In the Object List, click Application.

6. Click Create an Object with an AOT/AXT File, and then click Next.

7. Browse to the directory where you have stored the AOT file and click it.

8. Click Open, and then click Next.

9. Verify your Source and Target paths, and then click Next and Finish.

10. Define the parameters for your application object by right-clicking the application object.

11. Click Details.

12. In the Application Icon field, rename the icon if necessary.

13. Click Path to Executable File, and type the UNC or drive mapping.

Remote Control

The Z.E.N.works Remote Control, found in NetWare Administrator, will connect to and manage workstations on the network. The User Agent is the client-side software (WUSER.EXE on Windows 3.1 and Windows 95 workstations and WUSER32.EXE on Windows NT workstations) and must already be installed on the workstations in order for Remote Control to work.

For Remote Control to operate, Z.E.N.works must be installed and workstation objects must be registered and imported into the NDS. The following User Agent application objects are placed on the NDS tree during the Z.E.N.works installation:

- REMOTE16 application object (for Windows 3.1 or Windows 95 workstations)

- REMOTENT application object (for Windows NT workstations)

- REMOTENTSECURE application object (for secure Windows NT workstations)

To run these User Agents on Windows workstations, use the Application Launcher application objects. These User Agent application objects are associated with user objects, user group objects, or container objects in order to make them functional on the workstations. To distribute the User Agents, follow the steps in Procedure 7.7.

To access the Application Launcher, you must have Read and File Scan system rights to the directory where the Application Launcher and the User Agent reside. The default directory for both of these is SYS:PUBLIC.

PROCEDURE 7.7

Distributing User Agents

1. Go to the application object and right-click the Details window.

2. Choose Associations to associate the User Agent application object with another object.

PROCEDURE 7.7 (CONTINUED)

3. Highlight the object to which you associated the User Agent object.

4. Go to the Application property page. In the list of associated objects, mark the box for Force Run for the User Agent Application Object.

5. To launch the Force Run option, you must run Application Explorer to launch the User Agent applications. To automatically launch Application Explorer, add the following command to the parent container that is associated with the User Agent application object:

   `@\\servername\SYS\PUBLIC\NALEXPLP.EXE`

6. This will automatically launch Application Explorer and place the User Agent applications on the workstations.

On Windows NT workstations, the REMOTENT application object will launch NTSTACFG.EXE from the SYS:PUBLIC directory. The Novell WUSER Agent service is then registered with Windows NT. The WUSER.EXE application will run on Windows 3.1 and Windows 95 workstations from the SYS:PUBLIC directory. You can see that Remote Control is running on the workstation on the Windows Status bar.

When the Z.E.N.works remote client is installed on the workstation, the User Agent is installed in the Startup folder. This lets the agents activate when a user logs in to the network from each workstation.

The User Agent for Windows NT will run automatically after installation. You must specifically choose to run the User Agents for Windows 3.1 or Windows 95 through a login script, the Desktop Management Scheduler, or the Z.E.N.works Application Launcher.

To place the User Agent application in a login script, you should place a command to run the WUSER agent in a container login script that will run for the workstation objects. This method is preferred because the WUSER agent must run every time the workstations reboot.

You can go to the container login script by accessing the container object's Details in NetWare Administrator and adding the following lines:

```
IF "%PLATFORM"="W95" THEN begin @ wuser.exe
end
IF "%PLATFORM"="WIN" THEN begin @ wuser.exe
end
IF "%PLATFORM"="WNT" THEN begin @ ntstacfg.exe
end
```

You only need to install NTSTACFG.EXE once on a Windows NT workstation. After the initial installation, the service will run automatically every time the Windows NT workstation boots.

Remote Control will run with the NetWare Administrator utility (NWADMIN32) on servers running NetWare 4.11 or NetWare 5. The workstations must have the Z.E.N.works client installed, and they must be connected to the network through NDS.

Remote Control Security

When you attempt to remotely access a workstation using Z.E.N.works Remote Control, the workstation's User Agent application checks out the security restrictions in the workstation object. Any workstation policy packages (if they exist) are then checked for security restrictions.

Finally, the User Agent application checks for any Remote Control restrictions in the user object or in any policy packages associated with the user. If all of these NDS points of control allow it, a remote session can then begin.

The Z.E.N.works Remote Control user agents use NDS authentication to allow you to take remote control of a workstation. You need the necessary NDS and File System rights to access and control the workstations.

Remote Control Rights Requirements

The specific NDS rights you must have to remotely control a workstation are:

- Browse right to workstation object
- Read rights (from Public) to the wm:network address attribute of the workstation object
- Write right to the DM:Remote Control attribute of the workstation object

Remote Control Security Parameters

Workstation objects are created with Remote Control access enabled by default. You can use NetWare Administrator to set security parameters to grant or restrict access to workstations.

If Remote Control security applies only to a few users or administrators on your network, you can easily configure those parameters through the user or workstation objects on NDS. Use the page shown in Figure 7.5 to grant or restrict Remote Control access by a user. To configure Remote Control with User or Workstation objects, follow the steps in Procedure 7.8.

PROCEDURE 7.8

Configuring Remote Control with User or Workstation Objects

1. To configure these security parameters, go to the workstation or user object and access the Details of the user or workstation object.

2. Click the object's Remote Control button.

3. To restrict Remote Control access for this workstation or user, unmark the box for Enable Remote Control.

4. If you want to enable Remote Control and choose the type of prompt you want for a Remote Control session, keep the box marked.

5. To enforce these settings, check the box for Use These Settings and Ignore Workstation Remote Control Policy.

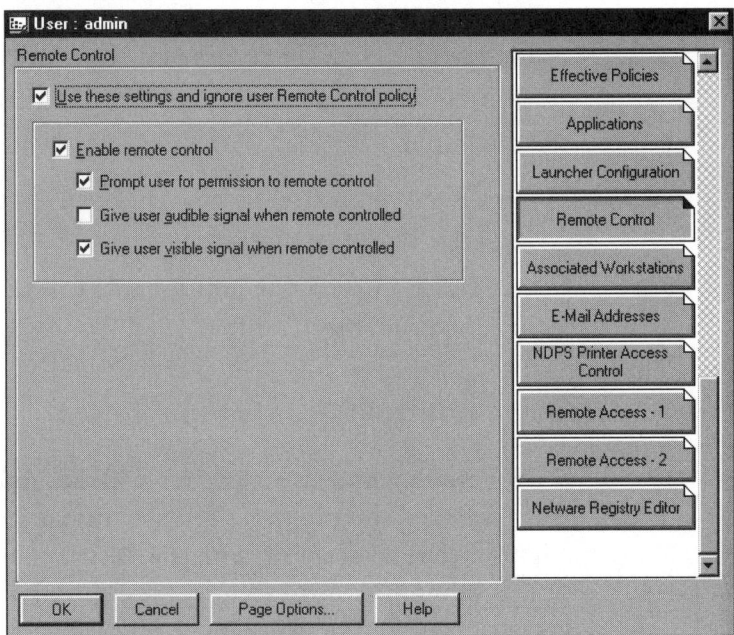

FIGURE 7.5

Remote Control page
of a user object

Remote Control for Multiple Users or Workstations   If you need to set up Remote Control for many users or workstations, you should set up the Remote Control policy in a policy package. (See Procedure 7.9.) To do this, you must:

- Make a workstation or user policy package in the NDS tree.

- Enable the policy package's Remote Control policy, and then configure the security parameters.

- Finally, associate the policy package with the objects (container, user, user group, workstation, or workstation group) for which the parameters are to be implemented.

PROCEDURE 7.9

Using a Policy Package to Configure Remote Control for Multiple Users

1. From NetWare Administrator, create a user or workstation policy package object with the correct workstation platform.

PROCEDURE 7.9 (CONTINUED)

2. Mark the box for Enable Remote Control and choose Prompt User for Permission to Use Remote Control.

3. Mark the box for Use These Settings and Ignore the Remote Control Policy.

4. If you do not want this workstation to be accessed by Remote Control, mark the box for Disable Remote Control.

5. Make certain that you then associate this policy package object with the object(s) to which you want these policies applied.

To configure the Remote Control security parameters, you can go to the Remote Control page in a workstation or user policy package object or you can access the Remote Control page in a workstation or user object. These parameters are displayed in Table 7.1.

T A B L E 7.1:   Remote Control Security Parameters

Parameter	Functionality
Audible Signal	This sends an audible alert signal to the workstation when it is being accessed by Remote Control.
Visible Signal	This sends a visible alert icon to the workstation when it is being accessed by Remote Control.
Prompt on Remote Control	This alerts the user at the workstation that a Remote Control session is being requested. The user must respond and confirm the session before the workstation can be remotely accessed. The user has 5 seconds to respond, or you must ask again. Train users to respond quickly if you choose this more polite option.
Disable Remote Control	This removes Remote Control as an option.

Using Remote Control

When a workstation needs attention, you can select its workstation object in the NDS tree and connect to it remotely with Z.E.N.works' Remote Control. To do this, use the NetWare Administrator.

Depending on how you alert or prompt the user, a remote session can then be established. You can view a representation of the target workstation's desktop on your own workstation through a Remote Control window.

You must have NetWare Administrator on the workstation from which you are working. The target workstation must be powered on, and it must be running the Z.E.N.works client software with IPX. As long as you have not disabled Remote Control, you can use it as described in Procedure 7.10.

PROCEDURE 7.10

Using Remote Control to Control a Workstation

1. Go to NetWare Administrator, and select the workstation object that represents the target workstation.

2. Go to Tools ➢ Remote Control Workstation and click.

3. To note the success of the connection, view the window showing the Remote Control connection status.

4. If successful, a window will appear on your desktop showing you the desktop of the target workstation. The following window (like any window) allows you to minimize it.

PROCEDURE 7.10 (CONTINUED)

5. To make selections as though you were at the target workstation, you can use the target workstation's Start button in the window. If your target workstation is a Windows 3.1 or Windows NT 3.5 workstation, use the Task List instead.

6. The Application Switcher button in the window's upper-right corner acts as an Alt+Tab keystroke to switch through applications on the target workstation.

7. Press the Tab key on your administrative workstation after you click the Application Switcher button to select an application.

8. The next button in the upper-right corner of the Remote Control window is the System Key Pass-Through button. This button toggles on and off. This allows you to use keyboard commands (like Control, Alt, or Enter) and have their functions pass through to the target workstation.

9. The next upper-right button in the Remote Control window is the Navigation button. When you click this button, a small window with the target workstation's desktop appears. When you move the red frame in this window, the view of the target workstation's desktop in your Remote Control window changes to match the area of the desktop that you have framed. You can enlarge specific features in a minimized window.

10. If the System Key Pass-Through button is turned off, you can make many other changes using the keyboard commands or hot keys on your administrative desktop. The functions that change the view of the Remote Control window are listed in Table 7.2.

T A B L E 7.2: Remote Control Window Hot Keys

Function	Hot Key Sequence	Function Description
Accelerated Mode	Ctrl+Alt+A	This will increase the refresh rate on your administrative workstation without changes being made to your target workstation.
Hot Key Enable	Ctrl+Alt+H	This will enable the Control Options Hot Keys on your target workstation.

T A B L E 7.2: Remote Control Window Hot Keys *(Continued)*

Function	Hot Key Sequence	Function Description
Full Screen Toggle	Ctrl+Alt+M	This will size the Remote Control window to the full size of your screen without any Windows borders.
Refresh Screen	Ctrl+Alt+R	This will refresh your target workstation's screen.
System Key Routing Toggle	Ctrl+Alt+S	This will pass all keyboard commands through to the target workstation.
Restart Viewer	Ctrl+Alt+T	This will reconnect you to the target workstation and refresh the Remote Control window.
Stop Viewing	Left-Shift+Escape	This will release control of the target workstation and enable you to move on to your next task.

If you don't have a photographic memory or you lose this book, you can view these Hot Key Sequences by selecting Hot Keys in the Remote Control window's pull-down menu. From the Hot Key window that appears, you can assign new stroke sequences to these functions. This feature could be useful with software that uses some of these sequences.

To make a Hot Key change, select the keystrokes in the Hot Keys window you want to change and hit the new keys you want to add.

There are three ways to disconnect from a Remote Control viewing session. They are:

- Use the Hot Key sequence for Stop Viewing (or new ones if you have changed them) in Table 7.2.

- Press Alt + F4 (the System Key Pass-Through button must be on for this to work).

- Open the pull-down menu of the Remote Control window and select Close.

Help Requester

Help Requester is an application that facilitates communications concerning technical support for users on their applications, workstations, servers, and networks. It is designed to use e-mail, but it will also deliver context and contact information if e-mail is not available.

Help Requester Distribution with Application Launcher

You can move Help Requester to client workstations with Application Launcher. When the Application Launcher window or the Application Explorer appears on the desktop, Help Requester will appear as a clickable icon.

Two platform-specific Help Requester applications are found in SYS:PUBLIC:

- HLPREQ16.EXE (Windows 3.1 workstations)

- HLPREQ32.EXE (Windows 95 and Windows NT workstations)

When Z.E.N.works is installed, application objects are created and mapped to these two executable files. The application objects are then available on the NDS tree and can be distributed to users with the Application Launcher. These application objects are:

- HELPREQ16 (Windows 3.1 workstations)

- HELPREQ32 (Windows 95 and Windows NT workstations)

These application objects must be associated with the usual suspects: container objects, user or user group objects, and workstation or workstation group objects. To distribute Help Requester using the Application Launcher, follow the steps in Procedure 7.11.

PROCEDURE 7.11

Using Application Launcher to Distribute Help Requester

1. Make sure the NAL.EXE wrapper is in a directory that users will be able to access, such as SYS:PUBLIC.

2. Go to the container in which you want to work, and add one of the following lines to the container login script:

   ```
   @\\servername\SYS\PUBLIC\.EXE or
   #\\servername\SYS\PUBLIC\.EXE
   ```

3. Associate one of these two application objects with the user, workstation, group, or container object of your choice. The next time the affected users log in, the Help Requester icon will appear in their Application Launcher window or Explorer window.

Help Requester Requirements

As with other Z.E.N.works components, Help Requester will run on NetWare 4.11 or NetWare 5 networks. Workstations must have the Z.E.N.works client installed and be connected to the network through NDS. They must be registered with NDS and have a workstation object on the NDS tree.

Users do not need to have any assigned NDS rights in order to access applications. By default, Read and Compare rights to All Property rights are assigned to all objects you associate with an application object. You will need Supervisor rights to the [Root] of the NDS tree to distribute the Help Requester application with the Application Launcher.

Users will need Read and File Scan system rights to the directory that contains the Help Requester application and the directory that contains the Application Launcher. SYS:PUBLIC is the default directory for both.

You must have the Z.E.N.works NetWare Administrator (NW-ADMIN32) installed on your administrative workstation to use Help Requester.

Using Help Requester

Help Requester policies apply to users and do not apply to workstations in Z.E.N.works. Therefore, you can configure them in the user policy packages. In the Help Desk policy's Configuration page, you must mark the box for "Allow User to Send Trouble Ticket" if you want your users to be able to report problems via e-mail. This will determine whether or not the Mail button appears on the Help Requester application window. You need to determine if you want help requests to come to help desk personnel via e-mail.

To e-mail help requests, you must have either GroupWise or a MAPI-compliant message service defined in the user policy package. You can choose Subject Line Topics for Help Messages, and you must provide information (such as name, phone number, and e-mail address) about the designated help technician if you choose to use e-mail.

After you distribute the Help Requester with the Application Launcher and set up an associated and configured policy package object, your affected users can launch the Help Requester application and report problems they are having.

The Help Requester window (see Figure 7.6) will appear when your users double-click their Help Requester icon in the Application Launcher or Explorer window.

FIGURE 7.6

The Help Requestor window

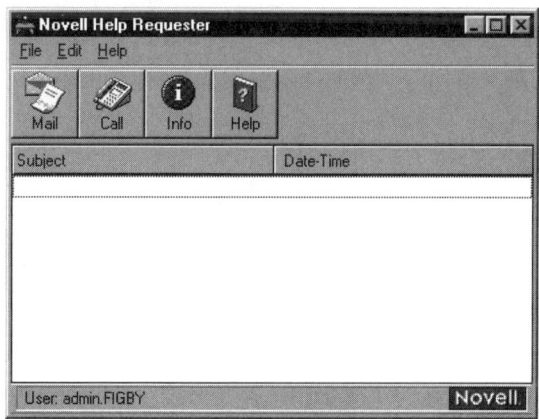

If the Mail button is included on your users' Help Requester application, they will have four buttons from which to choose:

- Mail

- Call

- Info

- Help

Using the Mail Button

The Mail button helps users with either GroupWise or a MAPI-compliant message service report problems via e-mail. After clicking the Mail button, users can select one of your preconfigured categories of workstation problems in the subject field's pull-down menu.

The Mail for Help window (see Figure 7.7) lets users see information about their workstation context. Through it, users send information to the designated help technician.

FIGURE 7.7

The Mail for Help
window in
Help Requester

In the Message tab section of the Mail for Help window, the user can write or cut-and-paste a more detailed description of the problem. Information about the workstation context, tree, and address is displayed in the User tab section of the Mail for Help window.

After users send messages through Help Requester, they can view a list of all their previous messages in the order they were sent. The messages are listed with the chosen subject lines. By double-clicking those subject lines in the list, users can bring up previous messages to view.

Using the Call Button

The Call for Help window opens when a user clicks the Call button. This will display the information about the designated help technician that was configured in the user policy package. The User Context, Workstation ID, Phone, Location, and Network Tree are all displayed in the User tab.

The Call for Help window (see Figure 7.8) appears when the Help Requester's Call button is clicked. This may be the first button if you choose not to enable e-mail reporting with the Mail button.

FIGURE 7.8

The Call for Help window

Call for Help

Contact: Michael Moncur
Phone: (801) 555-1234

User

User context: admin.FIGBY
Workstation ID: Workstation not registered
Phone:
Location:
Network tree: FIGBY_TREE

Close   Help

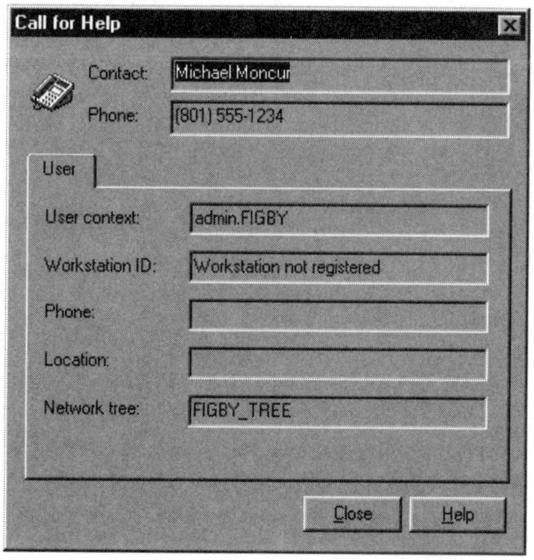

Using the Info Button

When the Info button is clicked, the User and Help Desk tabs display information regarding the workstation and information concerning the designated help technician. It can also include an e-mail address for help personnel and the Help Desk policy associated with the user.

Using the Help Button

The Help button may be the last button to which a frustrated user turns. By clicking the Help button, he or she can review instructions for using Help Requester. (See Figure 7.9.) Procedure 7.12 walks you through the process of using the Help Requester.

FIGURE 7.9

The Help dialog box
for Help Requester

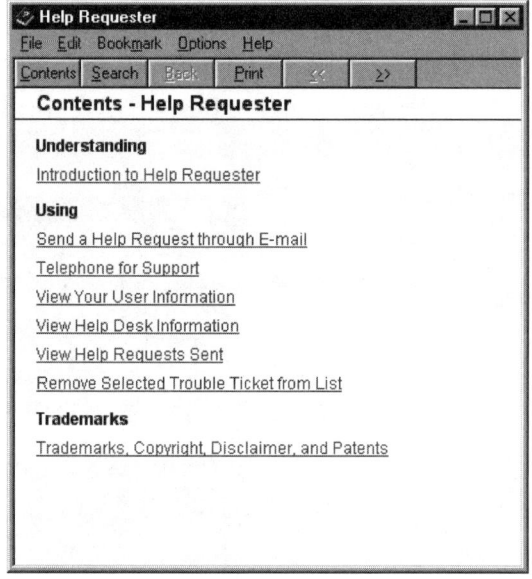

PROCEDURE 7.12

Using Help Requester

1. Go to NetWare Administrator and double-click the User Platform policy package in the container in which you choose to work.

2. In the User policy package, place a check in the Help Desk policy box and click Details.

3. Click Information and enter yourself as the designated contact and Admin.

4. Enter your e-mail address, assuming you have the required messaging service.

5. Enter your phone number in the correct field.

6. Click Configuration and select your messaging application service in the Trouble Ticket Delivery Mode field.

7. Click Add (which appears to the right of the Trouble Ticket Delivery Mode field).

8. In the Add Item window, click Add.

9. Enter **Application Problems** and click OK.

10. Repeat the process and type **Hardware Problems**. Click OK.

11. Close the Add Item window by clicking OK.

12. Mark the Allow User to Launch Help Request box and the Allow User to Send Trouble Tickets box.

13. Click OK twice.

14. In NetWare Administrator, associate the Help Requester application object with the container with which you are working.

15. Choose the name of a user in that container. Choose Start ➢ Shutdown.

16. Log in as the user you chose in step 15.

17. Double-click the Help Requester icon in the Application Launcher window.

PROCEDURE 7.12 (CONTINUED)

18. Click the Mail button and click the Hardware Problems topic.

19. Enter an imaginary hardware problem message and click Send.

20. Click the Call button. Observe the user and workstation context. Then click Close.

21. Choose Start ➢ Shutdown.

22. Log in as Admin.

23. Open your messaging application and retrieve the e-mail sent by Help Requester. Note the user and workstation context information in the e-mail.

Review

In this chapter, we extended our view of the powerful Z.E.N.works tools. We studied Z.E.N.works other three components:

- Application Launcher
- Remote Control
- Help Requester

Let's review what we learned about these three Z.E.N.works tools.

Application Launcher

Let's review the major features of the Application Launcher. The two Application Launcher components for users are:

- Application Launcher window
- Application Explorer

The two Application Launcher components for administrators are:

- NetWare Administrator Application Launcher Snap-In

- snAppShot

The Application Launcher window uses a *wrapper* technology with a wrapper executable file (NAL.EXE). We saw how these applications can work together to distribute software to users and to communicate about and fix problems across the network.

Remote Control

We saw how Novell's new Remote Control solves the problems that previously prohibited Remote Control solutions. The power of NDS enables Remote Control to work without the advertising traffic that made navigating so unattractive. We also saw how you can configure Remote Control to signal the start of a remote session or alert and request a remote session from the user.

We saw how the User Agent application objects must be associated with the appropriate user, workstation, container, or group objects to work. We learned that the following User Agent application objects are placed on the NDS tree during the Z.E.N.works installation:

- REMOTE16 application object (for Windows 3.1 or Windows 95 workstations)

- REMOTENT application object (for Windows NT workstations)

- REMOTENTSECURE application object (for secure Windows NT workstations)

Help Requester

We saw how Help Requester can facilitate a minimum required communication between a distressed user and help personnel. Users just need to double-click their Help Requester icon in the Application Launcher or Explorer window to make the Help Requester window appear.

We learned that e-mail responses must be configured for the Mail button to appear on Help Requester. If it does appear, the user will have four buttons to choose from:

- Mail

- Call

- Info

- Help

We learned how to associate policy package objects and application objects with user, workstation, and container objects in order to automate many previously tedious tasks.

We were introduced to the new standard in desktop management, and we practiced a number of network procedures. Let's move on and test our recall of these three Z.E.N.works components!

Z.E.N.works Practice Questions

1. The two administrative components of the Application Launcher are _____ and _____.

2. The wrapper file in the Application Launcher window is:

    A. NAL32.EXE

    B. NAL16.EXE

    C. NAL.EXE

    D. NALW.EXE

3. SnAppShot changes the file extensions on all application files to what extension?

   A. .SPS

   B. .FIL

   C. .BE4

   D. .PIC

4. Application Explorer will *not* deliver applications to which of the following? (Choose two.)

   A. The Start menu

   B. The Batch file

   C. The Desktop

   D. The Application Explorer window

   E. The Windows Explorer

   F. The System Tray

   G. The Kernel

5. SnAppShot will *not* take the "before" picture of the workstation's configuration for which of the following? (Choose two.)

   A. CPU

   B. Application files

   C. Text files

   D. Virtual memory

   E. Windows shortcuts

   F. DLLs

   G. INI files

   H. Registry

6. To access the Application Launcher and the User Agent, you must have which of the following file system rights?

   A. Write and Create

   B. Read and File Scan

   C. Supervisor

   D. Read and Erase

7. The login script will continue executing while the # command is being processed. The @ command instruction must be completed before the login script can continue. (True or False.)

8. The Prompt on Remote Control parameter sends the target workstation which type of signal in Remote Control?

   A. Audible tone

   B. Visible signal

   C. Remote Session Request

   D. Apology

9. Remote Control access is disabled by default. (True or False.)

10. Which of the following statements is true?

   A. Help Requester will run on NetWare 4 or NetWare 5.

   B. To e-mail help requests, Help Requester requires Group-Wise or a MAPI-compliant message service.

   C. Help Requester requests apply to workstations and not users; therefore, you must configure workstation policy packages.

   D. Help Requester always has four buttons in its main window to help the user.

11. The four buttons in Help Requester are:

A. Info

B. Help

C. Mail

D. Context

E. Address

F. Call

CHAPTER

8

Netscape FastTrack Server

Roadmap

This chapter covers Netscape FastTrack Server, the Web server that is included with NetWare 5.

Topics Covered

- Understanding Web servers and FastTrack Server
- Netscape FastTrack Server installation
- Configuring FastTrack Server
- Tuning and troubleshooting FastTrack Server

Skills You'll Learn

- Understand the way Web servers function
- Learn to install FastTrack Server
- Learn forms management with Server Manager
- Understand FastTrack Server configuration
- Learn the parameters that will affect FastTrack Server functionality

N ovell and Netscape formed a joint-venture company called Novonyx that was principally owned by Novell to develop the Web server product that became Netscape FastTrack Server. Novonyx became a division of Novell, and the Netscape FastTrack Server for NetWare became part of NetWare 5. A Web server is used to publish documents and files on the Internet or on a corporate intranet. The Netscape FastTrack Server is an entry-level Web server that you can use to design, build, and administer your Web sites to grow with your needs.

If your company has more complex Web server needs, you can easily upgrade Netscape FastTrack Server to Netscape's more robust

Enterprise Server. The move to Enterprise Server can evolve as your Web presence evolves.

FastTrack Server is easily managed from a browser anywhere on an intranet or through the Internet, thereby simplifying administration. Its administration interface is the same one that is used with all Netscape Suitespot servers.

FastTrack Server is reported to deliver high performance and reliability in its core Web engine through optimized caching, advanced use of kernel threads, HTTP 1.1 support, and sophisticated memory management. FastTrack Server also supports Secure Sockets Layer (SSL) 3, the widely accepted Internet security standard that encrypts information between server and client.

In this chapter, you will learn how to install FastTrack Server. You will learn to understand the services that FastTrack Server provides. You will learn to configure FastTrack Server by using Server Manager in the Administration Server. You will also learn to troubleshoot and fine-tune Netscape FastTrack Server for NetWare.

Understanding Netscape FastTrack Server

A FastTrack server functions in a client/server relationship similarly to the way a NetWare network functions. A client program, such as a Web browser, requests information or files from the server, which is physically connected to a TCP/IP-based network (the Internet). The Web server receives requests and serves files through HyperText Transfer Protocol (HTTP).

Most of the Web pages you see on the Internet are written in HyperText Markup Language (HTML), although some new alternatives are growing in popularity. HTML uses ASCII text characters in various combinations to tag blocks of text to employ various functions (e.g., formatting the text as either **bold** or *italics*). Because it utilizes ASCII, HTML is versatile and useful on many different platforms. HTML code can act as a link to another location, request user input, and store it in useful forms.

Web servers can distribute HTML files and other types of files, including:

- Compressed (.ZIP)
- Audio (.AU or .WAV)
- Video (.AVI or .MOV)
- Graphics (.JPEG, .GIF, etc.)
- Executable (.EXE)

Netscape FastTrack Server for NetWare adds Web server functionality to a NetWare 5 server. The FastTrack Server is comprised of a set of NLMs that run on the NetWare 5 server.

FastTrack Server Installation

To install FastTrack Server, you must have two computers: one serving as a client and the other as the server. The server must have NetWare 4.11 or NetWare 5 running and TCP/IP bound and configured. There must be a minimum of 64MB of RAM and at least 100MB of free space on the SYS volume. Long Name Space Support must be loaded on SYS and on any other volumes that will hold Web content.

Long Name Space Support is added by default to NetWare 5 volumes when a server is installed. This is not the case, however, for servers that have been upgraded to NetWare 5 from an earlier version. In these cases, it will be necessary to load Long Name Space Support on all volumes that will have FastTrack Server files.

The client workstation you use for the installation must have either Windows 95 or Windows NT running, and the new NetWare client must be installed and configured. A Netscape 3.x or higher browser should also be installed and configured. The workstation will need a CD-ROM drive (assuming you are installing from the FastTrack Server disk that ships with NetWare 5). You will need 100MB of free disk space on the client workstation as well.

Before you begin to install FastTrack Server, you must also:

- Have a registered IP address for Internet access or a unique address for intranet applications.

- Have Supervisor rights to the SYS volume.

- Know the DNS hostname for your server if DNS is running. If DNS is not running, you will need to use IP addresses.

FastTrack Server Files

When you install Netscape FastTrack Server, a file called NSWEB .NCF is created. This file has all of the LOAD commands necessary to start FastTrack Server. Similarly, a file named NSWEBDN.NCF containing the UNLOAD commands is created. NSWEB is created and added to the AUTOEXEC.NCF file during installation. This will load the FastTrack Server NLMs whenever NetWare Server is brought up.

FastTrack Server Directories

You can install FastTrack Server at any time after the installation of NetWare 5. (It is not included in the basic installation.) FastTrack Server installs a document directory for all of the files that the Fast-Track server will serve to its clients. This directory is named SYS:\ NOVONYX\SUITESPOT\DOCS. All files or documents served by the FastTrack server will come from here or a subdirectory of this directory.

To install FastTrack Server, follow the steps in Procedure 8.1. You will need to have the FastTrack Server CD that ships with NetWare 5.

PROCEDURE 8.1

FastTrack Server Installation

1. Before you install FastTrack Server, go to Windows Explorer and map a drive to the root of the SYS volume where you are going to install FastTrack Server. (By default, drive F: is mapped to this volume.)

2. On your client workstation, choose Start ➢ Run. In the Open field, type the address of the FastTrack Server installation file. (If you are installing FastTrack Server from the CD, this .EXE file will be on the disk at /PRODUCTS/WEBSERV/SETUP.EXE.) You will see the initial dialog for the FastTrack Server Installation Wizard as shown here.

3. After the installation files are unpacked, click Next in the Welcome dialog.

4. The license agreement for FastTrack Server is displayed, as shown in the figure. Click Yes to accept the agreement and continue the installation.

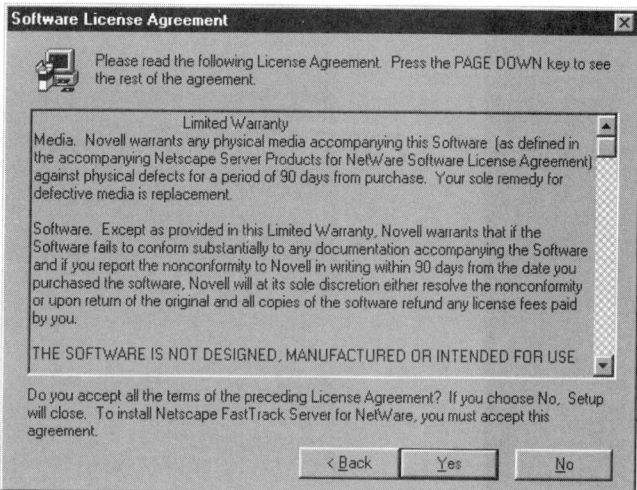

5. At the Choose Destination Location screen, browse to the drive you previously mapped, browse to the root of the SYS volume you have chosen to install on, and then click Next.

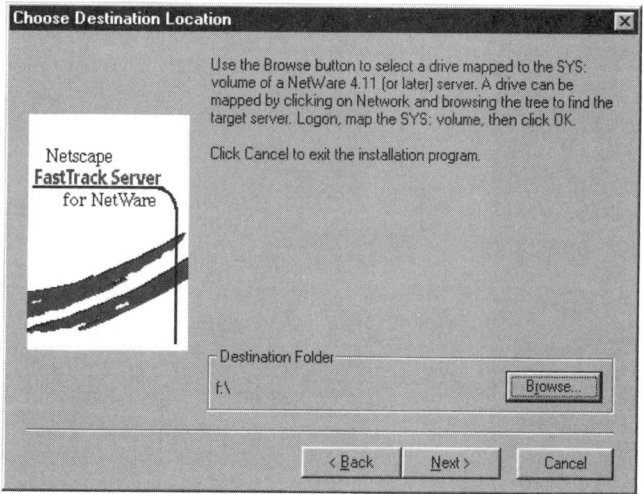

6. The next step in the installation prompts you for addressing information for the server. In the Address field of the Configure Server screen, enter the IP address of your NetWare server.

7. In the same dialog, enter the host name for your NetWare server, and click Next.

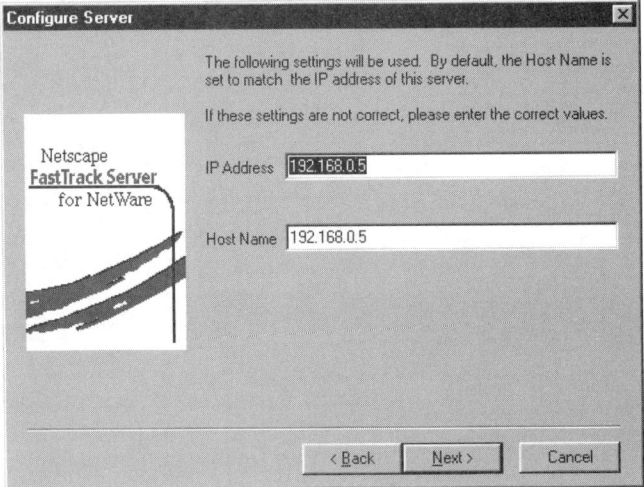

8. At the Web Configuration screen, specify the IP port number for FastTrack Server and click Next. This port, typically 80, will be used to answer HTTP requests.

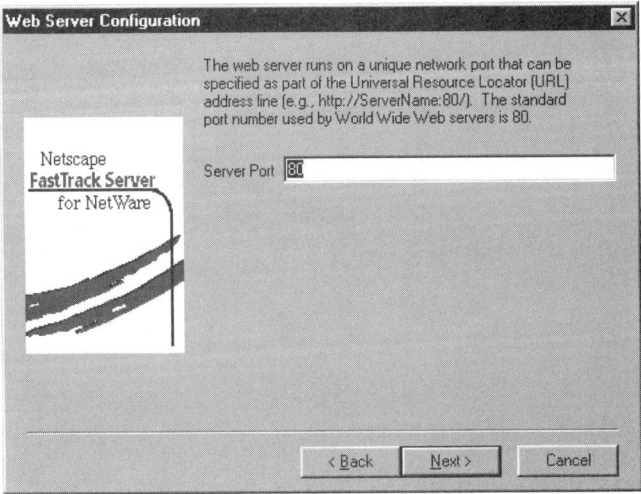

9. At the Administration Server Port Configuration screen, specify an Admin Port number. By default, a random port number is used. As an administrator, you can access the server at this port number to display administrative Web pages. Click Next to continue.

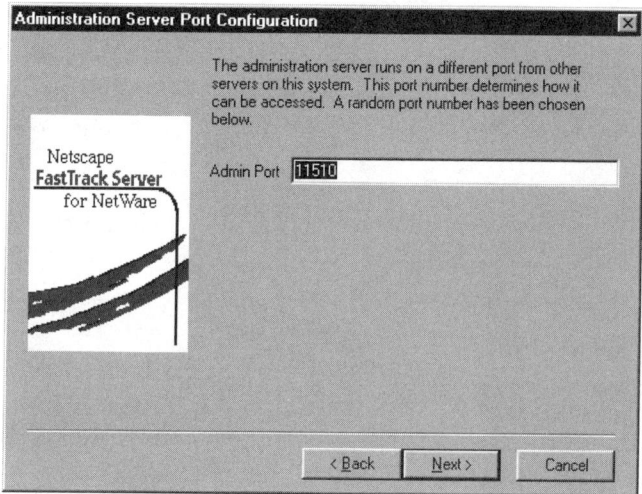

This box is followed by a dialog box that reminds you to remember the IP Address and Admin Port (see graphic). Remember to write down the Admin Port number; you cannot configure FastTrack Server without it.

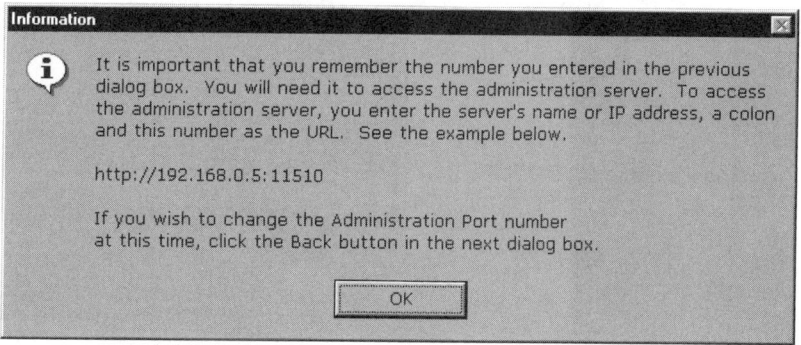

10. At the Administration Server Authentication screen, enter a username (Admin is the default), specify a password for administrative access to the server, and then click Next. This will create an Admin user in the FastTrack Server directory apart from NDS. The username and password are case-sensitive.

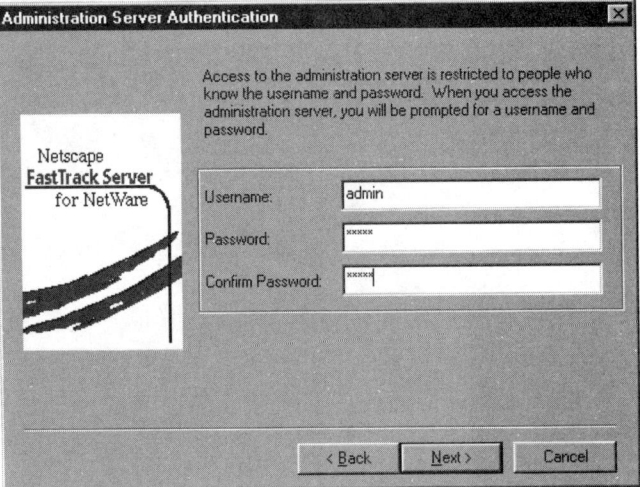

11. This box is followed by a box that queries whether you would like to keep the Netbasic files or to update them, as shown in this graphic:

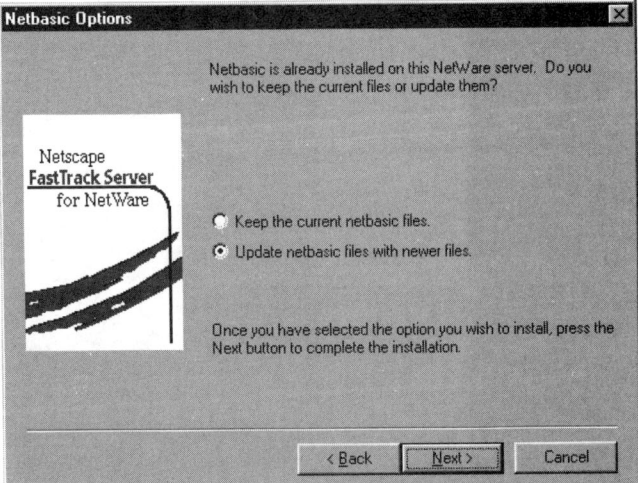

12. When you are prompted that you can use LDAP with FastTrack Server, click Next.

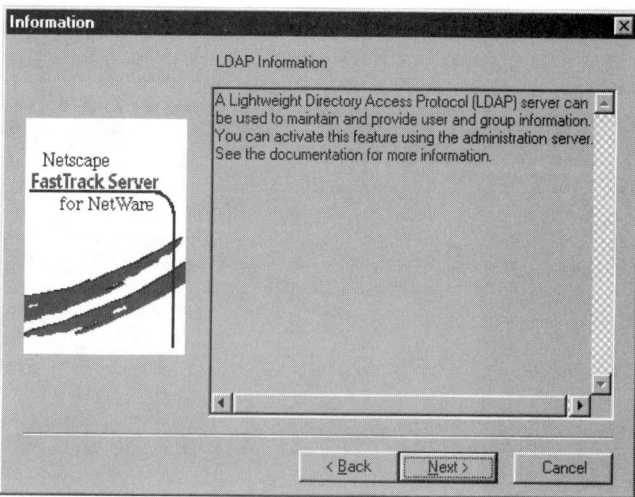

13. At the Autoexec.ncf Options screen, place a check in the Change the Autoexec.ncf File box. Click Next. This adds only one line to the autoexec.ncf file, which runs the NSWEB batch file to start the Web server.

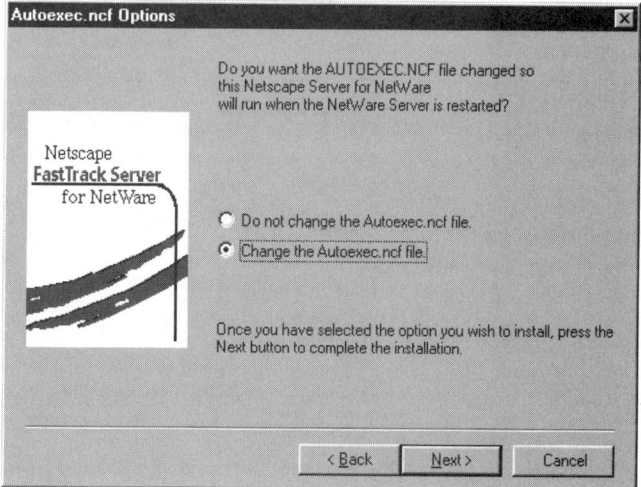

14. The Start Copying Files dialog, shown in the figure, summarizes your installation choices. Click Next and wait for the files to copy.

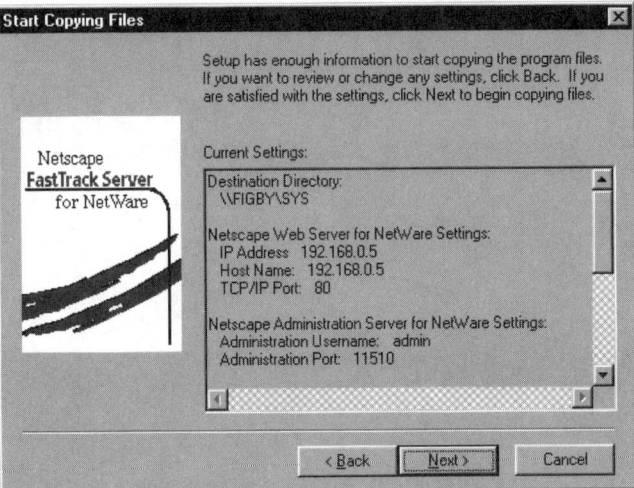

15. At the Setup Complete screen, place checkmarks in the View the Read Me File and Launch Server boxes. Click Finish.

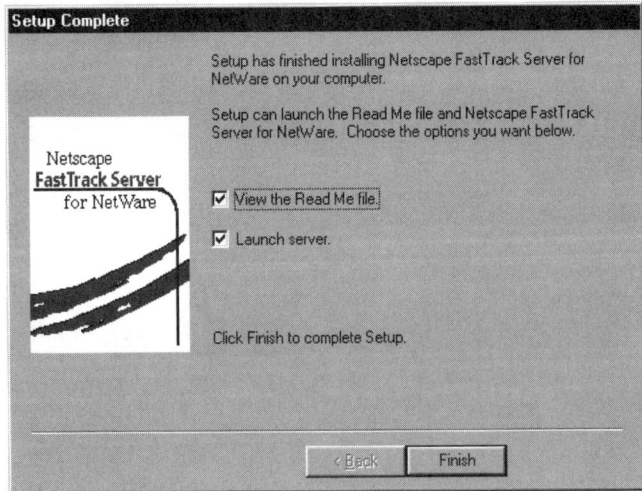

16. Verify that the Netscape FastTrack Server home page loads in your browser.

FastTrack Server Documentation

Product documentation for Netscape FastTrack Server can be found at:

`hhtp://hostname/Netscape scripting.htm` for scripting information

`hhtp://hostname/readme.htm` for a Netscape FastTrack Server Readme file

(The *hostname* is the name or IP address of the server where you installed FastTrack Server.)

For additional help information, click on the context-sensitive Help button that appears at the bottom of each administration page when you are configuring the server.

Configuring and Managing FastTrack Server

To configure and manage FastTrack Server, you must use two services:

- Administration Server
- Server Manager

Administration Server

When they are installed, the commands to launch the Administration Server are placed in the NetWare server's AUTOEXEC.NCF file. If you need to manually bring up the Administration Server, enter **ADMSERV** or **NSWEB** at the server console. The Administration Server is a series of NLMs running on the NetWare server that let you configure and manage the FastTrack server from the Administration Server home page.

From anywhere on the Internet or from within a corporate intranet, you can access the Administration Server by going to:

```
http://hostname:admin_port_number/
```

The `admin_port_number` is the number of the port you configured during the installation. When you access the Administration Server, you will need to enter the same Admin name and password you used in the installation (see Procedure 8.1). After authentication, the Administration Server home page in Figure 8.1 will appear.

FIGURE 8.1

The Administration Server home page will appear after you log in to Netscape Administration.

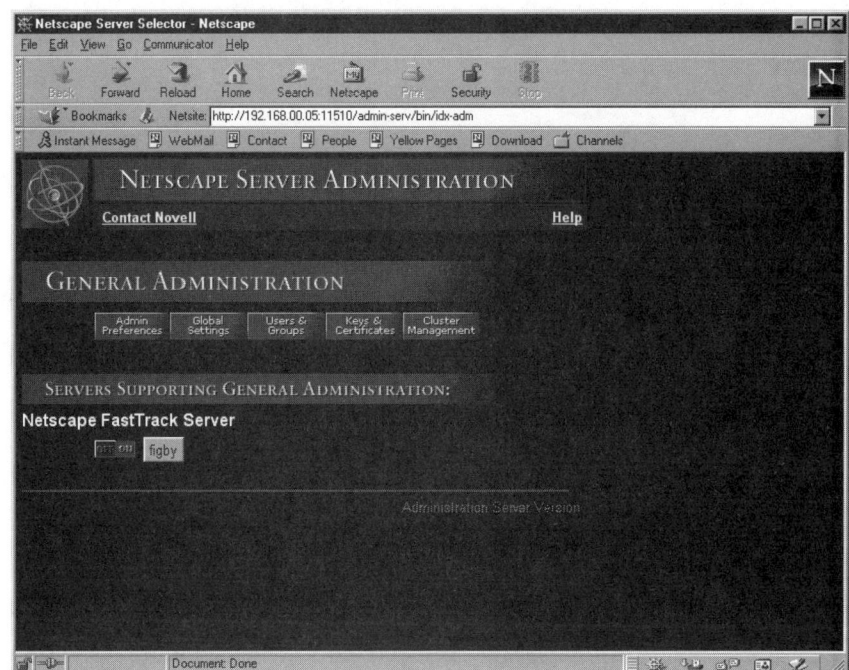

The Administration Server home page will list all of the Netscape servers you have installed. To access Server Manager, you must click the button of the Netscape FastTrack server you want to manage.

Server Manager

When the Server button is clicked, the Server Manager page will appear (as shown in Figure 8.2). The Server Manager is a set of forms you will use to manage and configure your FastTrack server.

FIGURE 8.2

The Server Manager page is used to manage and configure the FastTrack server.

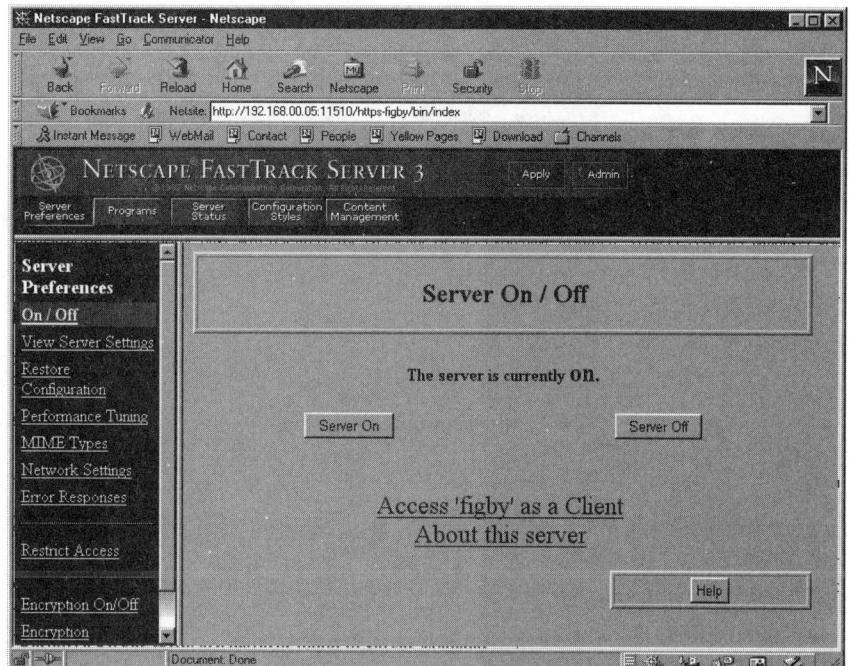

Server Manager forms are used to configure changes to individual files or directories and larger changes to the entire FastTrack server. The drop-down list in the Administration Server is used to choose which resources to configure. You can track usage, for example, with the Log Preferences form, as shown in Figure 8.3.

The drop-down list also includes many forms that permit you to specify wildcard patterns to represent one or more specific characters. Wildcard patterns allow you to find single or repetitive occurrences of specific and/or variable strings or substrings of characters. Table 8.1 lists the wildcard symbol and the pattern it is used to find.

FIGURE 8.3

The Log Preferences form of the Server Status page allows you to track usage.

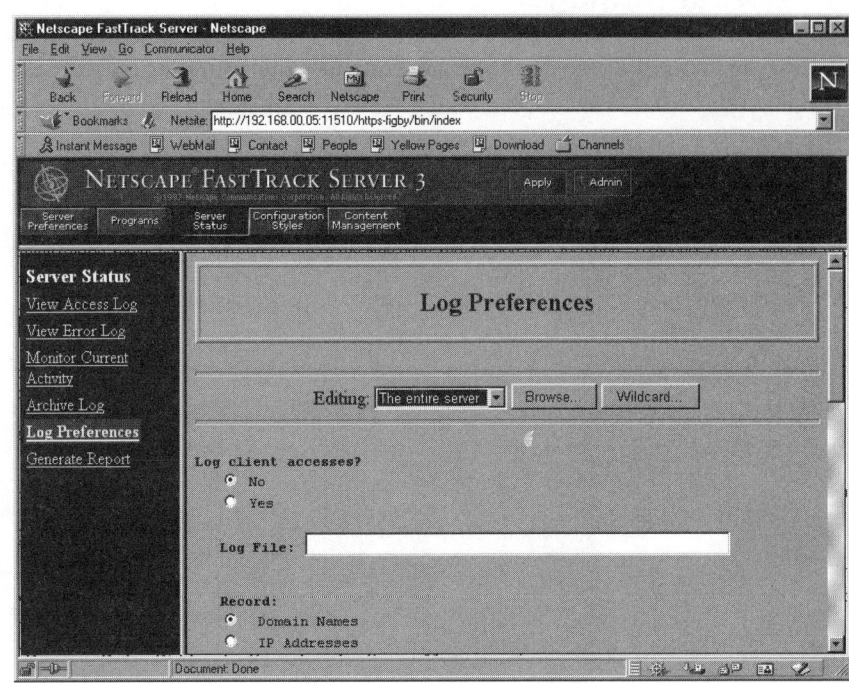

TABLE 8.1

The Drop-Down List Wildcard Patterns Found in Server Manager

Wildcard Symbol*	Pattern It Is Used to Find
*	This will match any number of characters (including zero).
*~	This symbol followed by any expression will remove that expression wherever it appears.
[abc]	This will match one occurrence of the characters a, b, or c.
[a-z]	This will match one occurrence of a character from a to z.
[^az]	This will match any single character other than a or z.
?	This will match specifically one occurrence of any character.

T A B L E 8.1 *(cont.)* The Drop-Down List Wildcard Patterns Found in Server Manager	**Wildcard Symbol***	**Pattern It Is Used to Find**
	|	This means "or." This symbol can be used with other symbols like * or ?. The substrings need to be enclosed in parentheses, but the parentheses cannot be nested: (abcd) but not (ab(cd)).
	$	This means to match the end of the string. This can be useful when using the pipe expressions (|).

Note: If you need to use one of these wildcard symbols without its wildcard significance, use the backslash (\) character preceding it.

FastTrack Server Configuration

Many different configuration options are available by using Server Manager to configure your FastTrack server. In this chapter, we are going to cover some basic configuration steps that you should know. We will cover the following configuration details:

- How to start and stop a FastTrack server

- How to configure the server port number

- How to set and change the primary document directory

- How to configure your document preferences

- How to restrict FastTrack server access

How to Start and Stop a FastTrack Server   On the Administration Server home page, a green light next to the On icon and the name of your FastTrack server indicates that the FastTrack server is running. You can turn on or turn off the FastTrack server by clicking the appropriate icons. After a FastTrack server is installed, it will run indefinitely, waiting for and responding to requests.

You can also down and restart a FastTrack server from the server console. To down a FastTrack server at the server console, enter

NSWEBDN. To restart a FastTrack server from the server console, enter **NSWEB**.

A third way to turn on or turn off a FastTrack server is to use Server Manager. For this method, you must go to Server Preferences in Server Manager and click On/Off. Then click Server On or Server Off.

Configuring the Server Port Number The port number of a Web server is the TCP port that the FastTrack server monitors for HTTP requests. It can be any port from 1 to 65535. The nonsecure Web server standard port number is 80. The secure Web Server standard port number is 443.

You can choose any port number; however, if you don't choose the standard secure or nonsecure port numbers, your users will need to know what port number to put in the URL (Ultimate Resource Locator). A Network Settings form under Server Preferences in Server Manager will let you change the server port number (as shown in Figure 8.4.)

FIGURE 8.4

The Network Settings form can be used to change the server port number.

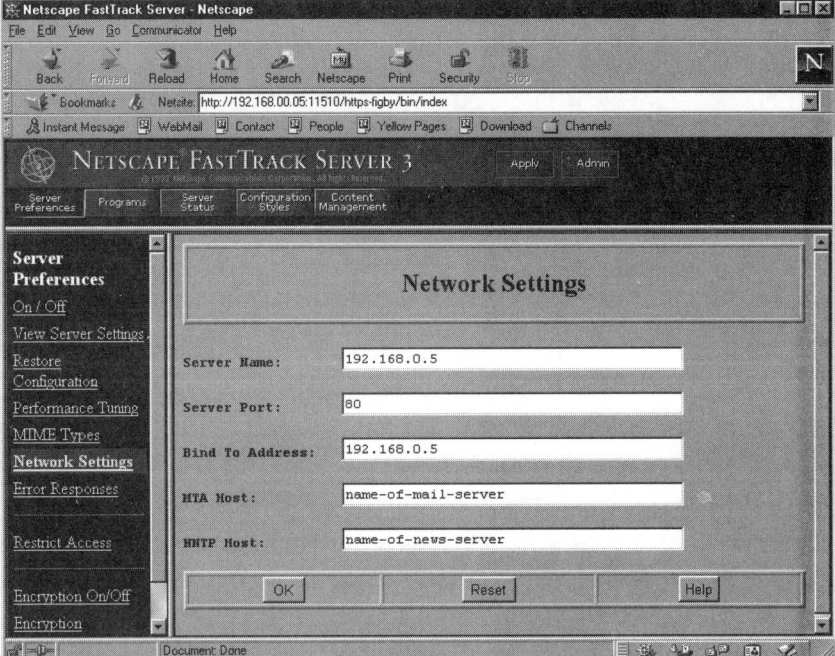

After you make the necessary changes, be sure to save and apply those changes.

If your hostname is `www.mycompany.com` and you choose to use port number 2002, a browser-equipped user will need to go to the following URL to get to your FastTrack server:

```
http://www.mycompany.com:2002
```

Setting and Changing the Primary Document Directory   The primary document directory, or document root, and its subdirectories are the locations to which the URL will map when documents are requested. By default, the primary document directory for the FastTrack Server is located at: SYS:\NOVONYX\SUITESPOT\DOCS.

All FastTrack Server documents will be delivered from this location (the home page) or a subdirectory (linked pages, files, etc.). Filenames that are added to an HTTP request will take the user to that specific subdirectory of the primary document directory.

Assume that the port number is set to the nonsecure standard number 80. If you want to provide an index to all of your Web information from the default primary document directory, you can easily link some text on your home page to the subdirectory index.html.

1. Go to Server Manager and click Content Management.

2. Click Additional Document Directories.

3. In the URL prefix field, enter the home page URL addition. Add index.html to `http:\\www.mycompany.com/`.

4. Enter the path to this document in the Map to Directory field.

Now, when users click on this link or go to `http:\\www.mycompany` `.com/index.html`, they will go to the documents at `SYS:\NOVONYX\` `SUITESPOT\DOCS\INDEX.HTML`.

If you choose to create a new location for your primary document directory, you can easily go to the forms in Server Manager to change it. This will send all HTTP requests to the new location. To accomplish this change:

1. Go to Server Manager and click Content Management.

2. Click Primary Document Directory.

The form in Figure 8.5 will appear. You can use this form to set a new location. Type the full pathname of a new location, and save and apply the changes.

F I G U R E 8.5

The Primary Document Directory form in Server Manager lets you set a new location for your primary document directory.

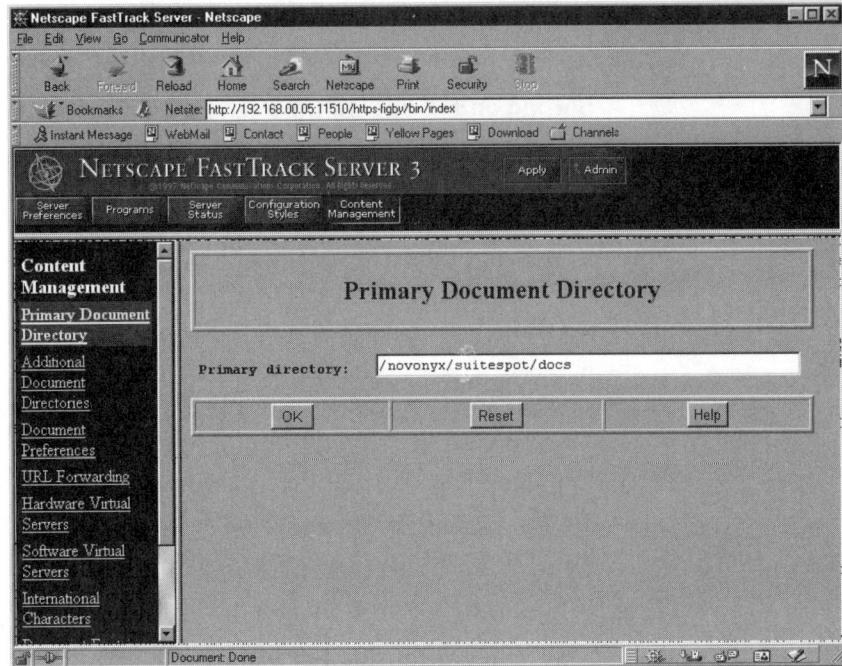

Configuring Your Document Preferences   In Server Manager, go to Content Management and click Document Preferences. This form will allow you to configure your preferences for your FastTrack Server documents.

First, you must enter the index filename, which is the file your Fast-Track server will display when a specific filename is not requested in a user's URL. The default filenames are index.html and home.html. If you place more than one filename here, FastTrack Server will attempt to display the files in the order they appear until a file is found.

Three choices appear under directory indexing: Fancy, Simple, and None. *Fancy directory indexing* displays a graphic for each type of file, along with other pertinent data including the last time the file was modified and the size of the file. *Simple directory indexing* lists the available files and uses less time to build the directory. The None option, of course, does not generate an index.

The FastTrack server will automatically develop an index as follows:

1. The FastTrack server will search for an index file that you may have generated.

2. If an index is not found, a file is created with all of the files found at the document root or the primary document directory.

3. The file that is created will be generated in either Fancy or Simple format, depending on which option you chose. If you chose None, you will not have a directory index list.

If you want a home page other than the files specified in the Index filenames field, mark the radio button next to Home Page, and enter the filename for the desired home page. Remember to save and apply your changes.

Restricting FastTrack Server Access   FastTrack Server is easily accessed by anyone with a browser. By default, access to all documents in the primary document directory or any subdirectories is unrestricted. This works fine for public access Web servers. However, FastTrack Server is also useful in situations where restricted access to sensitive documents is desirable.

To restrict access, you must bind the FastTrack server to NDS and create access restrictions. This extends NDS and allows its powerful security features to manage access to the files in the FastTrack server. File system trustee requirements will then govern access, and NDS will authenticate users' access.

To bind FastTrack server to NDS, follow these steps:

1. Open the Administration Server.

2. Specify that the FastTrack server use NDS.

3. Choose and state the NDS contexts that will be searched.

4. Down and restart the Administration Server and FastTrack Server.

After binding the FastTrack server to NDS, you can restrict access to FastTrack Server files by making trustee assignments. You will need to assign Read and File Scan rights at a minimum. These rights can be assigned for the container, group, or user objects to which you choose to restrict access. When they are accessed, restricted files or directories will display a box for a username and password.

Tuning and Troubleshooting the FastTrack Server

You can tune your FastTrack server's performance by configuring various options to match the load and demands of your network. The configurable options include:

- Enabling the Domain Name System Lookups parameter
- Configuring the Maximum Simultaneous Request parameter
- Configuring the Listen-Queue Size parameter
- Configuring the HTTP Persistent Connection Timeout parameter
- Configuring the Maximum Packet Receive Buffers parameter
- Configuring the Maximum Physical Receive Packet Size parameter
- Limiting Web server file size

Let's look at each of these parameters and determine how they can best be configured.

Enabling the DNS Lookups Parameter

By default, DNS lookups are not enabled. If you want a log of DNS hostnames that make requests instead of just listing IP addresses, you may want to enable DNS lookups. This feature can make your Fast-Track server run slowly. If speed becomes an issue, disable DNS lookups. When this parameter is enabled, each hostname is looked up and hostname restrictions work. If this parameter is disabled, you will only see logs of IP addresses and hostname restrictions will not function. You can enable this parameter in Server Manager's Performance Tuning page shown in Figure 8.6.

FIGURE 8.6

The DNS lookups are disabled by default.

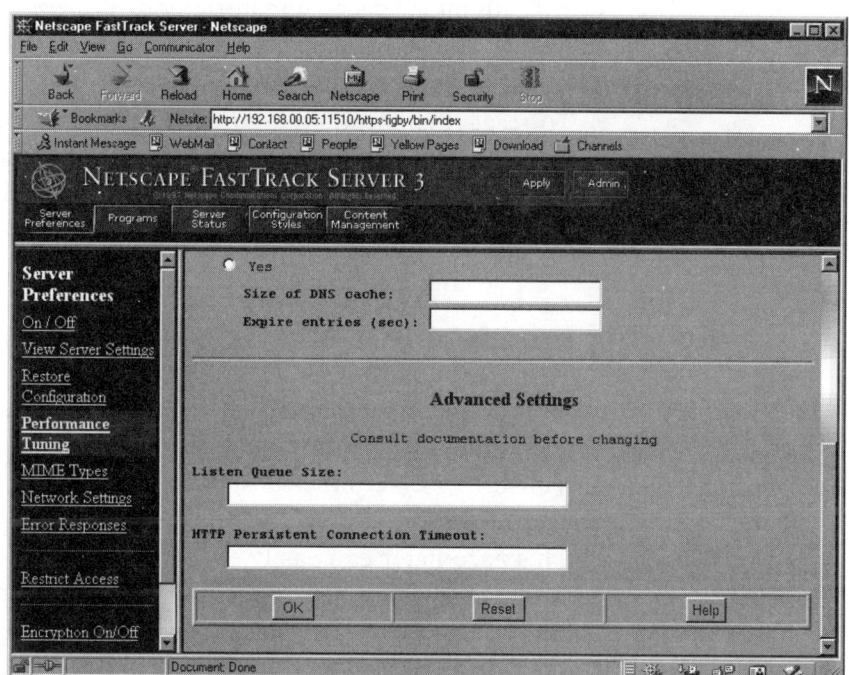

Configuring the Maximum Simultaneous Request Parameter

By default, your FastTrack server will set the Maximum Simultaneous Request parameter to 48. The number 48 refers to how many active requests are allowed to be processed by the server at any one time. The FastTrack server counts the number of active requests, and it will quit responding to requests once the set value is exceeded.

With responses taking place in as little as 5 milliseconds, HTTP requests usually have a very short duration. This means 48 requests could be responded to in a quarter of a second.

However, some users connect to the server and do not finish their requests until they are timed out. A FastTrack server can wait 30 seconds or more before timing out. Some Web sites have users who transact large downloads taking over a minute or more. Because of this variability, you may want to adjust your Maximum Simultaneous Request parameter up or down to fine-tune your FastTrack server.

To reset this parameter, go to Server Manager and click Server Preferences. Click Performance Tuning, and then enter the new number of Maximum Simultaneous Requests. Click OK and then Save and Apply.

Configuring the Listen-Queue Size Parameter

By default, the Listen-Queue Size parameter is set to 100 incoming connections. The Listen-Queue Size parameter is a socket-level measurement that determines how many incoming connections are allowed for the socket.

This parameter can easily exceed the hardware capacity of your server in a busy Web environment. If you are already overloaded at the default setting (or whatever setting you have) with too many incoming connections, you will need to upgrade the hardware before increasing this parameter. Otherwise, an increase in connections can further degrade server performance.

Your system will have a maximum Listen-Queue size apart from the value you enter in the Server Manager form. Your FastTrack server will ultimately default to this system maximum, even if the form compels the server to request a larger number.

Configuring the HTTP Persistent Connection Timeout Parameter

HTTP 1.1 includes a function with which a connection can be set to be persistent. You must still set a timeout parameter, so persistent connections don't consume all of your system resources. To change the HTTP Persistent Connection Timeout parameter, go to Server Manager and click Server Preferences. Click Performance Tuning. In the HTTP Persistent Connection Timeout field, enter a new number of seconds and click OK and Save and Apply.

Configuring the Maximum Packet Receive Buffers Parameter

The default for the Maximum Packet Receive Buffers parameter is 100 on a NetWare Server. This parameter configures the maximum amount of memory available to accommodate incoming packets. The range of possible values is between 500 and 4,294,967,295.

This parameter can be increased from the default amount so your FastTrack server will be able to handle more HTTP requests. To make this change responsibly, you must calculate the memory that is being used by other demands on the server.

To perform this calculation, let X = the product of the maximum physical receive packet size multiplied times the *current* maximum packet receive buffers.

Then let Y = the product of the maximum physical receive packet size multiplied times the *desired* maximum packet receive buffers.

Subtract X from Y to calculate the memory required for the *desired* change.

For clarity, the formula is:

$Y - X$ = memory required

To check to see if you have enough memory available to make your desired change, enter **Monitor** at the server console. Go to Server Parameters and press Enter. Then choose Communications and press

Enter. Choose Maximum Packet Receive Buffers and press Enter. If you have enough memory, enter this new number now. Press Enter and then press Escape twice. You must then exit MONITOR and restart the server to make the change.

Configuring the Maximum Physical Receive Packet Size Parameter

The Maximum Physical Receive Packet Size parameter determines the largest client packet size that your server will accept. Your network board driver has a capacity limitation that will specify the largest packet size it will handle.

In general, the rule is to set this parameter at the largest packet size you are likely to see with the topology you are using. Make sure you consider routers and variability of maximum sizes at different places on the network.

The default Maximum Physical Receive Packet Size parameters for some common topologies are shown in Table 8.2.

T A B L E 8.2 Default Maximum Physical Receive Packet Size Parameters for Different Topologies	Topology	Maximum Packet Size Default
	Ethernet	1514
	Token Ring (4Mbps)	4202
	Token Ring (16Mbps)	4202

To set or change the Maximum Physical Receive Packet Size parameter, go to the server console and enter **MONITOR**. Choose Server Parameters and press Enter. Choose Communications and press Enter. Choose the Maximum Physical Receive Packet Size and press Enter. Type the desired packet size and press Enter. Press Escape twice. Exit MONITOR and restart the server to effect the changes.

Limiting Web Server File Size

FastTrack server performance can be adversely affected by the size of the files that are requested from it. Usually, text files are not very large, but image files, audio files, and video clip files can be large enough to stop other server functions. The larger the file, the slower it will be to transfer.

Audio and video files that are 20MB or larger can clog up your server traffic, causing user packets to be dropped and server connections to be severed. If your FastTrack server is distributing large files and traffic becomes a problem, consider increasing your hardware capacity or limiting the file sizes.

HTML features can also require server processing time. For example, image maps and CGI scripting can eat up system resources. If server response time becomes sluggish or packets are being dropped, consider limiting your content with file sizes and scripts and image maps.

Review

In this chapter, we looked at Netscape FastTrack Server and how it works as a Web server. We practiced the steps involved in installing FastTrack Server. We looked at various ways to configure FastTrack Server through Administration Server and the forms in Server Manager. We learned how to configure FastTrack Server from anywhere on a network with browser access.

FastTrack Server Basics

FastTrack Server is an entry-level Web server that facilitates building a presence on the Internet or within a company intranet. Its features include:

- Kernel threads
- HTTP 1.1 Support

- Secure Sockets Layer (SSL) 3 Support
- Ability to bind to NDS security and management

Installing FastTrack Server

We learned that to install the FastTrack Server you must have two computers:

- One serving as a client
- One serving as the server

The server must have NetWare 4.11 or NetWare 5 running, and TCP/IP must be bound and configured. There must be a minimum of 64MB of RAM and at least 100MB of free space on the SYS volume. Long Name Space Support needs to be loaded on SYS and on any other volumes that will hold Web content.

We learned that the client workstation used for the installation must have either Windows 95 or Windows NT running. The new NetWare client must be installed and configured. A Netscape 3.*x* or higher browser must also be installed and configured.

Configuring and Managing the Server

We learned that FastTrack Server can be managed from anywhere through a browser by accessing the Administration Server page and by configuring the forms with the necessary choices in Server Manager.

We reviewed the drop-down list Wildcard patterns that permit us to search for data and strings and substrings of characters. We reviewed five basic processes:

- How to start and stop the FastTrack server
- How to configure the server port number
- How to set and change the primary document directory
- How to configure your document preferences
- How to restrict FastTrack server access

Tuning and Troubleshooting

We looked at tuning and troubleshooting the FastTrack server. We covered the various parameters you need to monitor:

- Enabling the Domain Name System Lookups parameter
- Configuring the Maximum Simultaneous Request parameter
- Configuring the Listen-Queue Size parameter
- Configuring the HTTP Persistent Connection Timeout parameter
- Configuring the Maximum Packet Receive Buffers parameter
- Configuring the Maximum Physical Receive Packet Size parameter
- Limiting Web server file size

These parameters help you adjust server performance and will sometimes indicate when you need to increase your hardware capacity.

If your company needs more capacity than Netscape FastTrack Server can supply, you can easily upgrade to Netscape's more robust Enterprise Server. For most small and midsize companies, Netscape FastTrack Server provides an easy-to-manage track into an Internet or intranet presence while providing functionality that can grow with your company.

FastTrack Server Practice Questions

1. Novonyx is best described as:

  A. A Netscape company that markets its FastTrack Server

  B. A joint venture by Novell and Netscape

  C. A division of Novell that works with the Netscape Fast-Track Server for NetWare

  D. A filename in FastTrack Server

2. The protocol through which a Web server requests and serves files is called:

A. IP

B. TCP/IP

C. IPX

D. HTTP

3. FastTrack Server is comprised of a set of NLMs that will run on a NetWare 5 server. (True or False.)

4. Long Name Space Support is added by default to all servers that are upgraded to NetWare 5. (True or False.)

5. A file with UNLOAD commands is automatically created when you install FastTrack Server. This file is called _____.NCF.

6. The drop-down list Wildcard Symbol (|) can be used with other symbols and it means _____.

7. The steps you perform to bind FastTrack Server to NDS include all but which of the following? (Choose one.)

A. Open the Administration Server

B. Specify that the FastTrack Server use NDS

C. Specify the Tree and Context for FastTrack Server

D. Choose and state the NDS contexts that will be searched

E. Down and restart the Administration Server and FastTrack Server

8. Find three ways to turn off the FastTrack Server.

    A. Click the Off icon on the Administration Server home page.

    B. Click the Server Off button in Server Preferences in Server Manager.

    C. Disable the server in the primary document directory.

    D. Type **NSWBDN** at the server console.

9. The default for the Maximum Packet Receive Buffers parameter is:

    A. 50

    B. 75

    C. 100

    D. 200

10. The parameter that determines the maximum number of incoming connections is called _____.

    A. The Domain Name System Lookups parameter

    B. The Maximum Simultaneous Request parameter

    C. The Listen-Queue Size parameter

    D. The HTTP Persistent Connection Timeout parameter

    E. The Maximum Packet Receive Buffers parameter

    F. The Maximum Physical Receive Packet Size parameter

    G. The Web Server File Size parameter

CHAPTER

9

Name Resolution with DNS

Roadmap

This chapter covers DNS (Domain Name Service) and describes how to install and configure NetWare 5's DNS features.

Topics Covered

- Introduction to DNS

- Components of the DNS System

- NetWare 5's DNS Support

- Installing and Configuring DNS

Skills You'll Learn

- Install DNS Support in NetWare 5

- Configure DNS zones and other features

- Understand how DNS is integrated with NDS

- Manage the DNS Server

- Import external data into the DNS server

As you probably know by now, one of the most important new features of the NetWare 5 operating system is native support for TCP/IP. To go with this, NetWare 5 also includes a number of TCP/IP-related features, including support for DNS (Domain Name Service).

DNS is a service that allows you to use friendly alphanumeric names to refer to nodes on a TCP/IP network. TCP networks, including the Internet, have two types of addressing:

- IP (numeric) addresses

- Domain names

DNS translates between these two systems. In this chapter, you'll learn how DNS works, learn about the components involved in its operation, and learn how to install, configure, and manage NetWare 5's DNS support.

Internet Naming

TCP/IP uses a system of IP addresses to refer to nodes on the network. IP addresses are 32-bit binary numbers, represented as four 1-byte octets. Although numeric addresses make it easy for computers to refer to each other, they don't necessarily make it easy for humans.

To simplify things for those of us who deal better with words than numbers, the Internet authorities created a system of alphanumeric names, known as *host names* or *domain names*. These names use a hierarchical method to refer to a machine on a network or the Internet.

If you've used the Internet, you're probably familiar with host names. They usually consist of two or more words separated by periods, such as `www.sybex.com`. The portions of a host name refer to different ways of locating a machine on the network, as described in the following sections.

Top-Level Domains (TLDs)

The last part of a host name is typically a three-letter code that indicates the type of organization that owns the domain, such as .com or .org. These organizations are called top-level domains, or TLDs. Each host on the Internet is assigned to one of the top-level domains based on its ownership.

Within the United States, TLDs are chosen based on the type of organization, such as .com for a private company or .gov for a government entity. For other countries, the standard two-letter code for the country name is used as the TLD. A secondary-level domain may also be included. For example, commercial organizations in the United Kingdom typically have names ending in .co.uk.

Table 9.1 describes the common top-level domains and their typical meanings.

TABLE 9.1	TLD	Description
Internet Top-Level Domains (TLDs)	COM	Companies
	ORG	Private or nonprofit organizations
	NET	Internet providers and network transport providers
	EDU	Universities, schools, and other educational institutions
	GOV	U.S. government departments
	MIL	U.S. military organizations
	US, UK, CH, etc.	International country-based domains

The two-letter codes used in country-based names are standardized by the ISO (International Standards Organization). The abbreviations are usually based on the country's name in its native language. For example, US is the United States, DE is Germany (Deutchland), and AU is Australia.

A committee is currently evaluating choices for a new system of top-level domains, because just about all of the names available in the popular .com domain are taken. The new system will further subdivide the top-level names in an effort to deal with the growing Internet.

Domain Names

To the left of the TLD in a host name is the domain name. This is usually the name of the company that owns the domain. For example, the sybex.com domain is owned by the publisher of this book.

Aside from the top-level domain, the domain owner can manage the namespace under their domain as they see fit. Additional subdomain names can be created to further divide the naming hierarchy. For example, the company.com domain might have subdomains called sales.company.com and personnel.company.com.

In a network without Internet connectivity, you can assign domain names as you please. On the Internet, domain names are assigned and managed by the InterNIC (Internet Network Information Center). You can register a domain name after you have a machine with an IP address. There is a small yearly fee (currently $70.00 for the first two years) for domain registration.

To find out more about the domain registration process or to register a domain of your own, contact the InterNIC at their Web site: http://www.internic.net/.

Machine Names

The leftmost part of an Internet host name is the *machine name*, or the name assigned to the actual computer that responds to requests for the host name. For example, in the machine name www.sybex.com, www is the machine name. (This is a common name for Web servers, although any name can be used.)

In organizations with a single machine, the domain name and the machine name are the same. For example, company.com could refer both to a domain owned by a company and to the server that handles requests for that domain.

Each machine name corresponds to a single IP address. Domain names correspond to a range of one or more IP addresses. The DNS service provides a bridge between these two types of names assigned to machines.

How DNS Works

DNS is a client-server protocol. Clients (usually workstations) that need to refer to a machine by name send a request to their local DNS server. If this server knows the IP address for the host, it returns it to the client. Otherwise, a higher-level server is contacted. This process is called *name resolution*.

Because DNS is an Internet standard, it works the same way whether the DNS server is running under UNIX, Windows NT, or NetWare. In the following sections, we will look at the way DNS organizes domain names. We will also examine the available types of DNS servers and how they communicate and synchronize information.

DNS Zones

DNS servers use a database of host names and IP addresses to perform their duties. The database is divided into *zones*. Each zone includes the naming and addressing information for a particular section of the hierarchy, beginning with a domain or subdomain name and including all of the machines or subdomains under the name.

In a small company, a server will typically use a single zone containing information for the entire domain. Larger organizations typically use separate zones for each subdomain within the organization (or for each of several domain names owned by the same organization).

A zone can also be divided into subzones. These are smaller zones that each handle a portion of the hierarchy under the main zone. The server with the main zone's database sends requests to subzone servers if it does not have information for that part of the hierarchy in its own database. Zones and subzones in DNS are similar to partitions in the NDS directory.

> The NetWare 5 DNS database uses NDS to store some data, but it does not correspond directly with the NDS hierarchy. In other words, you don't need to use host names that correspond to NDS distinguished names.

NetWare 5's DNS server supports three types of zones: standard zones, reverse DNS zones, and IP version 6 zones. These are explained in detail in the following sections.

Standard Zones

Standard zones are the most commonly used DNS zones. A standard zone's database contains a list of host names and their corresponding IP addresses, and it can be used to answer requests to resolve host names to IP addresses.

The zone database stores information about any subzones and the servers to be contacted to resolve names within them. It also includes a pointer to a higher-level server, or *root* server, which will be contacted for names that aren't within the current zone.

Reverse DNS Zones

When the client already knows the IP address and needs to know the host name for the machine, it is necessary to perform the opposite of a typical DNS request. NetWare 5's DNS server supports reverse zones, also known as IN-ADDR.ARPA zones, for this purpose.

These zones also store a database of host names and IP addresses, but they are designed to be looked up using the IP address. In most network configurations, you will not need this type of zone.

IP Version 6 Zones

As you learned in Chapter 4, IP addresses are quickly running out. The larger classes of address (A and B) are all taken, and the smaller Class C addresses are becoming scarce.

To resolve this problem, the Internet authorities have developed a new IP addressing standard, known as version 6 or IPv6. This standard allows for a larger number of networks, and it removes the class structure that limited the number of available networks in the previous version.

The NetWare 5 DNS server includes a zone type called IP6.INT. These zones are designed to work with the new IPv6 standard, and they can be used if your network uses the new addressing scheme.

DNS Components

DNS is designed to be a distributed system. Your network can use a single DNS server, or it can use a number of DNS servers for added speed and reliability. If the network is connected to the Internet or a larger network, DNS servers communicate with servers elsewhere on the network to resolve external names.

There are three types of machines involved in DNS: master servers, replica servers, and clients. The following sections examine each of these components of a DNS system in detail.

Master Servers

The master server stores the main copy of the zone's database, also known as the *authoritative database*. In a small network, the master server is usually the only server. The master server is the one you must access in order to configure the names and addresses in the zone database.

Replica Servers

If the master server for a zone is unavailable, a *replica server* can handle the request. These servers periodically contact the master server and synchronize their copy of the database to keep it current. While replica servers store the same information as master servers, you can't modify the zone using the replica server's database.

Replica servers serve two main purposes:

- To substitute for the master server when it is down or cannot be reached

- To distribute the load of name resolution and relieve the burden on the master server

DNS Clients

Clients are the third component in the DNS system. Most computers that are connected to the Internet or another IP network are DNS clients. Each client is configured with the IP address (not the host name, for obvious reasons) of the DNS server.

DNS clients are also known as *resolvers*. When a client needs to resolve a name, the following steps are performed:

1. The client sends a name resolution request to its default DNS server.

2. The server consults its local database to resolve the name. If the address for the name is found in the local database, the server sends the address back to the client.

3. If the address for the name was not found in the local database, the server contacts another server (a subdomain or root server) to resolve the name.

4. If the external server is able to resolve the domain, it returns the IP address to the local server. The server then sends the IP address to the client. If the address is still unresolved, the external server may contact another server.

NetWare 5's DNS Support

NetWare 5 includes a full-featured DNS server. This DNS server is included as part of Novell DNS/DHCP Services, which also acts as a server for the DHCP protocol. The following sections describe the services included with NetWare 5, and the NDS objects used to configure the DNS server.

DNS and DHCP Services

Novell DNS/DHCP Services is a single software component for NetWare 5 servers that acts as a server for two Internet protocols:

- DNS (Domain Name Service)
- DHCP (Dynamic Host Configuration Protocol)

DHCP is a protocol that stores a database of available IP addresses and dynamically assigns IP addresses to clients when they are initialized. You will learn more about DHCP in Chapter 10.

DNS and NDS

The NetWare 5 DNS server stores its data in the NDS (NetWare Directory Services) database. NDS includes a feature that allows the structure of the database, called the *schema,* to be extended to include additional objects.

The installation of DNS/DHCP services adds several objects to the NDS schema. The first three objects are the DNS/DHCP Group, DNS/DHCP Locator, and RootServerInfo Zone. Only one of each of these objects can exist in the NDS tree. These objects are described in the following sections.

DNS/DHCP Group

The DNS/DHCP Group object is actually an ordinary NDS Group object; it does not use the extended part of the NDS schema. This object is used to manage security and administration for the various DNS and DHCP objects.

The other DNS and DHCP objects are assigned as trustees of the Group object. Any user who is a member of this group can manage the DNS and DHCP databases. Servers that are running DNS and DHCP server software are also assigned as members of this group; this allows them to access the database information required to run the server.

DNS/DHCP Locator

The DNS/DHCP Locator object is used to store a central directory of resources related to the DNS and DHCP services. It maintains a list of all of the servers in the network and the DNS zones they contain. DNS servers and management utilities use this object to locate these resources without searching the entire NDS tree.

The Locator object also stores the global defaults and options for the DNS and DHCP services. This object is added to the NDS schema during the installation of DNS/DHCP services.

RootServerInfo Zone

The RootServerInfo Zone object stores pointers to root NDS servers. NDS server computers use these servers to resolve names that are not part of the local domain. The root servers may be on the Internet or elsewhere in a large organization's network. This object is added to the NDS schema during the installation process.

Other NDS Objects

Along with the basic NDS objects previously described, several others are added to the NDS schema. You will need to create and manage these objects to configure the DNS server. The various objects are described in the following sections.

Along with the following objects, a number of objects relating to the DHCP protocol are also added to the schema. They are described in detail in Chapter 10.

DNS Name Server

The DNS Name Server object stores information about a DNS server. It includes a DNS zone served by the server and a pointer to the NDS Server object representing the server running the DNS server software.

These objects are used to cross-reference between DNS zones and NetWare servers. The server that handles name resolution for a DNS zone is called the *designated server* for the zone.

NetWare supports two types of DNS zones: primary and secondary. A primary zone maintains its own database of names and IP addresses. A secondary zone synchronizes with an external server (an NDS server other than NetWare) and maintains a copy of its zone database.

DNS Zone

The DNS Zone object is a container object that represents a single DNS zone. Its properties store basic information about the zone. The Zone object can contain one or more child objects that define additional information about the zone; these include Resource Record objects and Resource Record Set objects.

Resource Record

The Resource Record object stores the actual host names and addresses for the DNS server. It can contain various types of records; the types used depend on the type of zone and the name resolution methods in use. You can create these objects only under the DNS Zone container object for the appropriate zone.

Resource Record Set

The Resource Record Set object acts as a sort of container for Resource Record objects. When you create Resource Records, they are automatically placed in a record set. This is not a true NDS container object.

Installing and Configuring DNS

The DNS/DHCP Server software is included with NetWare 5, and it can be installed on any NetWare 5 server. The following sections describe how to install the service and how to configure it for use.

Installing DNS Services

You can choose DNS/DHCP Services as an option when you install NetWare 5. If you have done this, you do not need to install any additional software to use the services. If you have not already installed DNS/DHCP Services, you can add it to the server. Follow the steps in Procedure 9.1 to install these services.

PROCEDURE 9.1

Installing DNS/DHCP Services on a NetWare 5 Server

1. Insert the NetWare 5 CD into the server's CD-ROM drive.

2. From the NetWare GUI, select Install from the Novell menu.

3. A dialog is displayed listing the currently installed products. Click the New Product button.

4. You are now prompted for the path to the installation files. Choose the NetWare 5 directory on the CD.

5. A list of products that can be installed is displayed. Check the box next to Novell DNS/DHCP Services, and click Next.

6. You are prompted for a name and password to authenticate to NDS. Enter the Admin account name and password.

7. Specify NDS contexts for the three DNS/DHCP objects. These default to the server's context.

8. A summary of the installation options is displayed. Click the Finish button to complete the installation.

Configuring the DNS Server

You can configure the NDS objects for the DNS server using the DNS/DHCP Management Console utility. This is a Java-based utility that runs at a workstation. To install the Management Console at a workstation, follow the directions in Procedure 9.2. This requires that the server already be installed, as described in Procedure 9.1.

PROCEDURE 9.2

Installing the DNS/DHCP Management Console

1. Boot the workstation to Windows 95/98 or NT, and log in to the NetWare 5 server.

2. Run the SYS:PUBLIC\DNSDHCP\SETUP.EXE program.

3. A Welcome screen is displayed. Click Next to continue.

4. You are prompted for the destination directory for the Management Console utility, as shown in Figure 9.1. Choose a directory on the workstation, and click Next.

5. A dialog prompts you to choose whether to copy the NDS snap-in files, as shown in Figure 9.2. These files allow NWADMIN to work with the new objects. Choose the path to NWADMIN (usually SYS:PUBLIC\WIN32), and click Next.

6. Click OK to complete the installation.

FIGURE 9.1

Select a destination directory for the Management Console files.

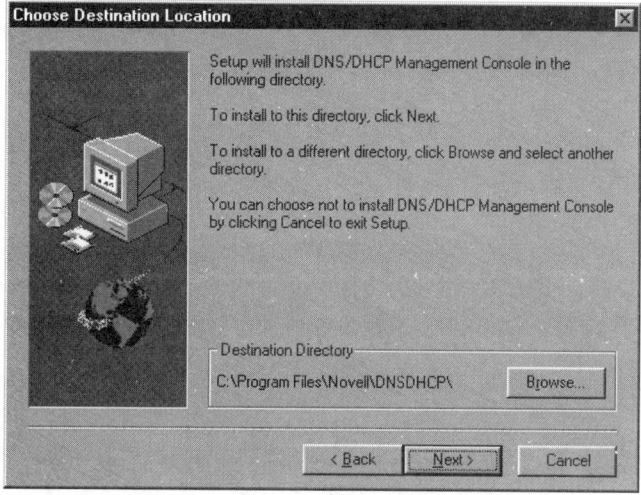

FIGURE 9.2

Choose whether to install the snap-in files.

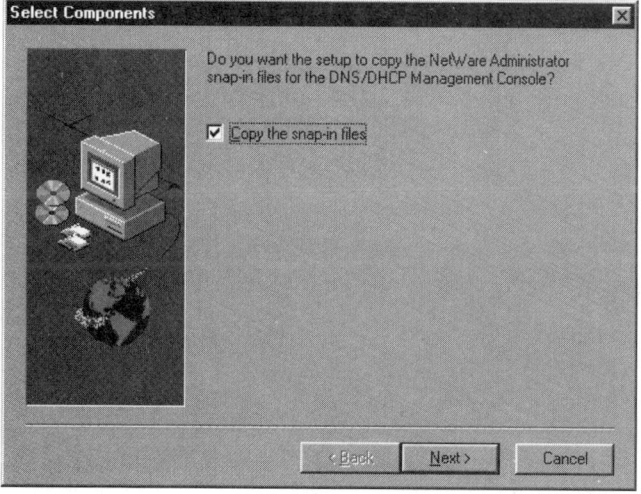

Once the Management Console is installed, you can run it from an icon in the Start menu. When you first run the Management Console, it prompts you for an NDS tree to use to manage objects (see Figure 9.3). Choose the appropriate tree, and click the Launch button to start the utility.

FIGURE 9.3

The Management Console prompts you for the NDS tree to manage.

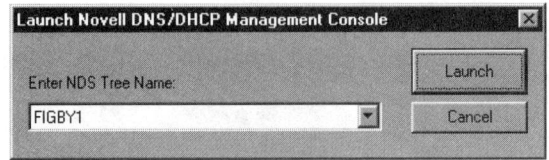

After you have specified the NDS tree and launched the program, the main Management Console screen should be displayed (see Figure 9.4). Choose DNS Service from the tabs at the top of the screen to display and manage DNS objects.

FIGURE 9.4

The main DNS Management Console screen

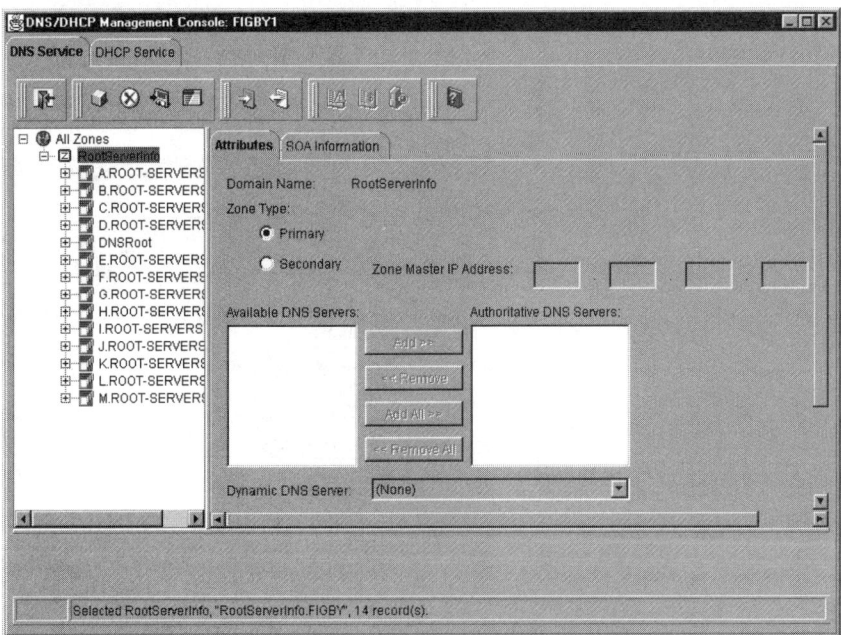

Creating NDS Objects

Once you have installed the DNS Management Console, you can use it to create the required objects for the DNS server. The following sections explain how to create each of the objects.

 **NOTE** Although you can view these objects in NetWare Administrator, you must use the DNS Management Console to create them and manage their properties.

DNS Server

You must create a DNS Server object for each NetWare 5 server that will run the DNS Server software. To create these objects, follow the steps in Procedure 9.3.

PROCEDURE 9.3

Creating a DNS Server Object

1. Click the Create button (the second icon from the left) in the DNS Management Console toolbar.

2. You are prompted for the type of object to create, as shown in Figure 9.5. Choose DNS Server.

3. Enter the details for the DNS Server object (see Figure 9.6), and click the Create button to create the object.

FIGURE 9.5

Choose the type of object to create.

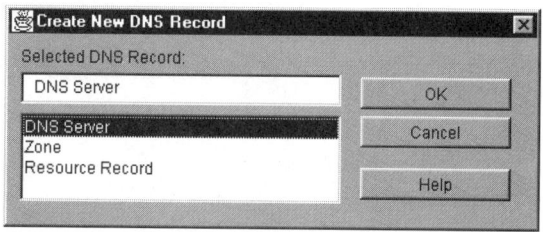

FIGURE 9.6

Enter the details for the DNS Server object.

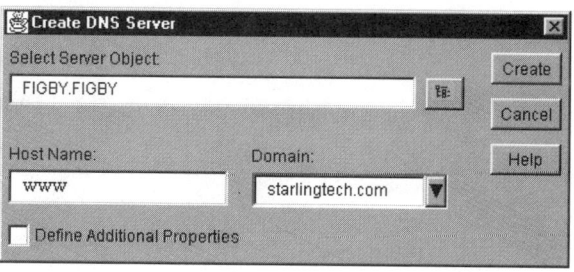

DNS Zone

You will need at least one DNS Zone object to run the DNS server. A single zone is created by default when you install the server software. To create an additional zone, follow the steps in Procedure 9.4.

PROCEDURE 9.4

Creating a DNS Zone Object

1. In the DNS Management Console, highlight the All Zones container for a standard zone, or the parent zone for a subzone.

2. Click the Create button in the Management Console toolbar.

3. You are prompted for the type of object to create. Choose DNS Zone.

4. You are prompted for the details of the DNS Zone object, as shown in Figure 9.7. After entering this information, click Create to create the zone.

FIGURE 9.7

Specify the details to create a DNS Zone object.

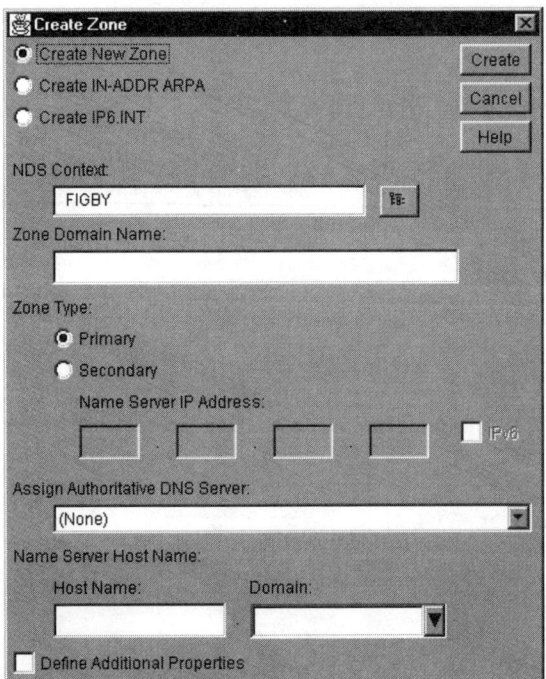

Resource Records

After you create a zone, you can create one or more resource records to link host names to IP addresses. These records are created as leaf objects under the DNS Zone container. Resource Record Set objects are created automatically to correspond with the record types you have entered. To create a DNS Resource Record, follow the steps in Procedure 9.5.

PROCEDURE 9.5

Creating DNS Resource Records

1. Highlight the DNS Zone object.

2. Click the Create button on the Management Console toolbar.

3. You are prompted for the type of object to create. Select Resource Record.

4. The Create Resource Record dialog is displayed (see Figure 9.8.) Specify the information for the Resource Record object, including the resource type, IP address, and host name.

5. Click Create to create the resource record.

FIGURE 9.8

Specify the details to create a Resource Record object.

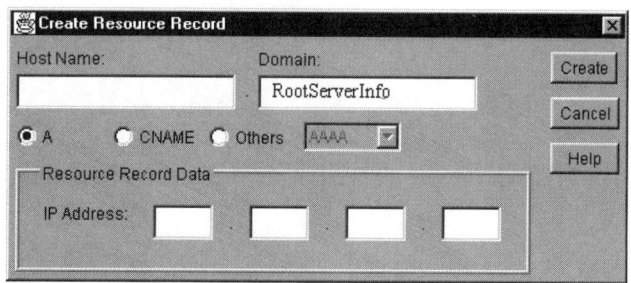

Configuring DNS Clients

Once the DNS server is running, you can configure clients to access the server. To do this, specify the DNS server's IP address in the TCP/IP stack configuration. The exact process involved depends on the client operating system. Procedure 9.6 explains how to configure a client under Windows 95 or 98.

PROCEDURE 9.6

Configuring a DNS Client Under Windows 95 or Windows 98

1. From the Windows 95/98 Desktop, right-click the Network Neighborhood icon and select Properties.

2. Select TCP/IP from the list of protocols and services, and click the Properties button.

3. Select the DNS Configuration tab.

4. Choose the Enable DNS option. Specify the DNS server's IP address, and click Add. This dialog is shown in Figure 9.9.

5. Click OK to complete the configuration.

FIGURE 9.9

Specify the DNS properties in Windows 95.

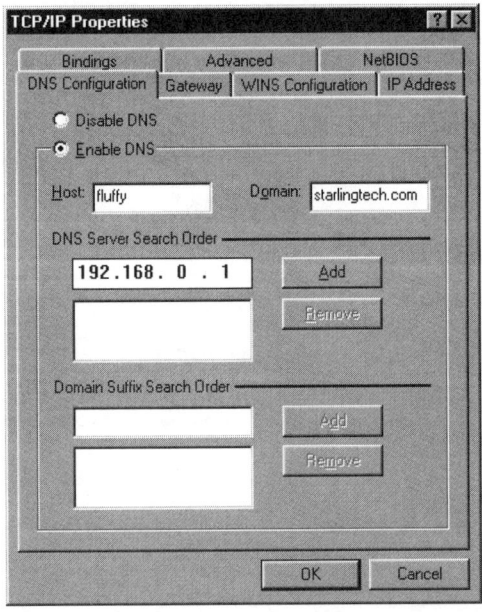

Importing and Exporting DNS Data

The NetWare 5 DNS server includes the ability to export and import data. This includes a zone's database of host names and IP addresses as well as configuration information about the server. You can use this feature to create a duplicate server for another location or to export data to be used by a non-NetWare server.

The configuration and zone data is stored in a file called the BIND master file. The following sections describe how to export data to this file and how to import the file from another server.

Creating a Master File

To export DNS data, you create a BIND master file. Procedure 9.7 explains how to export DNS data.

PROCEDURE 9.7

Creating a DNS Master File

1. In the DNS Management Console, highlight the DNS Zone object to be exported.

2. Click the Export button (the eighth icon from the left) in the Management Console toolbar.

3. You are prompted for a filename to export to, as shown in Figure 9.10. Enter the filename, and click the Export button to complete the export.

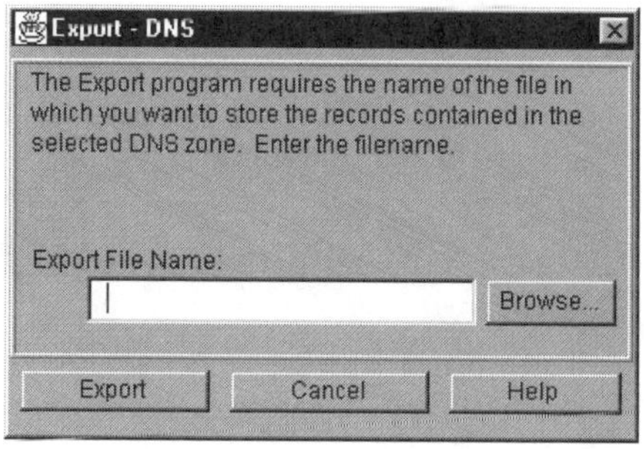

FIGURE 9.10

Enter the filename for the exported master file.

Importing a Master File

The Management Console also allows you to import an existing master file. To import DNS data from a master file, follow the steps in Procedure 9.8.

PROCEDURE 9.8

Importing DNS Data

1. In the DNS Management Console, click the Import button in the tool-bar (the seventh icon from the left).

2. You are prompted for a file to import from, as shown in Figure 9.11. Enter the filename, and click Next.

3. Specify the NDS context for the new zone, and click Next.

4. Select the DNS Server object to correspond with the zone. Click the Next button to continue.

5. A summary dialog is displayed. Click the Import button to complete the import process.

FIGURE 9.11

Enter the filename from which to import.

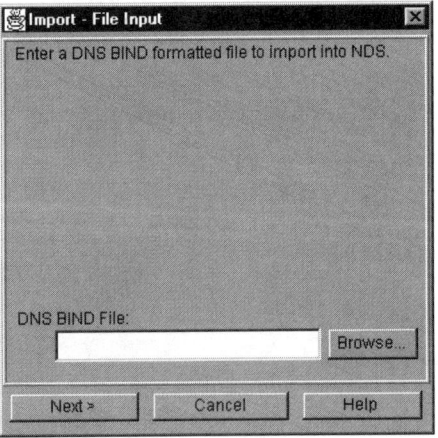

Review

In this chapter, you learned about the DNS (Domain Name Service) and configured NetWare 5 to act as a DNS server.

Internet Naming

Machines on an IP network can be referred to with two names: a host name and an IP address. DNS translates between these two formats. Internet host names include three components:

- A TLD (top-level domain) such as .com or .org

- A domain name and optional subdomain names

- A machine name

How DNS Works

DNS servers maintain a list of host names and corresponding IP addresses. A client sends a request to the DNS server when it requires name resolution. The server either answers the request directly or forwards it to another server when external hosts are involved.

DNS server databases are divided into zones, which are sections of the naming hierarchy. NetWare 5 supports three types of zones: standard zones, reverse zones, and IP version 6 zones.

DNS in NetWare 5

DNS is handled by the DNS/DHCP Server component of NetWare 5. DNS data is stored in four types of NDS objects:

- DNS Server is a pointer to a server running the DNS software

- DNS Zone stores information about a zone

- Resource Records store IP addresses and host names

- Resource Record Sets group similar types of resource records

Name Resolution Practice Questions

1. A partition within the DNS hierarchy stored on a single server is referred to as a _____.

2. Which types of organizations use domains in the top-level domain NET?

   A. Any company on the Internet

   B. Network providers

   C. Network users

3. DNS clients are also referred to as _____.

4. A DNS zone can be divided into _____.

5. Which of the following are DNS zones supported by NetWare 5? (Choose one or more.)

   A. Standard zone

   B. IPv6 zone

   C. DHCP zone

   D. IN-ADDR.ARPA zones

6. A _____ is a type of DNS server that stores a copy of the DNS database that cannot be modified directly.

7. Which of the following are true of DNS clients? (Choose one or more.)

   A. Special client software is required.

   B. The name of the DNS server should be specified.

   C. The IP address of the DNS server should be specified.

   D. The host name of the client should be specified.

8. If a local DNS server is unable to resolve a request and sends it on to a root server, which server sends the resolved address back to the client?

A. The local server

B. The root server

9. Where do you install the DNS/DHCP Server software?

A. On any NetWare 5 server

B. On a Workstation

C. On a separate machine

10. Which of the following NDS objects is *not* automatically created when you install the DNS server?

A. DNS/DHCP Group

B. RootServerInfo Zone

C. Resource Record

D. DNS/DHCP Locator

CHAPTER

10

IP Addressing with DHCP

Roadmap

This chapter covers DHCP (Dynamic Host Configuration Protocol) and describes how to install and configure NetWare 5's DHCP features.

Topics Covered

- Introduction to DHCP
- DHCP's features and advantages
- How NetWare 5 supports DHCP
- The NDS Objects used with DHCP
- Managing the DHCPs

Skills You'll Learn

- Install DHCP support in NetWare 5
- Choose DHCP configurations
- Manage DHCP server
- Create and manage NDS objects for DHCP

Now that NetWare 5 includes direct support for the TCP/IP protocol, IPX isn't necessarily the best choice for your network. However, there is still an obstacle to moving to TCP/IP: quite a bit of administrative work, including configuring the network and assigning IP adressess, needs to be done in a TCP/IP network.

Fortunately, the TCP/IP suite includes tools that make this process easier. One of the most important is the DHCP (Dynamic Host Configuration Protocol). DHCP servers can dynamically assign IP addresses to clients. This not only simplifies administration, but it allows a large number of computers to share a smaller pool of addresses.

NetWare 5 supports DHCP as part of Novell DNS/DHCP Services, included with NetWare 5. In this chapter, we will explore the capabilities of DHCP and NetWare's DHCP server and describe the process of configuring and managing DHCP.

Introduction to DHCP

In the early days of networking, computers without their own disk drives (*diskless workstations*) were common. These computers loaded their operating system software from the network. This setup allowed administrators to tightly control the software and settings for workstations.

Because multiple diskless workstations used the same disk image to boot, the image couldn't be set up with a specific IP address. For this reason, the BootP protocol was developed. This protocol assigns IP addresses to workstations automatically from a range of available addresses.

DHCP (Dynamic Host Configuration Protocol) is a newer and more sophisticated protocol based on BootP. Although it can be used with diskless workstations, it is more commonly used to manage IP addressing on ordinary workstations.

DHCP is a client-server protocol. The server maintains a database of available IP addresses and doles them out automatically to clients. This provides two administrative benefits:

- You don't need to assign IP addresses yourself.

- You can use a small pool of addresses to support a larger number of computers. For example, if your company has been assigned a range of 10 IP addresses on the Internet, you can still configure 20 computers to obtain addresses with DHCP. (However, only 10 of the computers can be used at a time.)

DHCP Features

DHCP is typically used to assign addresses temporarily. When a machine boots, it is assigned an address and continues to use that address until a time limit expires, or until it is turned off. In DHCP terminology, an address with a time limit is referred to as a *lease*.

DHCP actually supports three different types of address assignments. They are described in the following sections.

Dynamic Addressing

This is the most common type of DHCP addressing. Addresses are assigned to clients on a first-come, first-serve basis. When a machine reboots or allows its address lease to expire, it must request a new address.

This type of addressing is commonly used by Internet providers. When you dial in to the Internet, you might have a different IP address each time. The disadvantage of this method is that some protocols need to know a specific IP address, so a nondedicated address can be inconvenient.

Automatic Addressing

This method assigns addresses, but it does not expire leases. This means that once a machine has obtained an IP address, the address is reserved for the machine, and it is assigned each time the machine boots.

This method doesn't allow machines to share a pool of addresses. It simply provides a convenient way to add workstations to the network without manually assigning them IP addresses.

Reserved Addresses

By using a reserved address you can specify a particular IP address for a particular machine. This is known as a manual address assignment or a *reservation*. To reserve an address, you specify the IP address and the hardware address of the computer's network card. This machine will be assigned the address each time it boots.

One reason to reserve addresses is for machines that will be used as servers. For example, a machine acting as a DNS server needs to have the same IP address at all times, because workstations will be configured to contact a particular address.

How DHCP Works

DHCP is an Internet standard protocol, and it works the same way whether it is running under NetWare, Windows NT, or another system. The following sections describe the workings of the TCP/IP protocol.

How DHCP Servers Handle Requests

When a client that has been configured to use DHCP boots, it sends a DHCP request. The following steps are involved in the communication between the DHCP client and server:

1. The client sends a DHCP request message over the network. This is a broadcast message, and it is not addressed to a particular server.

2. The DHCP server for the current subnet receives the broadcast. If an IP address is available and the client is authorized to obtain one, the server returns an IP address with a lease time limit directly to the client.

3. The client configures itself with the received IP address. When the lease time is half over, it sends a renewal request to the server to renew the address.

4. The server renews the lease with a new time limit. If the lease expires because the client is turned off or is unable to contact the DHCP server, it attempts to request a new address the next time it is booted.

DHCP Routing

Because DHCP request messages are broadcasts, they are not forwarded by routers between different subnets. You can remedy this problem by using a single DHCP server per subnet. As an alternative, you can use the same server for multiple subnets with a DHCP relay agent.

A relay agent receives DHCP broadcasts on one subnet, and forwards them to a server in another subnet. The relay agent can be hardware (for example, some routers include this feature) or software. NetWare 5 includes an NLM that allows a NetWare server to act as a DHCP relay.

DHCP Support in NetWare 5

NetWare 5 supports DHCP with the Novell DNS/DHCP Services component, introduced in Chapter 9. This can be installed during the NetWare 5 installation or added to the server after installation.

When you install DNS/DHCP services, three items are installed: the NetWare server software for the services, the client installation files, and an extension to the NDS schema that supports DNS and DHCP objects.

NDS and DHCP

Like DNS, NetWare 5 uses a variety of NDS objects to store DHCP information. These objects are added to the NDS schema when you install DNS/DHCP Services. Some of the objects are created automatically; you must create others manually. The available objects are described in the following sections.

DHCP Server

This object represents a NetWare 5 server that is running the DNS/ DHCP server software. Its properties point to the NDS Server object for an existing server. The object also stores a pointer to each of the ranges of subnet addresses managed by the server (represented by Subnet Address objects).

Subnet

This object represents a subnet in the network. It is a Container object, and it can contain Subnet Address Range and IP Address objects. A DHCP server can be linked to one or more subnets.

Subnet Address Range

This object is a child of the Subnet object. It stores the specifics for a range of IP addresses that will be available to DHCP clients in the subnet. You will need to create at least one of these objects to configure the DHCP server.

IP Address

This object is similar to the Subnet Address Range object, but it stores only a single IP address. It is also a child of the Subnet object. IP Address objects can be used to make single IP addresses available. They can also be used to create exceptions (addresses that fall within the subnet address range, but should not be available to clients).

When you create a Subnet Address Range object, two IP Address objects are created automatically. These are exceptions for the addresses ending in .0 and .255. Some network equipment does not support addresses ending with these numbers.

Subnet Pool

This object is similar to an NDS Group object. While a Group object groups users, a Subnet Pool object groups subnets. You can group two or more subnets using a Subnet Pool object if you need to keep multiple subnet addresses (for example, an Internet address and an internal network address) for DHCP clients.

Installing and Configuring DHCP

NetWare 5 includes a DHCP server as part of Novell DNS/ DHCP Services. This is the same component used to provide DNS (Domain Name Service) services. The following sections describe the process of installing and managing DHCP support in NetWare 5.

Installation

You can install DNS/DHCP Services as part of the NetWare 5 installation. If you did not install these services during installation, you can add them using the Install program in the NetWare 5 GUI console. Follow Procedure 10.1 to install DNS/DHCP Services.

The installation is identical whether you plan to use DNS, DHCP, or both. You may have already installed these services while working with DNS in Chapter 9.

PROCEDURE 10.1

Installing DNS/DHCP Services on a NetWare 5 Server

1. Insert the NetWare 5 CD into the server's CD-ROM drive.

2. From the NetWare GUI, select Install from the Novell menu.

3. A dialog is displayed listing the currently installed products. Click the New Product button.

PROCEDURE 10.1 (CONTINUED)

4. You are now prompted for the path to the installation files. Choose the NetWare5 directory on the CD.

5. A list of products that can be installed is displayed. Check the box next to Novell DNS/DHCP Services, and click Next.

6. You are prompted for a name and password to authenticate to NDS. Enter the Admin account name and password.

7. Specify NDS contexts for the three DNS/DHCP objects. These default to the server's context.

8. A summary of the installation options is displayed. Click the Finish button to complete the installation.

The Management Console

As with DNS, you can manage NetWare 5's DHCP support using the DNS/DHCP Management Console software. This is a Java-based GUI application that runs on a workstation.

If you have not already installed the Management Console on a workstation, you can do so using the NetWare 5 CD-ROM. This process is described in detail in Chapter 9.

After you have installed the console, it is available from the Start menu on the workstation. When you run the console, choose the appropriate NDS tree to manage, then select the DHCP tab at the top of the window. The main DHCP console should be displayed, as shown in Figure 10.1.

You can also run the Management Console by selecting DNS/DHCP Management Console from the Tools menu in NetWare Administrator.

FIGURE 10.1

The main DHCP
console window

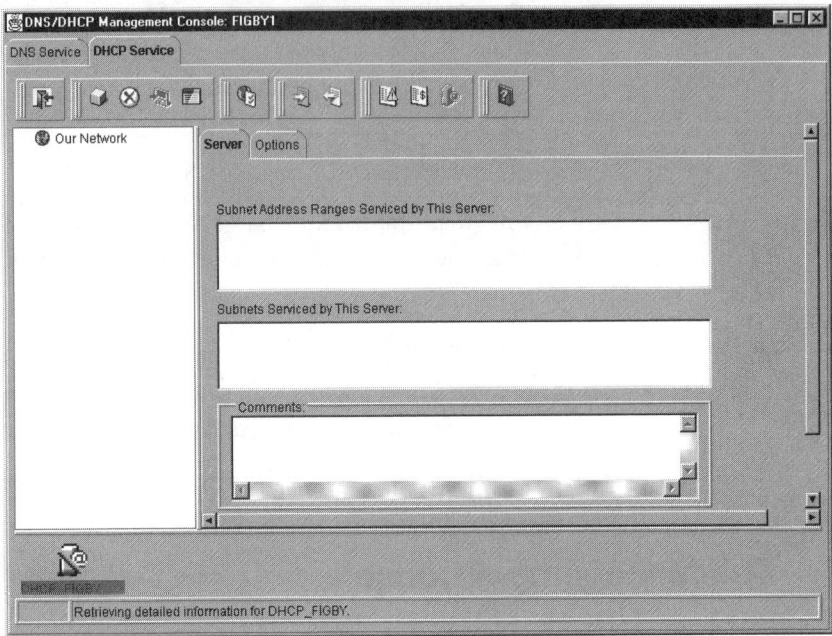

Creating NDS Objects

In order to maintain DHCP settings and IP address pools, you can create and manage the properties of the NDS objects related to DHCP. The following sections describe how to create each object type.

You cannot modify these objects using NetWare Administrator, although you can view them and some of their properties. You must use the DNS/ DHCP Management Console to manage DHCP objects.

DHCP Server Objects

You will need to create a DHCP Server object for each NetWare 5 server that will act as a DHCP server. A default DHCP Server object is created when you install DNS/DHCP Services. To create a DHCP Server object, follow the steps in Procedure 10.2.

PROCEDURE 10.2

Creating a DHCP Server Object

1. From the Management Console window, click the Create button (the second button from the left) in the toolbar to create a new object.

2. You are prompted for the type of object to create (as shown in this figure).

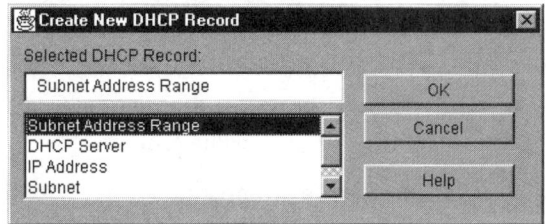

Select DHCP Server, and click the OK button.

3. The Create DHCP Server dialog is displayed, as shown in the following figure.

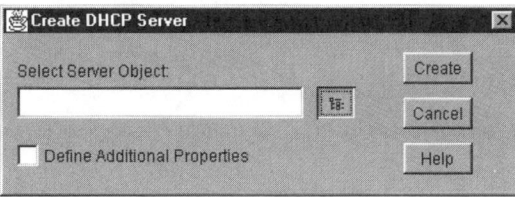

Specify the NDS Server object of the NetWare 5 server that you will use as a DHCP server.

4. If you are unsure of the name or context of the Server object, click the button to the right of the Server field to browse the NDS tree, as shown in the following figure.

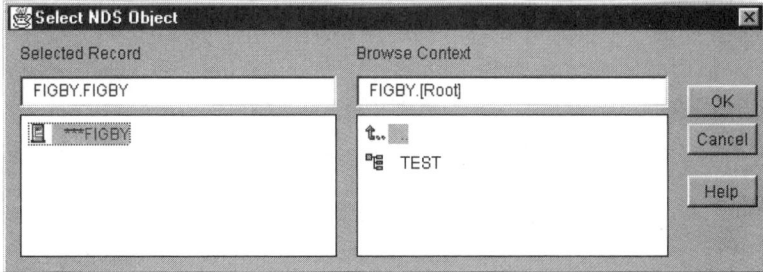

5. Click the Create button to create the object.

Subnet Objects

You can create any number of Subnet objects; you should create one for each physical subnet in the network. Follow the steps in Procedure 10.3 to create a Subnet object.

PROCEDURE 10.3

Creating a Subnet Object

1. Click the Create button (the second button from the left) in the Management Console toolbar.

2. You are prompted for the type of object to create. Select Subnet, and click the OK button.

3. Next, you are prompted for the required properties of the Subnet object, as shown in the following figure.

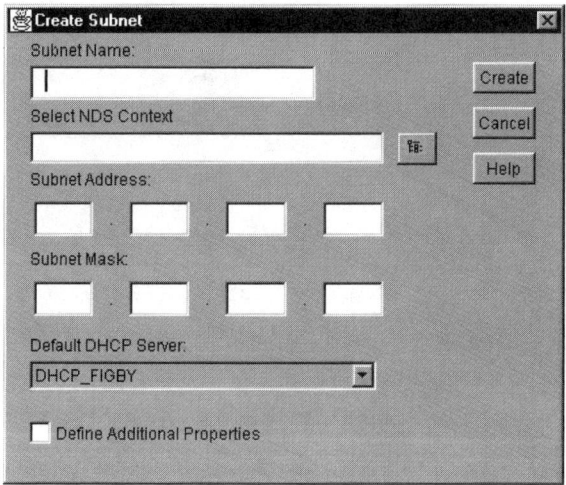

Specify the following information:

- The name of the subnet

- The NDS context in which to create the Subnet object

- The subnet's network address and subnet mask

- The DHCP server that will handle the subnet

4. Click the Create button to create the Subnet object.

Subnet Address Range Objects

Each Subnet object can contain one or more Subnet Address Range objects. To create a subnet address range, follow the steps in Procedure 10.4.

PROCEDURE 10.4

Creating a Subnet Address Range

1. Highlight a Subnet object under which to create the address range.

2. Click the Create button (the second button from the left) in the Management Console toolbar.

3. You are prompted for the type of object to create. Choose Subnet Address Range and click the OK button. (This choice is not available unless you have highlighted a Subnet object.)

4. You are prompted for the required properties for the Subnet Address Range object, as shown in the following figure.

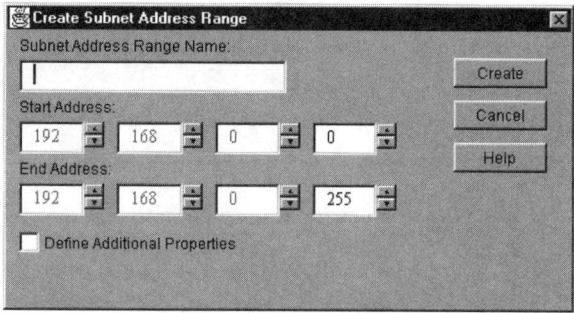

Specify a name for the address range, the starting address, and the ending addresses.

5. Click the Create button to create the object.

IP Address Objects

You can use IP Address objects to assign a single IP address, either as a single available address or an exception to an address range. This object is also created under the Subnet object. Follow the steps in Procedure 10.5 to create an IP Address object.

Creating an IP Address Object

1. Highlight the Subnet object under which to create the address.

2. Select the Create button (the second button from the left) in the Management Console toolbar.

3. You are prompted for the type of object to create. Choose IP Address and click OK. This choice is available only if you have highlighted a Subnet.

4. You are prompted for the required properties for the object, as shown in the following figure.

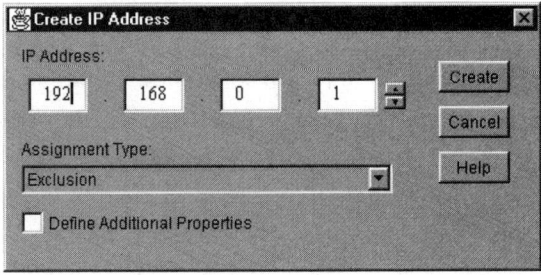

These include the IP address and the assignment type (manual address or exclusion)

5. Click the Create button to create the IP Address object.

Subnet Pool Objects

The final object you can create is a Subnet Pool object. This object groups Subnet objects into a pool of subnet addresses that all point to the same physical subnet. This object can be created under any NDS container. To create a Subnet Pool object, follow the steps in Procedure 10.6.

PROCEDURE 10.6

Creating a Subnet Pool Object

1. Select the Create button (the second button from the left) in the Management Console toolbar.

2. You are prompted for the type of object to create. Choose Subnet Pool, and click OK.

3. You are prompted for the object's required properties, as shown in the following figure.

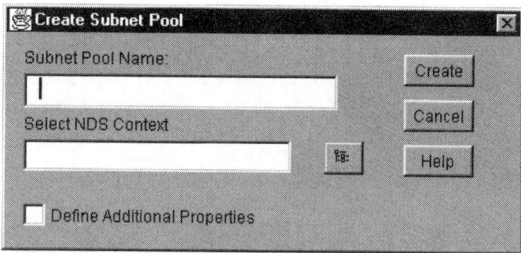

Specify a name for the subnet pool, and choose an NDS container under which to create the object.

Once you have created this object, highlight it to modify its properties, and add one or more Subnet objects to the list of subnets in the Details property screen.

Running the DHCP Server

Once you have installed the DNS/DHCP Server component and configured the NDS objects, you can begin running the DHCP server on the NetWare 5 server. The DHCP server is handled by a NetWare loadable module, DHCPSRVR.NLM.

To start the DHCP server, type **DHCPSRVR** at the console prompt. (You will need to exit the GUI to type this command.)

Although DHCP and DNS are installed as part of the same software component, they are handled by separate NLMs. You will need to load both DHCPSRVR.NLM and NAMED.NLM if you want to run both of these services. See Chapter 9 for more information about the DNS server.

Configuring DHCP Clients

Like DNS, DHCP does not require any special client software. Because DHCP requests are broadcasts, you do not need to specify the DHCP server's address to clients. The only client configuration necessary is to enable the client's DHCP option. This process depends on the operating system. As an example, Procedure 10.7 explains how to enable DHCP support in Windows 95 or 98.

PROCEDURE 10.7

Configuring a Windows 95/98 Workstation for DHCP Support

1. Right-click the Network Neighborhood icon and select Properties. A list of protocols and services is displayed. Select TCP/IP from the list and click the Properties button.

2. Choose the IP Address tab, as shown in the following figure.

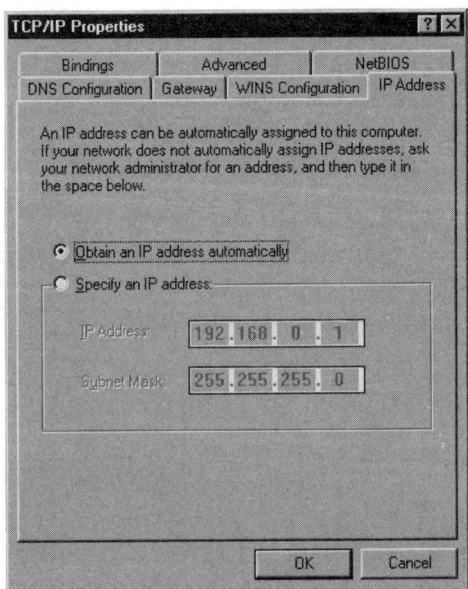

PROCEDURE 10.7 (CONTINUED)

Then select the Obtain an IP Address Automatically option.

3. Click OK to finish the configuration. You will need to restart the computer to obtain an IP address from the DHCP server.

Review

IP addressing is one of the most difficult tasks for IP network administrators. DHCP (Dynamic Host Configuration Protocol) automates the assignment of IP addresses. This allows you to avoid manually assigning addresses. Additionally, it can be used in some circumstances to reduce the number of IP addresses needed for a network.

How DHCP Works

DHCP is a client-server protocol. DHCP servers maintain a pool of available IP addresses. When a client sends a DHCP request broadcast, the server assigns it an address. There are three types of address assignments:

- Dynamic addresses are assigned for a limited duration (leased).

- Automatic addresses are assigned permanently to the machine to which they are first assigned.

- Reserved addresses are manually configured to match a specific hardware address with a specific IP address.

NetWare 5's DHCP Support

NetWare 5 supports DHCP as part of Novell DNS/DHCP Services, a component included with NetWare 5. Once this software is installed, the NetWare server can act as a DHCP server. Additionally, several NDS objects for DHCP are added to the NDS schema:

- *DHCP Server objects* represent NetWare 5 servers that run DHCP server software.

- *Subnet objects* are containers that represent subnets of the network.

- *Subnet Address Range objects* are stored under a Subnet object and specify a range of available IP addresses.

- *IP Address objects* are stored under a Subnet object and make a single IP address available or exclude it from a subnet address range.

- *Subnet Pool objects* group together two or more Subnet objects that represent the same physical subnet.

Installation and Administration

Like DNS, DHCP services can be managed using the DNS/DHCP Management Console utility. This utility is Java-based and can be installed at a workstation.

While the DHCP information is stored in NDS objects, you cannot manage them with NetWare Administrator. Instead, you can use the Management Console to work with these objects.

IP Addressing Practice Questions

1. What is the primary purpose of the DHCP protocol?

    A. To convert IP addresses to domain names

    B. To convert domain names to IP addresses

    C. To assign IP addresses dynamically to clients

    D. To allow several clients to use the same IP address at the same time

2. DHCP stands for _____.

3. DHCP is based on what Internet standard protocol?

   A. DNS

   B. BootP

   C. PPP

   D. NDS

4. You are using DHCP to assign addresses, and your company has been assigned a pool of 10 IP addresses for the Internet. There are two shifts, day and night, with no overlap between the two. The day shift employees use different computers than the night shift employees. How many total employees could you support with DHCP?

5. An address assigned by DHCP to a client with a limited duration is known as a _____.

6. Which type of DHCP addressing assigns addresses dynamically, but always uses the same address for a client each time it boots?

7. An IP address manually assigned to a specific computer in DHCP is also known as a _____.

8. Which hardware or software component is required in order to use the same DHCP server in two subnets of a network?

   A. An address pool

   B. A DHCP relay agent

   C. A BootP server

   D. A router

9. The Subnet Address Range and IP Address objects are child objects of which NDS container object?

   A. Organization

   B. DHCP server

   C. IP address pool

   D. Organizational unit

   E. Subnet

10. Which utility would you use to create an IP Address object?

   A. NWADMIN

   B. DNS/DHCP Management Console

   C. ConsoleOne

   D. INSTALL

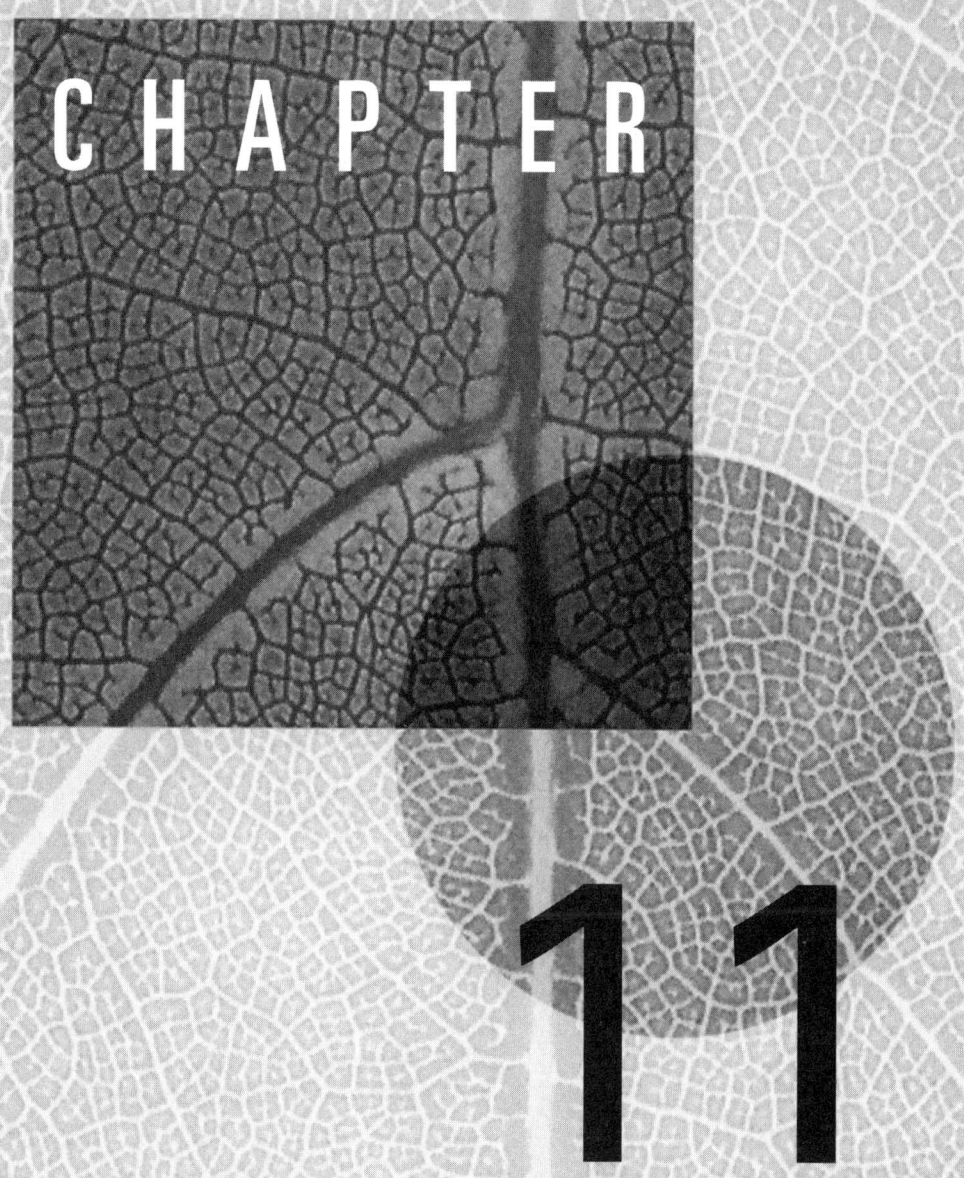

CHAPTER

11

SLP and Mobile Users

Roadmap

This chapter covers the Service Location Protocol (SLP) and mobile user administration.

Topics Covered

- Understanding SLP and its function of infrastructure service provider discovery

- Understanding how SLP functions as a compatibility facilitator with IPX and SAP

- Understanding server and client SLP configurations

- Understanding mobile user administration

- Understanding mobile user strategies and design

Skills You'll Learn

- Understand the traffic considerations involved in locating services and how to weigh your location strategy choices

- Understand SLP parameters

- Design strategies for mobile users

- Set up a contextless login

In real estate, there is an important parameter called *location/ location/location*. In a network environment, we need to find the location of various infrastructure services on the network and we need to know how users can access the network from locations both inside and outside the network.

In this chapter, we will look at how services are located across increasingly complex networks and at how mobile users can access the network from any location.

We will also look at the Service Location Protocol (SLP) that discovers infrastructure services across the network and encapsulates SAP broadcasts in an IPX Compatibility Mode network. SLP will discover infrastructure services such as NDS servers, NDPS registration servers, DNS servers, DHCP servers, and assorted protocol gateways.

We will then look at mobile user administration, which can be achieved by:

- Client configuration

- Knowledgeable user login

- Alias object

- Login script

- Contextless login

By understanding these different strategies and their implications, you will be better prepared to decide which mobile user strategy will work best for your network.

Service Location Protocol (SLP)

Service Location Protocol is an Internet Standard protocol (RFC2165) that is used on NetWare 5 to perform two primary functions. The first is to discover, or locate, assorted infrastructure service providers across the network. The second function is to encapsulate the network clogging SAP broadcasts in an IPX Compatibility Mode environment. Let's look at the locating or discovery function of SAP.

Infrastructure Service Discovery

Any infrastructure service can be registered into the NDS name base either manually or automatically through NDS system calls written into the software. IPX-based applications that advertise their services through SAP are registered in the bindery container of NDS and can be accessed through a bindery call. SLP works with NDS to coordinate information about IP infrastructure resources in one place. This eliminates the constant SAP advertising that eats up so much bandwidth.

In the previous IPX versions of NetWare through NetWare 4.11, each machine had a bindery and SAP was global. This SAP/Bindery architecture could pick up a SAP packet from any service that was then recognized globally across the network.

As networks became more complex, many network administrators created even more NDS trees. Each tree put out a SAP advertisement that was saved in the router tables on each NetWare server. A NetWare client could then access this information from the server. SAP was created in the early network days when WANs were not prevalent.

SAP messages refresh themselves every 60 seconds regardless of whether anything has changed. The continuous updates were convenient for Plug and Play on a LAN, but they generated too much traffic for WAN links.

Network administrators paid the price for this service visibility in reduced bandwidth and subsequent corrective responses, e.g., filtering out service visibility to reduce line congestion.

SLP takes advantage of the information NDS has about IP infrastructure services, including:

- NDS trees

- NDPS service registries

- NCP servers

- DNS servers

- Protocol gateways

NDS objects are not created for these services, but the NDS information is collected and stored in the single SLP database. The NetWare 5 client can access this information to connect to these infrastructure services.

In NetWare 5, NDPS gets automated management in the IP environment from SLP. NDPS can function without SLP, but the automated management function is reduced.

IPX Compatibility Mode Encapsulation

In NetWare 5, both SAP/Bindery-based applications and IPX-based applications will continue to work in an IP environment because of SLP. SLP accomplishes this by letting the Compatibility Mode drivers translate SAP packets into SLP packets that are then passed to other Compatibility Mode servers. The SLP packets are then returned to the router tables.

Directory Agents

Directory Agents are SLP entities that provide scalability and service visibility across the enterprise. Smaller networks (20–30 servers) do not need Directory Agents. These networks have User Agents and Service Agents that are loaded automatically and don't require any configuration. In larger networks, the frequency and location of Directory Agents is dependent upon the overall design and traffic strategy that you develop.

SLP Scopes

SLP scopes are a filtering method that reduces traffic outside of chosen network segments. In the largest networks, a "flat" SLP implementation may not be effective for traffic management and scalability. One way to configure such networks is to use *SLP scopes* to subdivide the network.

For example, your Marketing department may have a number of services that are registered in and used only by that department. You could configure a scope attribute of MTG to be added to each of the Marketing department's services. These services would then become visible only when requests included the SCOPE=MTG attribute. Subdividing with scopes is one filtering method you can use. If you choose not to use this method, your SLP implementation is said to be *unscoped*.

Service Visibility

As with our Marketing department example, every service does not need to be visible everywhere across the enterprise. Because of IPX packet filtering at routers, SAP broadcasts were not always visible across earlier versions of NetWare. A parallel effect could be achieved with NetWare 5 by disabling the IP Multicast and configuring a number of Directory Agents across the network. These Directory Agents can be regionally configured so that each contains different data and each services different areas of the network.

Fault Tolerance

Although a single Directory Agent could function effectively for fairly large companies, it would establish a single point of failure. By using multiple Directory Agents, this risk is minimized but a need to synchronize these Directory Agents results. You must weigh these choices as an administrator.

NDS Replication

You can use NDS replication to synchronize the data in various Directory Agents across the network. This system works better in a LAN environment. Employing this method over a WAN link can be expensive and use up your bandwidth. You can look further into NDS deployment and replication and your own system capacity to evaluate this method for your network.

IP Multicasting

The SLP User Agent uses IP Multicasting to access the various SLP Service Agents by default in a local network segment environment. If IP Multicasting is made available across the network, then SLP will use your available bandwidth to find Service Agents. If you disable the IP Multicasting to reduce traffic, you can use DHCP to find non-local Service Agents for the User Agents.

You must also weigh the benefits of using multicast technology in your network. It works best on local segments. When configured across routers, multicast technology can quickly grow to a consuming bandwidth. If properly configured, IP Multicasting can globally distribute your network's information.

Organizational Density

Network topographies vary as greatly as the companies and departments they connect. Network infrastructures vary greatly, and no single service location strategy will work for all situations. Geographical situations with LAN segments and WAN links must be considered when you develop an SLP technology strategy. Concentrated LAN segments work well with IP Multicast and NDS replication. With WAN links, NDS replication with WAN management synchronization and/or locating services through DHCP and DNS might be attractive.

With WAN connections over a modem link, you could configure the local SLP and Service Agents to use DHCP to locate a corporate SLP Directory Agent. Another solution would be to have a static configuration send clients to a specific tree or Directory Agent.

SLP Strategies

The SLP strategy you choose will depend most on the size of your network. Let's take a look at three general size categories:

Small networks (less than 30 servers in a multicast radius)   A small network with 20–30 servers doesn't benefit from having a Directory Agent (DA). If you don't have limiting WAN links, you can do quite well with smaller networks using the SLP Service, User Agents, and IP Multicasting. This default setup will let network clients have dynamic discovery of NDS trees, NDPS Service Registries, NCP servers, and other infrastructure services like gateways.

Medium networks (more than 30 servers but not quite a large enterprise network)   In most cases, a medium-sized network will benefit from using Directory Agents. If the network is generally flat, eliminating IP Multicasting and using DHCP to find the DAs for the User Agents might be the best setup. Service information can be kept in NDS containers and replicated across the network for other Directory Agents to use.

Large networks (many servers in a large enterprise implementation) Large, complex enterprise situations require a planned combination of SLP Directory Agents, NDS replication, DHCP, and local IP Multicast. The DAs will acquire information from the local Service Agents. This information is loaded into a container and copied through NDS replication with information from other DAs across the network. The traffic in WAN links throughout the enterprise must be considered. Letting Service Agents use DHCP to locate DAs can reduce traffic.

Server SLP Configuration Parameters

The SLP options discussed in this chapter can be configured from the server console using the SET command in the STARTUP.NCF file. The following parameters are available:

SLP DA Discovery Options A set of one-bit binary flags that control the behavior of SLP discovery. This value can range from 0 to 8, and it defaults to 3.

SLP Multicast Radius Specifies the radius for SLP multicasts. This value can range from 0 to 32, and it defaults to 32.

SLP Debug A set of binary flags that can be used to enable SLP debugging. The default is 0.

SLP MTU Size Specifies the maximum transfer unit (MTU) size for SLP transmissions. This value can range from 0 to 4,294,967,255, and it defaults to 1,472.

SLP Rediscover Inactive Directory Agents Specifies the minimum time SLP will wait (in seconds) before attempting to rediscover an inactive Directory Agent. This value can range from 0 to 4,294,967,255, and it defaults to 60.

SLP SA Default Lifetime   Specifies the default time a service register will last. This value can range from 0 to 4,294,967,255, and it defaults to 900.

SLP Event Timeout   Specifies the number of seconds SLP will wait before assuming a multicast packet request has ended. This value defaults to 53.

SLP DA Heartbeat Time   Specifies the frequency (in seconds) at which SLP sends out heartbeat packets, which are used by Directory Agents to monitor the server. This value defaults to 10,800.

SLP Close Idle TCP Connections Time   Specifies a timeout in seconds for TCP connections not currently in use. This value can range from 0 to 4,294,967,255, and it defaults to 300.

SLP TCP   This value can be set to OFF or ON. If this value is set to ON, SLP attempts to use TCP packets instead of UDP as often as possible.

SLP Retry Count   Specifies the number of times SLP will attempt to resend a transmission. This value can range from 0 to 128, and it defaults to 3.

SLP Broadcast   This value can be set to OFF or ON. If turned on, SLP uses standard broadcast packets instead of multicast packets. The default is OFF.

SLP Scope List   Specifies a comma-separated list of scope policies. This value can be up to 1,023 characters long.

SLP DA Event Timeout   Specifies a timeout in seconds for Directory Agent packet requests. This value ranges from 0 to 429, and the default is 5.

Client SLP Configuration Parameters

To configure the SLP interaction with the NetWare client, go to the Novell Client Configuration property page under the Advanced Settings. The General property category includes these settings:

SLP Multicast Radius   Describes the maximum number of subnets that an SLP Multicast will traverse. A value of 1 will confine the multicasts to the local segment only. This value ranges from 1 to 32, and it defaults to 32.

SLP Active Discovery   This value can be set to ON or OFF, and it defaults to ON. If set, SLP first attempts to look up Directory Agents. If none are found, it sends a multicast to Service Agents.

SLP Maximum Transmission Unit   Specifies the maximum UDP packet size for SLP transmissions. This value ranges from 576 to 4096, and it defaults to 1400. Extremely low or high values can decrease SLP's performance.

The SLP Times property category includes these settings:

SLP Default Registration Lifetime   Specifies a default lifetime for services registered by Service Agents. If the service provider specifies a lifetime value, it overrides this value. Services must be renewed or unregistered before this time expires; otherwise, they will be deleted. This value ranges from 60 to 60,000 seconds, and it defaults to 10,800.

SLP Cache Replies   Specifies the number of minutes SLP will wait after receiving a service request from a User Agent before sending a reply. Requests are cached during this period to prevent duplicates. This value ranges from 1 to 60 minutes, and it defaults to 1. Higher values will increase SLP's memory usage and may affect performance.

Mobile User Administration

As technology advances in modern society, users are becoming increasingly mobile. Administration for mobile users can be achieved through one of the following methods:

Alias object   If the number of mobile users on your network is small, you can create an alias object for each mobile user below the top organizational object in the tree. This alias object points to the user objects in the correct containers.

Login scripts   You can use login scripts to let mobile users access the network from wherever they log in.

Client configuration   You can set the preferred server and name context in the mobile users' clients. This is accomplished by placing the information in the NET.CFG file in DOS or Windows 3.1*x* or in the client properties screen in Windows 95 or Windows NT.

Knowledgeable user login   You can allow users to manually enter their distinguished name when they log in.

Contextless login   You can run NDS Catalog Services on your NetWare 5 server and configure your Novell clients to use contextless login. This allows users to log in without providing a context. NDS Catalog Services provides context information about mobile users.

Setting Up Contextless Login

When a user logs in and specifies a tree and a username, NDS Catalog Services can find the username and add a context automatically. If the username exists in multiple contexts in the tree and Contextless Login is configured to allow wildcards, Contextless Login will let a user pick a username and context pair.

To set up Contextless Login, repeat the steps in Procedure 11.1.

PROCEDURE 11.1

Setting Up Contextless Login

1. Install the latest Novell NetWare client software on the client.

2. Check to make sure that the LGNCON32.DLL file exists in the WINDOWS\ SYSTEM directory (Windows 95) or in the WINDOWS\SYSTEM32 directory (Windows NT).

   Also check to make sure that the DSCQRY32.DLL file is in the WINDOWS\ SYSTEM directory (Windows 95) or in the WINDOWS\SYSTEM32 directory (Windows NT).

PROCEDURE 11.1 (CONTINUED)

3. Log in as Admin from the client.

4. Check to make sure NDS Catalog Services was installed during the NetWare 5 installation. If it wasn't, install it.

5. In NetWare Administrator, create an object in NDS at your desired position in the tree and name it **CATALOG**.

6. Click the catalog object you just created, and then click Details.

7. Choose the Identification page, and click the Browse button to the right of Host Server. Browse to and select the server that is running Catalog Services.

8. In the Label section, click New. Enter **LGNCON** for the primary label and **Users** for the secondary label.

9. Next configure the Filter page by typing **"Object Class" = "User"** in the Filter field. Choose Search Subtree, and leave the Context field blank, which will let the entire tree be cataloged.

10. Configure the Attributes/Index page by clicking Selected Attributes, and then click Select Attributes. From the available list, choose Full Name and click Add.

11. Click Select Indexes. From the list, choose Full Name. Click Add and then OK.

12. Configure the Schedule page by clicking Manual. Click OK.

13. Assign Browse Object rights and Read and Compare Rights to All Properties to the CATALOG object.

14. Make [Public] a trustee of the CATALOG object with Browse object rights and Read and Compare rights to All Properties.

15. At the server console, load DSCAT.NLM.

16. When you are prompted that the dredge for CATALOG is finished, unload the DSCAT.NLM.

Once you've configured the server, you can set up the client for Contextless Login. Follow the steps in Procedure 11.2.

PROCEDURE 11.2

Setting Up the Client for Contextless Login

1. On the Windows 95/98 Desktop, right-click Network Neighborhood.

2. Click Properties, and then click Contextless Login.

3. Click Enabler, and click Wildcard Searching Allowed.

4. In the Tree field, enter the name of your NDS tree. In the Catalog field, enter **CATALOG**.

5. Click Add. Click OK twice.

6. Reboot your workstation.

To test the installation, run LOGINW32.EXE. In the Tree field, enter the tree name for an existing tree. In the Username field, enter a username for an existing user. The correct context for the user should appear in the Context field.

Using Encryption Services

Another new feature of NetWare 5 is its built-in support for encryption. Although this might sound like something that only government agencies and spies would use, it's actually being used in more and more networks—particularly because many networks are now connected to the Internet. One use for these features is to configure secure access to Web pages on the NetWare server.

NetWare 5's security features include the following:

- PKI (Public Key Infrastructure) allows the use of public-key encryption.

- CA (Certificate Authority) manages digital certificates.

- NICI (Novell International Cryptography Infrastructure) is a fundamental service used by the other components.

- SAS (Secure Authentication Services) is a service that authenticates applications.

These features are explained further in the following sections.

How Public Key Cryptography Works

If you've used the Internet much, you've probably heard of Public Key cryptography, but you may not know exactly what it means. Let's start with the basics: *cryptography* is the science of converting one (readable) document to another (unreadable) one to prevent unauthorized reading. There are many ways of doing this; the most common method uses a *key* to encrypt the document. Each character in the document is modified with an algorithm that uses the key to produce a new character.

Public key cryptography is a system that uses two keys: a public key and a private key. Each key can only be used one way, and the two keys complement each other. A document encrypted with a public key can only be decrypted with the private key, and a document encrypted with the private key can only be decrypted with the public key.

Although this sounds strange, it turns out to be very practical. Here's how you would use it to encrypt an e-mail conversation: You find out your pen pal's public key (which can be publicly posted) and use it to encrypt the message. Once your pen pal receives the message, she can decrypt and read it with her private key. She can also encrypt messages with your public key, and you can read them by using your private key.

On the other hand, you can encrypt a message with your own private key and send it. This provides a sort of digital signature, because anyone can decrypt the message with your public key, thereby proving that you sent it with your private key.

> A common implementation of public-key cryptography is PGP (pretty good privacy), which is widely used on the Internet.

NetWare Security Components

At the foundation of NetWare 5's cryptography features is NICI, or Novell International Cryptography Infrastructure. This software provides a set of services that can be used by any software on the NetWare server. NICI uses a modular system for its cryptography modules, so new modules can be added at any time to take advantage of new encryption schemes.

Next is PKI, or Public Key Infrastructure. This is a service that manages public-key encryption. PKI also handles digital certificates, which are authoritative documents that can be used to authenticate a message. Certificates are managed by certificate authorities, large companies with known reputations. NetWare 5 includes its own implementation of a certificate authority (CA), which can act as a local authority and can be authorized by a major authority.

Finally, SAS (Secure Authentication Services) is a service that authenticates applications. This service is required to use NICI and PKI on your NetWare 5 server. SAS uses the SSL (Secure Sockets Layer) protocol to enable secure communication between applications.

Configuring Security

To enable NetWare 5's encryption features, you must install three components:

- SAS (Secure Authentication Services)
- PKI (Public Key Infrastructure)
- NICI (Novell International Cryptographic Infrastructure)

You can install all of these using the NWCONFIG utility's Other Installation Items menu. The products are located on the NetWare 5 CD-ROM.

After the products are installed, the NDS schema is extended. A new object, Security Container, is added to the [Root] context in the NDS tree. A snap-in for NWADMIN allows you to manage this object. You can create two types of objects under the Security Container:

Certificate Authority   This object stores information for the local CA.

Key Material   This object stores information about public keys and digital certificates.

Once these components are installed and configured, the cryptographic services are ready for use. They can be used by any compatible software. Two NetWare 5 components that use these services are LDAP (Lightweight Directory Access Protocol) and Novell BorderManager.

Review

In this chapter, we saw how SLP uses a number of strategies to discover infrastructure service locations and how it encapsulates SAP packets to travel to Compatibility Mode servers across the network.

We looked at the different strategies and administrative options you can use to handle network logins by mobile users. The locations of the services and the locations of the users create problems to which there are no single, simple solutions.

Let's review the principal details we learned.

SLP

SLP functions on the network by allowing NetWare clients to query one database for information regarding IP infrastructure services and their locations. This method improves on the previous method of constantly advertising SAP broadcasts that consumed network bandwidth.

SLP accomplishes this function through User Agents that act for a client, by Service Agents that act for services, and by Directory Agents that function together in large complex networks. We looked at the SLP strategies that will work best with small, medium, and large networks.

We looked at the various parameters that must be considered when designing the SLP configuration including:

- Directory Agents

- SLP scopes

- Service visibility

- Fault tolerance

- NDS replication

- IP Multicasting

- Organizational density and location

We looked at the various configuration parameters for servers and clients.

Mobile Users

We looked at the principal methods for dealing with the ramifications that providing a workable login creates for mobile users. These approaches included:

- Alias objects

- Login scripts

- Client configurations

- Knowledgeable user logins

- Contextless logins

We looked at various strategies for different sizes of mobile user groups and different types of users. We looked at the steps to set up contextless logins and at how this solution will work in all the situations we studied.

Encryption Services

NetWare 5 includes a number of features that allow the use of cryptography and authentication for secure communications. These features include the following:

- PKI (Public Key Infrastructure) allows the use of public-key encryption.

- CA (Certificate Authority) manages digital certificates.

- NICI (Novell International Cryptography Infrastructure) is a fundamental service used by the other components.

- SAS (Secure Authentication Services) is a service that authenticates applications.

SLP and Mobile Users Practice Questions

1. What was the unifying theme of this chapter?

   A. Odds and ends

   B. Added page count

   C. Growing enterprise complexity

   D. Location/location/location

2. Which of the following is not an infrastructure service that would be kept track of by SLP?

   A. NDS servers

   B. NDPS registration servers

   C. NSS servers

   D. DHCP servers

   E. Protocol gateways

   F. DNS servers

3. SLP is which Internet Standard protocol?

  A. IEEE 802.3

  B. FDDI

  C. X.25

  D. RFC2165

  E. SMDS

4. Which of the following parameters would be the best way to confine network traffic to a certain department of your company whose services do not need to be seen elsewhere on the network?

  A. Directory Agents

  B. SLP scopes

  C. Service visibility

  D. Fault tolerance

  E. NDS replication

5. NDPS is automatically managed in the IP environment from SLP and can't function without SLP. (True or False?)

6. The integer value that represents the Multicast radius is:

  A. 0 to 32

  B. 60 to 60,000

  C. 0 to 8

  D. 0 to 4,294,967,255

  E. 0 to 128

7. Which client configuration parameter will hurt SLP performance if it is set at either extreme?

   A. SLP Maximum Transmission Unit

   B. SLP Multicast Radius

   C. SLP Cache Replies

   D. SLP Default Registration Lifetime

   E. SLP Active Discovery

8. You can set the preferred server and name context in the mobile users' clients by placing the information in the _____ file in DOS or Windows.

9. If Jlewis wants to log in with an alias object and his organizational object name is MTG, he should log in as:

   A. MTG.Jlewis

   B. MTG.Alias.Jlewis

   C. Alias.Jlewis.MTG

   D. Jlewis.MTG

10. Which executable did we use to check to see if our installation of Contextless Login was successful?

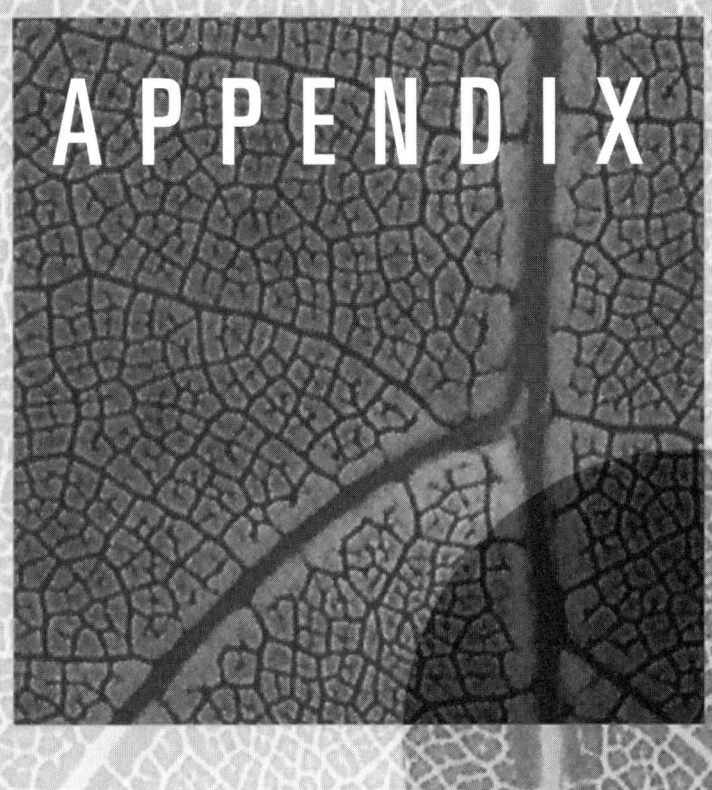

APPENDIX

Answers to Practice Questions

Chapter 1 Answers

1. Novonyx, the company that developed the FastTrack Server, is now owned by Netscape. (True or False.)

   Answer: False

2. What does the acronym DHCP stand for?

   Answer: Dynamic Host Configuration Protocol

3. From now on, all new Novell products will use a common installation architecture called *Novell Installation Services*. (True or False.)

   Answer: True

4. Which of the following security features is not included in Cryptographic Services?

   A. Authentication

   B. Nonrepudiation

   C. Integrity

   D. Digital certificates

   E. Confidentiality

   Answer: D

5. In general, if you choose IP as a core protocol, it will not do which of the following? (Choose two.)

   A. Require less hardware in routed environments

   B. Require less software in routed environments

   C. Save bandwidth

   D. Decrease remote user possibilities

E. Work well with the Internet

F. Run Compatibility Mode

Answer: D, F

6. Which Z.E.N.works feature includes snAppShot?

A. Desktop Manager

B. Help Requester

C. Application Launcher

D. Remote Control

Answer: C

7. What is the maximum size file that NSS (Novell Storage Services) can handle?

Answer: 8 terabytes

8. SRS eliminates the need for SAP (Service Advertising Protocol) by performing which of the following? (Choose one.)

A. Providing plug-and-print capability

B. Having the Print Device Subsystem retrieve information about printers

C. Letting Novell Printer Manager manage all Printer Agents

D. Keeping a list of all registered printers

Answer: D

9. What new NetWare 5 feature allows you to plug in new network cards while the server is running?

Answer: Hot Plug PCI

10. Novell Upgrade Wizard will work with either NetWare 3.1*x* or NetWare 4.*x* upgrades for across-the-wire installation. (True or False.)

Answer: False

Chapter 2 Answers

1. The size limit for a single file in the traditional NetWare file system is:

A. 1MB

B. 1GB

C. 2GB

D. 8TB

Answer: C

2. What is the minimum amount of RAM required for the installation of NetWare 5?

A. 12MB

B. 16MB

C. 32MB

D. 64MB

Answer: D

3. How much disk storage is required for the installation of NetWare 5, including the DOS partition?

A. 1GB

B. 230MB

C. 485MB

D. 2GB

Answer: C

4. If you upgrade a NetWare 4 machine to NetWare 5 without upgrading any hardware, it will run faster. (True or False.)

Answer: False

5. Which of the following hardware items are required for the installation of NetWare 5? (Select all that apply.)

A. CD-ROM drive

B. Network card

C. Network connection

D. Floppy drive

E. Mouse

F. Pentium-class processor

Answer: B, C, F

6. Which extensions are used for disk drivers in NetWare 5? (Select all that apply.)

A. DSK

B. DLL

C. NLM

D. HAM

E. CDM

Answer: D, E

7. Which of the following are advantages of the NSS file system? (Select all that apply.)

A. Less memory is required for large volumes.

B. Larger file sizes are possible.

C. It is compatible with older NetWare versions.

D. It has faster access to files.

Answer: A, B, D

8. If you buy a new machine to run NetWare 5 and replace the old server, you need to use the _____ upgrade method to install NetWare 5.

   Answer: Across-the-wire

9. Which program is used to migrate data to a new server?

   A. Migration Wizard

   B. MIGRATE.EXE

   C. MIGRATE.NLM

   D. Upgrade Wizard

   Answer: D

10. Which versions of NetWare can you upgrade to NetWare 5 by using the installation program? (Select all that apply.)

    A. NetWare 4.*x* only

    B. NetWare 3.1*x* or 4.*x*

    C. NetWare 2.*x* through 4.*x*

    D. Previous versions of NetWare 5 only

    Answer: B

Chapter 3 Answers

1. A plug-and-print printer on Novell Distributed Print Services is also called a _____Printer.

   Answer: Public Access

2. A printer capable of bidirectional communication on Novell Distributed Print Services is also called a _____ Printer.

   Answer: Controlled Access

3. The new intelligent element that becomes the individual brain of each network Printer is called:

    A. A print queue

    B. A print server

    C. The Printer Agent

    D. A print object

Answer: C

4. For how long does a single NDPS Broker function in the network?

    A. As long as the capture statement is functional

    B. As long as there are Controlled Access Printers on the network

    C. For three hops

    D. For all servers within two hops

Answer: C

5. Which of the three gateways uses a Setup Wizard?

    A. The Novell Gateway

    B. The Hewlett Packard Gateway

    C. The Epson Gateway

    D. The Xerox Gateway

Answer: D

6. Which of the following statements regarding a Public Access Printer is not true?

    A. It allows plug-and-print freedom.

    B. You cannot configure it for hierarchical usage.

C. It is managed through its NDS object.

D. Its print job status can't be directed.

Answer: C

7. Regarding a Controlled Access Printer, which of the following is true?

   A. A full range of NetWare security options is denied.

   B. Bidirectional communications are not allowed.

   C. Access to users in a container must be individually granted on NDS.

   D. It is managed through NetWare Administrator.

   Answer: D

8. Novell Printer Manager allows you to do which of the following? (Choose all that apply.)

   A. View a list of all print jobs

   B. Submit a job with a hold

   C. Access the real-time status of those jobs

   D. Pause, delete, or remove print jobs

   E. Change the printer gateway

   F. Access and upgrade the printer list

   G. Configure the spooling of print jobs

   H. Add printers to the list

   I. Check toner level

   Answer: A, B, C, D, F, G, H

9. List the four elements that make up NDPS.

A. _____

B. _____

C. _____

D. _____

Answer:

A. The NDPS Manager

B. The Printer Agent

C. The NDPS Broker

D. The three gateways

10. The minimum system requirements for an NDPS Server are 80MB of disk space and at least 8MB of RAM more than the minimum needed to run NetWare 5. (True or False.)

Answer: False. Only 4MB of RAM more than the minimum are required.

Chapter 4 Answers

1. The TCP and IP protocols are analogous to which NetWare protocols? (Select two choices.)

A. IPX

B. NFS

C. LPD

D. SPX

E. NCP

Answer: A, D

2. Which of the following protocols are considered to be connection-oriented? (Select one or more choices.)

A. TCP

B. UDP

C. SPX

D. IPX

Answer: A, C

3. Which of the following statements is *not* true of IP?

A. It is similar to IPX.

B. It resides in the Process/Application layer.

C. It performs routing functions.

D. It has a 32-bit address space.

Answer: B

4. Which of the following protocols relates to electronic mail?

A. SMTP

B. SNMP

C. TFTP

D. ARP

Answer: A

5. The Token Ring protocol resides at the _____ layer of the DOD model.

Answer: Network Access

6. Which of the following statements is *not* true of UDP?

   A. It is a connectionless protocol.

   B. It is rarely used.

   C. It doesn't require acknowledgments.

   D. It's more efficient than TCP.

   Answer: B

7. An IP address is how many bits long?

   A. 42

   B. 30

   C. 32

   D. Depends on the class of network

   Answer: C

8. In the IP address 164.33.103.4, the node address is _____.

   Answer: 103.4

9. Which of the following is the correct format for class A network addresses?

   A. Node.Net.Net.Net

   B. Node.Node.Net.Net

   C. Net.Net.Net.Node

   D. Net.Node.Node.Node

   Answer: D

10. What are the leading bits of a class B address?

A. 110

B. 10

C. 1

D. 011

Answer: B

11. Which of the following statements is true concerning NetWare 5?

A. IPX packets can be encapsulated within TCP/IP.

B. TCP/IP packets are encapsulated within IPX.

C. IPX is not supported at all.

D. TCP/IP requires IPX to work properly.

Answer: A

12. Which component allows you to set policies for NDS synchronization?

A. NTP.NLM

B. WAN Traffic Manager

C. Migration Agent

D. PX compatibility mode

Answer: B

13. Which server component (NLM) handles IPX Compatibility Mode?

Answer: SCMD.NLM

14. Which server component should be run on a Migration Agent server?

   A. A.SCMD.NLM

   B. B.WAN Traffic Manager

   C. C.MIGRATE.NLM

   D. D.Migration Gateway

   Answer: A

Chapter 5 Answers

1. The graphical Java console in NetWare 5 replaces the text-based console used in previous versions. (True or False.)

   Answer: False

2. Which two hardware devices are specifically required to run the GUI console in NetWare 5? (Select two.)

   A. VGA or better video card

   B. CGA or better video card

   C. Mouse

   D. 64MB of RAM

   E. 200MB of disk storage

   F. CD-ROM drive

   Answer: A, C

3. _____ are Java programs that are designed to run within a Web page.

   Answer: Applets

4. Which types of graphical applications can run under the NetWare 5 GUI console? (Choose one or more.)

  A. Java applets

  B. Java applications

  C. X Windows applications

  D. NetWare Loadable Modules (NLMs)

  E. Windows applications

  Answer: A, B

5. Which of the following statements is true of the Java language?

  A. Java creates programs for Windows platforms only.

  B. Java is compiled into machine language.

  C. Java classes can work on multiple platforms.

  D. NetWare 5 supports only Windows-based Java applets.

  E. All programs require an HTML document to launch.

  Answer: C

6. Which of these NetWare 5 tools allows you to view multiple server consoles, each in its own window in the server GUI?

  A. RConsoleJ

  B. Console Manager

  C. NWADMIN

  D. Install

  Answer: B

7. If you install a new video card in the NetWare server, which of the following is the correct command to set up the driver for the new card?

  A. VESA

  B. VESA_RSP

   C. INSTALL

   D. CONFIG

   Answer: B

8. Which of the following is *not* a function available in the ConsoleOne utility?

   A. View text-based consoles for the local server

   B. View text-based consoles for remote servers

   C. View graphic consoles for remote servers

   D. View properties of NDS objects

   Answer: C

9. Which of these file system operations are available from the ConsoleOne utility? (Choose one or more.)

   A. Delete a file

   B. Rename a file

   C. Salvage a deleted file

   D. Edit a text file

   Answer: A, B, D

10. You need to add a Java applet to the Novell menu in the server GUI. The applet is stored in the test.class file and referenced in the TEST.HTML document. Which of the following is the correct command to add to the menu configuration file?

   A. `+ "Test applet" Exec TEST.class`

   B. `+ "Test applet" Exec APPLET TEST.class`

   C. `+ "Test applet" Exec JAVA TEST.HTML`

   D. `+ "Test applet" Exec APPLET TEST.HTML`

   Answer: D

Chapter 6 Answers

1. Z.E.N.works stands for which of the following?

    A. Zinc Embedded Nexus

    B. Zero Entropy Networking

    C. Zero Effort Networking

    D. Zigzag Energy Network

    Answer: C

2. Which of the following is not a Z.E.N.works component?

    A. Novell Workstation Manager

    B. NetWare Application Launcher

    C. Z.E.N.works Scheduler

    D. Help Requester

    E. Remote Control

    Answer: C

3. Which of the following functions are not performed by Workstation Manager? (Choose two.)

    A. Manage workstation inventories in NDS with workstation objects and workstation group objects, without visiting the workstation

    B. Import network workstations into the NDS

    C. Distribute and update clients, applications, or print drivers to the client workstations

D. Choose a standard user interface or designate specific interfaces for individual users

E. Schedule functions on the workstation to occur during the evening or when users are logged off of the network

F. Install and configure Z.E.N.works components on the server

Answer: B, F

4. The Z.E.N.works Application Launcher enables you to do all except which of the following? (Choose two.)

A. Automate tasks that previously required a physical trip to a user's workstation

B. Grant file rights to users and assign access to them

C. Take "pictures" of a workstation's configuration before and after an application is installed with the snAppShot utility

D. Hierarchically situate application objects in the NDS tree through multilevel folders

E. Restrict application access through workstation-specific and user-specific policy packages

F. Allow registration with a secure Windows NT server through Windows NT Service Control Manager to make changes on the server or workstations

G. Associate application objects with workstation objects in NDS

H. Use an application suspension configuration to schedule times for an application's access to cease

Answer: E, G

5. Choose three types of policy packages.

  A. Container

  B. [Root]

  C. User Group

  D. Workstation

  E. Supervisor

  F. Organization

  Answer: A, C, D

6. The order in which policies are applied in policy associations is unimportant. (True or False.)

  Answer: False

7. The number of objects must never exceed:

  A. 750

  B. 1,000

  C. 1,500

  D. 2,000

  E. 2,500

  Answer: C

8. The server in a Z.E.N.works installation requires how many megabytes of available memory?

  Answer: 70

9. When you are installing Z.E.N.works, the best context in which to grant rights is generally which of the following?

  A. Workstation Group

B. User Group

C. Container

D. [Root]

Answer: D

10. For NT workstations, SETUPNW.EXE will work only for users in which two groups?

A. Power Users Group

B. Supervisor Group

C. Administration Group

D. Container Group

Answer: A, C

Chapter 7 Answers

1. The two administrative components of the Application Launcher are _____ and _____.

Answer: NetWare Administrator Application Launcher Snap-In and snAppShot

2. The wrapper file in the Application Launcher window is:

A. NAL32.EXE

B. NAL16.EXE

C. NAL.EXE

D. NALW.EXE

Answer: C

3. SnAppShot changes the file extensions on all application files to what extension?

   A. .SPS

   B. .FIL

   C. .BE4

   D. .PIC

   Answer: B

4. Application Explorer will *not* deliver applications to which of the following? (Choose two.)

   A. The Start menu

   B. The Batch file

   C. The Desktop

   D. The Application Explorer window

   E. The Windows Explorer

   F. The System Tray

   G. The Kernel

   Answer: B, G

5. SnAppShot will *not* take the "before" picture of the workstation's configuration for which of the following? (Choose two.)

   A. CPU

   B. Application files

   C. Text files

   D. Virtual memory

   E. Windows shortcuts

   F. DLLs

G. INI files

H. Registry

Answer: A, D

6. To access the Application Launcher and the User Agent, you must have which of the following file system rights?

A. Write and Create

B. Read and File Scan

C. Supervisor

D. Read and Erase

Answer: B

7. The login script will continue executing while the # command is being processed. The @ command instruction must be completed before the login script can continue. (True or False.)

Answer: False

8. The Prompt on Remote Control parameter sends the target workstation which type of signal in Remote Control?

A. Audible tone

B. Visible signal

C. Remote Session Request

D. Apology

Answer: C

9. Remote Control access is disabled by default. (True or False.)

Answer: False

10. Which of the following statements is true?

A. Help Requester will run on NetWare 4 or NetWare 5.

B. To e-mail help requests, Help Requester requires Group-Wise or a MAPI-compliant message service.

C. Help Requester requests apply to workstations and not users; therefore, you must configure workstation policy packages.

D. Help Requester always has four buttons in its main window to help the user.

Answer: B

11. The four buttons in Help Requester are:

A. Info

B. Help

C. Mail

D. Context

E. Address

F. Call

Answer: A, B, C, F

Chapter 8 Answers

1. Novonyx is best described as:

A. A Netscape company that markets its FastTrack Server

B. A joint venture by Novell and Netscape

C. A division of Novell that works with the Netscape Fast-Track Server for NetWare

D. A filename in FastTrack Server

Answer: C

2. The protocol through which a Web server requests and serves files is called:

A. IP

B. TCP/IP

C. IPX

D. HTTP

Answer: D

3. FastTrack Server is comprised of a set of NLMs that will run on a NetWare 5 server. (True or False.)

Answer: True

4. Long Name Space Support is added by default to all servers that are upgraded to NetWare 5. (True or False.)

Answer: False

5. A file with UNLOAD commands is automatically created when you install FastTrack Server. This file is called _____.NCF.

Answer: NSWEBDN

6. The drop-down list Wildcard Symbol (|) can be used with other symbols and it means _____.

Answer: OR

7. The steps you perform to bind FastTrack Server to NDS include all but which of the following? (Choose one.)

A. Open the Administration Server

B. Specify that the FastTrack Server use NDS

C. Specify the Tree and Context for FastTrack Server

   D. Choose and state the NDS contexts that will be searched

   E. Down and restart the Administration Server and FastTrack Server

Answer: C

8. Find three ways to turn off the FastTrack Server.

   A. Click the Off icon on the Administration Server home page.

   B. Click the Server Off button in Server Preferences in Server Manager.

   C. Disable the server in the primary document directory.

   D. Type **NSWBDN** at the server console.

Answer: A, B, D

9. The default for the Maximum Packet Receive Buffers parameter is:

   A. 50

   B. 75

   C. 100

   D. 200

Answer: C

10. The parameter that determines the maximum number of incoming connections is called _____.

   A. The Domain Name System Lookups parameter

   B. The Maximum Simultaneous Request parameter

   C. The Listen-Queue Size parameter

   D. The HTTP Persistent Connection Timeout parameter

   E. The Maximum Packet Receive Buffers parameter

F. The Maximum Physical Receive Packet Size parameter

G. The Web Server File Size parameter

Answer: C

Chapter 9 Answers

1. A partition within the DNS hierarchy stored on a single server is referred to as a _____.

Answer: Zone

2. Which types of organizations use domains in the top-level domain NET?

A. Any company on the Internet

B. Network providers

C. Network users

Answer: B

3. DNS clients are also referred to as _____.

Answer: Resolvers

4. A DNS zone can be divided into _____.

Answer: Subzones

5. Which of the following are DNS zones supported by NetWare 5? (Choose one or more.)

A. Standard zone

B. IPv6 zone

C. DHCP zone

D. IN-ADDR.ARPA zones

Answer: A, B, D

6. A _____ is a type of DNS server that stores a copy of the DNS database that cannot be modified directly.

Answer: Replica server

7. Which of the following are true of DNS clients? (Choose one or more.)

A. Special client software is required.

B. The name of the DNS server should be specified.

C. The IP address of the DNS server should be specified.

D. The host name of the client should be specified.

Answer: C, D

8. If a local DNS server is unable to resolve a request and sends it on to a root server, which server sends the resolved address back to the client?

A. The local server

B. The root server

Answer: A

9. Where do you install the DNS/DHCP Server software?

A. On any NetWare 5 server

B. On a Workstation

C. On a separate machine

Answer: A

10. Which of the following NDS objects is *not* automatically created when you install the DNS server?

A. DNS/DHCP Group

B. RootServerInfo Zone

C. Resource Record

D. DNS/DHCP Locator

Answer: C

Chapter 10 Answers

1. What is the primary purpose of the DHCP protocol?

A. To convert IP addresses to domain names

B. To convert domain names to IP addresses

C. To assign IP addresses dynamically to clients

D. To allow several clients to use the same IP address at the same time

Answer: C

2. DHCP stands for _____.

Answer: Dynamic Host Configuration Protocol

3. DHCP is based on what Internet standard protocol?

A. DNS

B. BootP

C. PPP

D. NDS

Answer: B

4. You are using DHCP to assign addresses, and your company has been assigned a pool of 10 IP addresses for the Internet. There are two shifts, day and night, with no overlap between the two. The day shift employees use different computers than the night shift employees. How many total employees could you support with DHCP?

Answer: 20 (10 in each shift)

5. An address assigned by DHCP to a client with a limited duration is known as a _____.

Answer: Lease

6. Which type of DHCP addressing assigns addresses dynamically, but always uses the same address for a client each time it boots?

Answer: Automatic addressing

7. An IP address manually assigned to a specific computer in DHCP is also known as a _____.

Answer: Reservation

8. Which hardware or software component is required in order to use the same DHCP server in two subnets of a network?

A. An address pool

B. A DHCP relay agent

C. A BootP server

D. A router

Answer: B

9. The Subnet Address Range and IP Address objects are child objects of which NDS container object?

    A. Organization

    B. DHCP server

    C. IP address pool

    D. Organizational unit

    E. Subnet

    Answer: E

10. Which utility would you use to create an IP Address object?

    A. NWADMIN

    B. DNS/DHCP Management Console

    C. ConsoleOne

    D. INSTALL

    Answer: B

Chapter 11 Answers

1. What was the unifying theme of this chapter?

    A. Odds and ends

    B. Added page count

    C. Growing enterprise complexity

    D. Location/location/location

    Answer: D

2. Which of the following is not an infrastructure service that would be kept track of by SLP?

A. NDS servers

B. NDPS registration servers

C. NSS servers

D. DHCP servers

E. Protocol gateways

F. DNS servers

Answer: C

3. SLP is which Internet Standard protocol?

A. IEEE 802.3

B. FDDI

C. X.25

D. RFC2165

E. SMDS

Answer: D

4. Which of the following parameters would be the best way to confine network traffic to a certain department of your company whose services do not need to be seen elsewhere on the network?

A. Directory Agents

B. SLP scopes

C. Service visibility

D. Fault tolerance

E. NDS replication

Answer: B

5. NDPS is automatically managed in the IP environment from SLP and can't function without SLP. (True or False?)

Answer: False

6. The integer value that represents the Multicast radius is:

A. 0 to 32

B. 60 to 60,000

C. 0 to 8

D. 0 to 4,294,967,255

E. 0 to 128

Answer: A

7. Which client configuration parameter will hurt SLP performance if it is set at either extreme?

A. SLP Maximum Transmission Unit

B. SLP Multicast Radius

C. SLP Cache Replies

D. SLP Default Registration Lifetime

E. SLP Active Discovery

Answer: A

8. You can set the preferred server and name context in the mobile users' clients by placing the information in the _____ file in DOS or Windows.

Answer: NET.CFG

9. If Jlewis wants to log in with an alias object and his organizational object name is MTG, he should log in as:

A. MTG.Jlewis

B. MTG.Alias.Jlewis

C. Alias.Jlewis.MTG

D. Jlewis.MTG

Answer: D

10. Which executable did we use to check to see if our installation of Contextless Login was successful?

Answer: LOGINW32.EXE

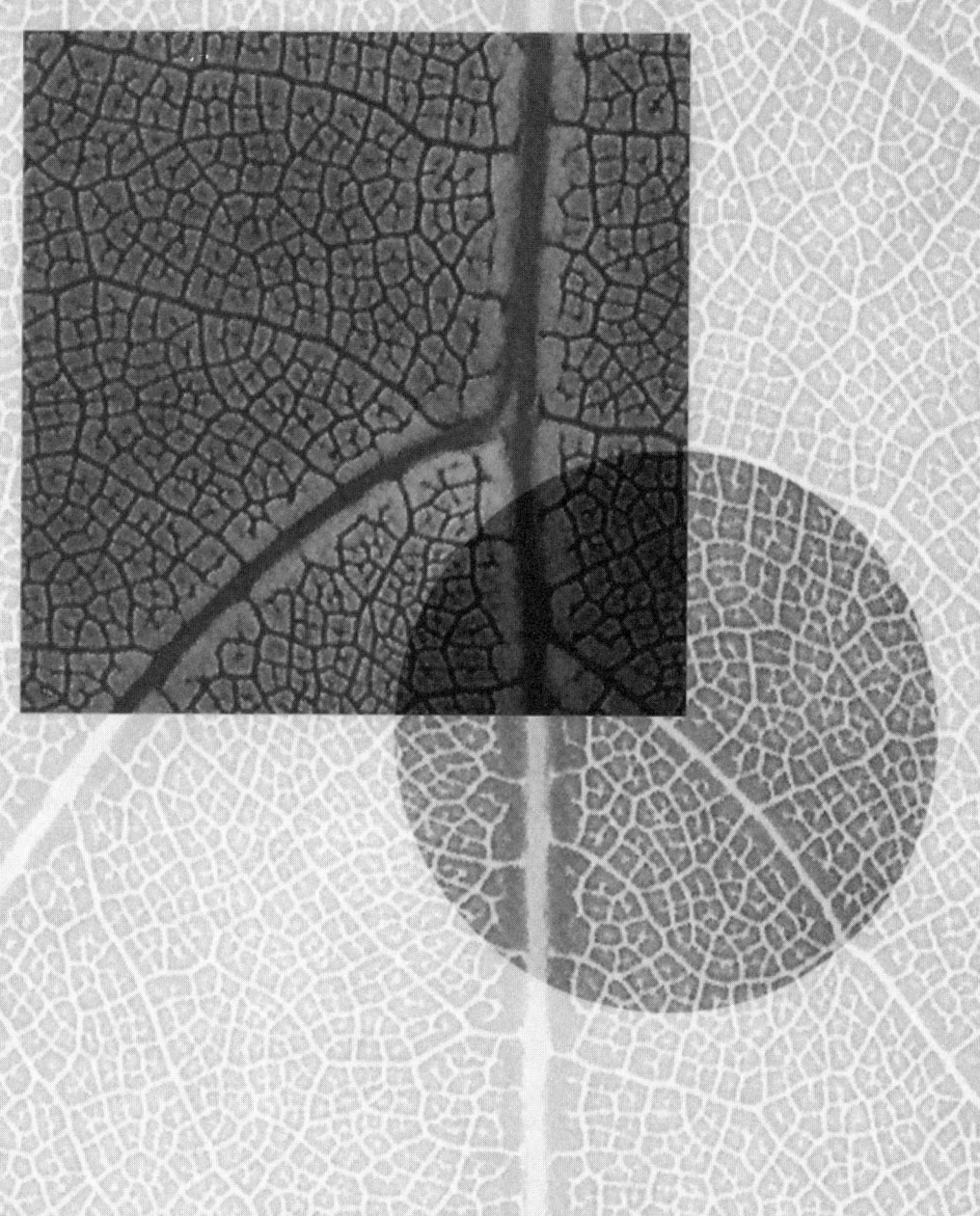

Glossary

Abend   Short for abnormal end. This is NetWare's term for a server crash. An abend is frequently caused by an application (NLM) writing to an area of memory that belongs to the operating system.

Access Control List (ACL)   The property of an NDS object that contains the list of *trustees* or other objects that have rights to the object.

Across-the-Wire Migration   One of the two possible migration strategies from NetWare 3.1*x* or 4.*x* to NetWare 5. In the across-the-wire strategy, a new NetWare 5 server is connected to the same network as the old server and data is copied over the network.

Additive Licensing   NetWare 4.11's licensing system, which allows you to add licenses when your network needs to allow more user logins. For example, you can add a 5-user license to a 25-user license for a total of 30 possible users. NetWare 5's system is similar, but it is not compatible with NetWare 4 licenses.

Address   In TCP/IP, an IP address is a 32-bit numeric identifier assigned to a node. The address has two parts, one for the network identifier and the other for the node identifier. All nodes on the same network must share the network address and have a unique node address. For networks connected to the Internet, network addresses are assigned by the Internet Activities Board (IAB).

Addresses also include IPX addresses—the internal network number and external network number—and the MAC address (Media Access Control) assigned to each network card or device.

Amplitude   In communications, the distance between the highest and lowest points in a wave. The amplitude controls the strength, or volume, of the signal.

Amplitude Modulation   A type of communications that modulates, or makes changes in, the amplitude of the wave in order to transmit bits of data.

Analog Data   Data that has an infinite number of possible states, rather than the simple 1s and 0s of a digital signal. Audio, video, and voice telephone signals, for example, can all be represented using analog signals.

AppleTalk   A networking system developed by Apple for use with Macintosh computers. The software for AppleTalk connectivity is built into the Macintosh operating system (MacOS or System 7). NetWare for Macintosh allows connectivity between AppleTalk and NetWare networks by emulating AppleTalk services on the NetWare server.

Asynchronous   A type of communication that sends data using flow control rather than a clock to synchronize data between the source and destination.

Attenuation   A communications term referring to a signal decreasing in volume (and amplitude) over a distance. The length of the cable and its resistance can affect the amount of attenuation.

Attributes   File attributes are stored for each file and directory on a server's file system. Attributes are used for security purposes and for status information for the file. For example, the read-only attribute prevents a file from being written to or erased, and the Can't Compress attribute indicates that NetWare was unable to compress the file.

NDS objects also have attributes. For clarity, these attributes are usually referred to as *properties*.

Auditing   A NetWare service that allows a user, or *auditor*, to monitor activities on the network. The auditor can monitor the file system or an NDS container. Auditing is done through the AUDITCON utility.

Authentication   Part of the login process, during which NDS verifies that the user's password, access rights, and other settings are correct. Authentication is handled by the nearest read/write or master replica.

Bandwidth   In network communications, the amount of data that can be sent across a wire in a given time. Each communication that passes along the wire decreases the amount of available bandwidth.

Baseband   A transmission technique in which the signal uses the entire bandwidth of a transmission medium.

Base Schema   The NDS base schema defines the structure of NDS—which objects are possible, which properties an object can have, and so forth. The NDS base schema is written to the server when NDS is installed. Third-party applications can extend, or add to, this schema using the NetWare API.

Batch File   A file containing a list of commands to be executed. DOS batch files have the extension BAT. Examples include AUTO-EXEC.BAT, which executes when the workstation is booted, and STARTNET.BAT, which is used to attach to the network.

Binary   The numbering system used in computer memory and in digital communication. All characters are represented as a series of 1s and 0s. For example, the letter *A* might be represented as 01000001.

Bindery   The database used to store information about users, printers, and other network objects in NetWare 3.1*x* and earlier versions. The bindery is a simple, flat database that is stored separately on each server. NetWare 4 and NetWare 5 replace the bindery with NDS, NetWare Directory Services.

Bindery Context   The context that will be provided as a simulated bindery by bindery services. You can set up to 16 separate contexts to serve as bindery contexts; these will be combined into a "bindery" that bindery-based clients can access.

Bindery Services   A service, available in NetWare 4 and NetWare 5, that allows the simulation of a bindery. This allows clients using older client software, such as the NetWare DOS Shell, to access the network. A branch of the NDS tree, the bindery context, is used as a simulated bindery.

Binding   The process of connecting a communication protocol, such as TCP/IP, to a LAN board driver, such as an Ethernet driver.

Bits   In binary data, each unit of data is a bit. Each bit is represented by either 0 or 1, and is stored in memory as an ON or OFF state.

Block   One of the divisions of a hard disk. NetWare stores files on the volume in terms of blocks. In NetWare 3.1x and earlier, entire blocks are always used. Block sizes are typically 4K for NetWare 3.1x and later.

Block Sub-Allocation   A NetWare 4 and NetWare 5 feature that allows smaller portions of disk blocks to be used. Each block is divided into 512-byte units that can be used instead of entire blocks. This allows for more efficient use of disk space.

Bridge   A device that connects two segments of a network and sends data to one or the other based on a set of criteria.

Broadband   A network transmission method in which a single transmission medium is divided and shared simultaneously.

Broadcast   In TCP/IP, a network transmission that is addressed with a network or node address containing only binary 1 digits. This indicates that the transmission is meant to be broadcasted to all networks or nodes.

Buffer   In communications, an area of memory used as temporary storage for data being sent or received. A NetWare 4.11 server uses packet buffers for this purpose. The term buffer can be used to refer to any area of memory in a computer.

Byte   The unit of data storage and communication in computers. In PC systems, a byte is 8 bits or an 8-digit binary number. A single byte can represent numbers between 0 and 255.

Cache Buffer   NetWare sets aside a portion of the server's memory as cache buffers. These buffers are used to cache information for the file system. The amount of cache buffers depends on the available memory.

Cache Hit   A statistical term used when data has been successfully read from the disk cache. A high percentage of cache hits indicates that the amount of cache buffers is sufficient and that the server is running smoothly.

Caching   A technique used by NetWare servers to increase disk performance. Data read from the disk drive is stored in a block of RAM memory, or *cache buffer*. When clients request this data, it can be read directly from the cache, avoiding the use of the disk. NetWare provides both read and write caching.

Carrier   In communications, a signal that is kept on the line at all times so that the device on the other end knows that it is connected.

Checksum   A number that is calculated based on the values of a block of data. Checksums are used in communication to ensure that the correct data was received.

Child Object   In NDS, an object that is under a container object. The container object is referred to as the *parent object*.

Circuit Switching   A type of communication system that establishes a connection, or circuit, between the two devices before communicating and does not disconnect until all data is sent.

Client   Any device that attaches to the network server. A workstation is the most common type of client. Clients run *client software* to provide network access. A piece of software which accesses data on a server can also be called a client.

Client/Server Network   A server-centric network in which some network resources are stored on a file server, while processing power is distributed among workstations and the file server.

Coaxial Cable   One of the types of cable used in network wiring. Typical coaxial types include RG-58 and RG-62. The 10base2 system of Ethernet networking uses coaxial cable. Coaxial cable is usually shielded. The Thicknet system uses a thicker coaxial cable.

Common Name   In NDS, the least significant portion of an object's name. This is the name given to the object when it is created. The common name is abbreviated CN in typeful naming. See *Typeful Naming*.

Container Administrator   An administrator who is given rights to a container object and all of the objects under it. A container administrator can be *exclusive,* meaning that no other administrator has access to the container.

Container Object   In NDS, an object that contains other objects. Container objects include Organization, Organizational Unit, and Country objects. The [Root] object is also a specialized kind of container object. Objects within a container can be other container objects, or *leaf objects*, which represent network resources.

Context   In NDS, an object's position within the Directory Tree. The context is the full path to the container object in which the object resides.

Current Context   The current position in the Directory Tree, maintained for a workstation connection. By default, objects are assumed to be in this context, unless you specify the full *distinguished name*. The current context is also called the *default context*.

Custom Device Module (CDM)   Part of the NetWare Peripheral Architecture (NPA) system of device drivers, the CDM provides an interface between the device and the Host Adapter Module (HAM). The HAM provides communication with the controller.

Data Packet   A unit of data being sent over a network. A packet includes a header, addressing information, and the data itself. A packet is treated as a single unit as it is sent from device to device.

Default Context   See *Current Context*.

Device Driver   A piece of software that allows a workstation or server to communicate with a hardware device. For example, disk drivers are used to control disk drives, and network drivers are used to communicate with network boards.

Digital Data   Data that uses 1s and 0s to store information. See also *Analog Data*.

Directly Connected Network Printer   A type of network printer allowed by NetWare 5. This type of printer is attached to the network rather than to a workstation or server. Directly connected printers can operate in either *remote mode* or *queue server mode*.

Directory   In NDS, the database that contains information about each of the objects on the network. The Directory is organized into a tree-like structure, the *Directory Tree*, with a *[Root] object* on top and *leaf objects* at the bottom. To distinguish it from disk directories, the name of the NDS Directory is always capitalized.

Directory Agent   In SLP, a component that manages service location for a larger network. Directory agents are used if no service agents respond to a user agent's broadcast.

Directory Map   A special NDS object that is used to map directories in the file system. The MAP command can specify the name of the Directory Map object rather than the exact directory name. The directory name is contained in a property of the Directory Map object.

Directory Tree   See *Directory*.

Distinguished Name   In NDS, the full name of an NDS object, which includes the object's *common name* and its *context*, or location, in the Directory tree. Also referred to as the *full distinguished name*.

DOD Networking Model   A four-layer conceptual model describing how communications should take place between computer systems. The four layers are Process/Application, Host-to-Host, Internet, and Network Access. DOD is the acronym for Department of Defense, the government agency that provided the original funding for the development of the TCP/IP protocol suite.

DOS Shell   The client software used for DOS workstations in NetWare 3.1*x* and earlier versions. The executable program for the DOS shell is NETX.COM. The DOS shell does not provide access to NDS, but it can be used with NetWare 4 or NetWare 5 via Bindery Services.

Down   To bring down a NetWare server, usually by using the DOWN command at the server console. Any users logged in to the server will be disconnected when it goes down.

Duplex   A way of classifying communication systems. Full duplex is full two-way communication; half duplex means that data can only travel in one direction at a time.

Effective Rights   The rights that a user (or other trustee) has in a file system directory or NDS object after all factors—explicit rights, inherited rights, the IRF, and security equivalencies—are considered.

Enterprise Networking   The type of networking required to connect an entire enterprise, or a large corporation. This usually implies a wide area network (WAN). NetWare 5 is suitable for enterprise networks (and smaller networks).

Events   In NetWare auditing, the types of activities that can be monitored by the auditor for a volume or NDS object.

Exclusive Container Administrator   A special type of *container administrator* who is given rights to a container and the objects within it. The IRF is used to prevent other administrators from having rights in the container.

Explicit Rights   In NDS or the file system, any rights that are given directly to a user for a directory or NDS object. Explicit rights override *inherited rights*.

Explicit Security Equivalence   In NDS, a method of giving one trustee the same rights as another. Explicit security equivalence can be assigned with group membership, an Organizational Role, or the trustee's Security Equal To property.

Fiber Optics   One of the media that can be used for network communications. Fiber optics uses a tiny glass or plastic fiber, and sends a light signal through it.

File Attributes   See *Attributes*.

File Compression   A NetWare 4 and NetWare 5 feature that automatically compresses files that are not in use. A compressed file can take as little as 33 percent of the space of the original file. Compressed files are uncompressed automatically when a user accesses them.

File Transfer Protocol (FTP)   A TCP/IP protocol that permits the transferring of files between computer systems. Because FTP has been implemented on numerous types of computer systems, file transfers can be done between different computer systems (e.g., a personal computer and a minicomputer).

Full Distinguished Name   See *Distinguished Name*.

Full-Duplex Transmission   Transmission in which there is full, two-way communication. See *Duplex*.

Group Rights   NDS or file system rights that a user receives because of membership in a Group object. This is an example of *implicit security equivalence*.

Half-Duplex Transmission   Transmission in which data is sent only one way at a time. See *Duplex*.

Handshaking   In network communication, a process used to verify that a connection has been established correctly. Devices send signals back and forth to establish parameters for communication.

Host   An addressable computer system on a TCP/IP network. Examples would include endpoint systems such as workstations, servers, minicomputers, mainframes, and immediate systems such as routers. A host is typically a system that offers resources to network nodes, similar to a NetWare server's function.

Host Adapter   A hardware device that allows communication with a peripheral, such as a disk or tape drive. The host adapter, also called a *controller*, is usually a card that is inserted into a slot on the server's motherboard.

Host Adapter Module (HAM)   One of the components of the NetWare Peripheral Architecture (NPA) device driver standard. The HAM provides communication with the *host adapter*.

Implied Security Equivalence   In NDS, an object is security equivalent to—receives the rights of—the object's parent object and its parents, leading up to the [Root] object. This is also called *container security equivalence*. The IRF does not affect this process.

In-Place Upgrade   One of the methods for migrating (upgrading) a server from NetWare 3.1*x* or 4.*x* to NetWare 5. In this method, the server is upgraded directly to the new NOS, leaving data files on the server intact. An alternative method is *across-the-wire migration*.

Inherited Rights   In NDS or the file system, inherited rights are rights that a trustee receives for an object because of rights to the object's parent (a directory in the file system or a parent object in NDS). Inherited rights can be blocked by an explicit assignment or by the *IRF*.

Inherited Rights Filter (IRF)   In the file system, the IRF is the list of rights that a user can inherit for a directory from directories above it. An IRF also exists for each NDS object, and it lists the rights that a trustee can inherit from the object's parents. In NetWare 3.1*x,* the IRF was called the Inherited Rights Mask (IRM) and applied only to the file system.

Internet   A global network made up of a large number of individual networks interconnected through the use of TCP/IP protocols. The individual networks comprising the Internet are from colleges, universities, businesses, research organizations, government agencies, individuals, and other bodies. The governing body of this global network is the Internet Activities Board (IAB). When the term "Internet" is used with an uppercase "I," it refers to the global network, but when written with a lowercase "i," it simply means a group of interconnected networks.

Internetworking   The process of connecting multiple local area networks to form a wide area network (WAN). Internetworking between different types of networks is handled by a *router.*

Intranet   A term for any network that makes Internet-related services, such as e-mail, FTP, and the Web, available to users of a local network.

IPX External Network Number   A number that is used to represent an entire network. All servers on the network must use the same external network number.

IPX Internal Network Number   A number that uniquely identifies a server to the network. Each server must have a different internal network number.

IPX/IP Gateway   A piece of software included with the Intranet-Ware (NetWare 4.11) package. This gateway allows TCP/IP traffic to travel over an ordinary IPX network. This allows clients on the network to use Internet/intranet services without directly supporting TCP/IP. In NetWare 5, IP is supported implicitly.

LAN   See *Local Area Network.*

Leaf Object   An object that cannot contain other objects, and that represents a network resource. Leaf objects include User, Group, Printer, Server, Volume, and many others.

License Disk   A disk included in the NetWare 5 package that contains licensing information. The license controls the number of users the network can have logged in at one time. Licenses are managed using NetWare Licensing Services (NLS).

Local Area Network (LAN) A network that is restricted to a local area—a single building, group of buildings, or even a single room. A LAN often has only one server, but it can have many, if desired.

Logical Ports In queue-based printing, ports used by the CAPTURE command to redirect a workstation printer port to a network print queue. The logical port has no relation to the port to which the printer is actually attached or the *physical port*.

Login Script A set of commands that are automatically executed when a user logs in. NetWare 5 includes Container, Profile, User, and Default login scripts. Up to three of these can be executed for each user. The login script consists of a special type of command called *login script commands*.

Login Security The most basic form of network security. A user-name and password are required in order to log into the network and access resources.

MAN See *Metropolitan Area Network*.

Master Replica The main replica for an NDS partition. The master replica must be available when major changes, such as partition merging and splitting, are performed. Another replica can be assigned as the master if the original master replica is lost.

Merging Directory Trees The process of combining two Directory trees into a single tree. The objects in the *source tree* are combined into the *destination* or *target* tree. The DSMERGE utility is used to merge trees.

Merging Partitions The process of combining an NDS partition with its parent partition, resulting in a single partition. The master replica of the partition must be available for this process.

Message Switching A type of network communication that sends an entire *message*, or block of data, rather than a simple packet.

Metropolitan Area Network (MAN)   A network spanning a single city or metropolitan area. A MAN is larger than a local area network (LAN), which is normally restricted to a single building or neighboring buildings, but smaller than a wide area network (WAN), which can span the entire globe.

Mobile User   A network user without a consistent network connection. This includes users with portable computers and users who routinely log in to the network from different locations.

Multicast   In TCP/IP, a type of packet that is addressed for delivery to a number of nodes at the same time. (This is similar to a broadcast, but it is not necessarily sent to all nodes on the network.)

Multi-Valued Property   In NDS, a property that can have multiple values. For example, a User object's Telephone Number property can store multiple telephone numbers.

Name Space   A service that you can install on a NetWare server volume to allow the use of different types of filenames. Name spaces are available for Windows 95, OS/2, NFS, and Macintosh naming. The default NetWare 5 name space supports DOS filenames only.

NetWare Directory Services (NDS)   The system NetWare 4.11 uses to catalog objects on the network—users, printers, volumes, and others. NDS uses a *Directory tree* to store this information. All of the NetWare 4.11 network's resources can be managed through NDS.

NetWare Distributed Print Services (NDPS)   The printing system supported by NetWare 5. NDPS provides a more efficient alternative to queue-based printing, supported by NetWare 4.*x* and earlier versions. NetWare 5 can also support queue-based printing.

NetWare Loadable Module (NLM)   An application or program that executes on the NetWare server. NLMs are used for device drivers, LAN drivers, and applications such as backup software. A variety of utility NLMs are provided with NetWare 5, and others are available from third parties.

NetWare Peripheral Architecture (NPA) A system supported by NetWare 4.11 and NetWare 5 for *device drivers,* used to control disk and tape drives. The driver is divided into two modules: a host adapter module (HAM) and a custom device module (CDM) for each device attached to the host adapter. Older device drivers use a single program with a .DSK extension. These can still be used in NetWare 4.11, but they cannot be used in NetWare 5.

Network Address A unique address that identifies each node, or device, on the network. The network address is generally hard-coded into the network card on both the workstation and server. Some network cards allow you to change this address, but there is usually no need to do so.

Network Interface Card (NIC) Physical devices that connect computers and other network equipment to the transmission medium used. When installed in a computer's expansion bus slot, a NIC allows the computer to become a workstation on the network.

Network Operating System (NOS) The software that runs on a file server and offers file, print, and other services to client workstations. NetWare 4.11 is a NOS. Other examples include NetWare 3.1*x,* Banyan VINES, and IBM LAN Server.

NIC See *Network Interface Card.*

Node In TCP/IP, an IP addressable computer system, such as workstations, servers, minicomputers, mainframes, and routers. In IPX networks, the term is usually applied to nonserver devices, such as workstations and printers.

Object In NDS, any resource on the network. Users, printers, and groups are examples of *leaf objects. Container objects* are used to organize other objects.

Open Systems Interconnect (OSI) A model defined by the ISO to conceptually organize the process of communication between computers in terms of seven layers, called *protocol stacks.* The seven layers of the OSI model provide a way for you to understand how communication across various protocols takes place.

Organization Object   Usually the highest-level container object used. Organizations are created under the [Root] or under the Country object if it is used. This object usually represents an entire organization or company. More than one Organization can be used in the same Directory tree.

Organizational Role Object   An object that is used to represent a role—an administrator or other specialized user—that requires access to certain NDS objects or files. This is often used for container administrators. The user assigned to the Organizational Role is called the *occupant* of the role.

Organizational Unit Object   The lowest-level container object. Organizational Units can be used to divide locations, divisions, workgroups, or smaller portions of the Directory tree. Organizational Units can be subdivided further with additional Organizational Units.

OSI   See *Open Systems Interconnect.*

Packet   The basic division of data sent over a network. Each packet contains a set amount of data along with a header, containing information about the type of packet and the network address to which it is being sent. The size and format of packets depends on the *protocol* and frame types used.

Packet Switching   A type of data transmission in which data is divided into packets, each of which has a destination address. Each packet is then routed across a network in an optimal fashion. An addressed packet may travel a different route than packets related to it. Packet sequence numbers are used at the destination node to reassemble related packets.

Parent Object   In NDS, an object that *contains* another object—
a container object. This is a relative term; a parent object also has
parent objects of its own, and is considered a child object from that
perspective.

Partition (In NDS)   A branch of the NDS tree that can be replicated
onto multiple servers. The partition includes a container object and
the objects under it, and is named according to the name of that
object. By default, a single partition—the [Root] partition—exists.

Partition (On a Disk)   NetWare uses disk partitions to divide a
hard disk. A disk can contain a single NetWare partition, which is
used to hold one or more NetWare volumes. In addition, it can have
a DOS partition, used to boot the server and hold the SERVER.EXE
program.

Peer-to-Peer Network   A local area network in which network
resources are shared among workstations, without the use of a file
server.

Physical Port   In queue-based printing, the port to which a printer is
actually attached. This differs from the *logical ports* used in the CAP-
TURE command for printer redirection.

Ping   A TCP/IP utility used to test whether another machine is online.
A ping program sends a request to the other machine, waits for a reply,
and displays the time the reply took to arrive. An implementation of
this utility, WinPing, is included with the IPX/IP Gateway software.
This command is named after the "ping" signals sent and received by
radar systems.

PPP   Stands for Point-to-Point Protocol. This protocol allows the
sending of IP packets on a dial-up (serial) connection. Supports compression and IP address negotiation.

Print Job A file that has been sent by a client for printing. Print jobs are stored in a *print queue* until they can be serviced by the print server.

Print Queue In queue-based printing, the area used to hold the list of print jobs that are waiting to print. The print queue is managed through the Print Queue object in NDS. Print jobs are sent from the print queue to the print server one at a time.

Print Server In queue-based printing, an NDS object used to manage printing. The print server itself can run on a NetWare server (PSERVER .NLM) or in a hardware device.

Profile Object A special NDS object that is used to assign the same login script to a group of users. The Profile login script is executed after the Container login script and before the User login script.

Properties In NDS, all of the possible information that can be entered for an object. The properties of a User object include login name, full name, and telephone number. The information in a property is the *value* of the property.

Protocol A method of communicating between NetWare servers and clients. The protocol is the "language" used for sending data. Data is divided into packets specified by the protocol. IPX is the typical protocol for NetWare networks.

Protocol Suite A collection of protocols that are associated with and that implement a particular communication model (such as the DOD Networking Model or the OSI Reference Model).

Relative Distinguished Name (RDN) A shortened version of an object's full distinguished name that specifies the path to the object from the current context. Relative distinguished names do not begin with a period. Periods can be used at the end of the RDN to move up the Directory tree.

Replica Ring   A group of NDS replicas that are synchronized. This includes a master replica and one or more other replicas.

Replication   The process of keeping copies of the NDS information on separate servers. Each *partition* in NDS has a set of replicas. These include the master replica—the original partition—and, optionally, read/write and read-only replicas.

RIP   Stands for Router Information Protocol. A distance-vector routing protocol used on many TCP/IP internetworks and IPX networks. The distance vector algorithm uses a "fewest-hops" routing calculation method.

Scope   In DHCP, a pool of IP addresses that are available and can be issued to DHCP clients. A scope can contain one or more consecutive ranges of IP addresses.

Security Equivalence   In NDS, any situation where an object, or trustee, receives the same rights given to another object. There are two types of security equivalence: *implied* and *explicit.*

Service Advertising Protocol (SAP)   The protocol used for various NetWare 4.11, as well as 2.*x* and 3.*x,* services. When using Pure IP communication, NetWare 5 encapsulates SAP broadcasts using SLP (Service Location Protocol).

Service Agent   In SLP, a component that receives broadcasts from user agents and responds with the location of a service.

Simple Network Management Protocol (SNMP)   A management protocol used on many networks, particularly TCP/IP. It defines the type, format, and retrieval of management information about nodes.

SLIP (Serial Line Internet Protocol)   A protocol that permits the sending of IP packets on a dial-up (serial) connection. Does not, by itself, support compression or IP address negotiation.

SLP (Service Location Protocol) A protocol supported by NetWare 5. SLP allows services (such as DNS or DHCP) to be located or discovered by clients.

SNMP See *Simple Network Management Protocol.*

Splitting Partitions The process of creating a new NDS partition. A container object within a current partition is specified, and that object and all objects under it are moved (split) to a new partition.

Storage Management Services (SMS) The NetWare 5 service that allows for backup services. SMS consists of several components, ranging from the device driver that handles access to the backup device, to the front end or *backup engine.*

Synchronization The process used by NDS to ensure that all replicas of a partition contain the same data. Synchronization is handled through *replica rings.*

Target Service Agent One of the components of the NetWare 5 Storage Management System (SMS). The TSA provides an interface to the device that will be backed up. Devices include servers, workstations, and the NDS database. A separate TSA is used for each one. The NetWare 5 client software includes a TSA component.

TCP/IP Stands for Transmission Control Protocol/Internet Protocol. Generally used as shorthand for the phrase *TCP/IP protocol suite.*

Telnet A TCP/IP terminal emulation protocol that permits a node, called the Telnet client, to log in to a remote node, called the Telnet server. The client simply acts as a dumb terminal, displaying output from the server. The processing is done at the server.

Trustee Any object that has been given rights to an NDS object or file. Trustee rights can include explicit, inherited, and effective rights.

Twisted Pair   A type of wiring used for network communications, which uses copper wires twisted into pairs.

Typeful Naming   The formal method of naming NDS objects, including name types for each portion of the name. For example, .CN=Terry.OU=Mktg.O=QAZ_CO.

Typeless Naming   The more common method of NDS object naming, which does not include name types. For example, .Terry .Mktg.QAZ.CO. Typeless naming is adequate for most uses within NDS utilities.

UDP   Stands for User Datagram Protocol. UDP uses a connectionless, unguaranteed packet delivery method. It resides at the Host-to-Host layer of the DOD Networking Model.

UNIX   A multitasking operating system, created by AT&T's Bell Labs, that is used on a wide variety of computers, including many Internet servers.

User Agent   In SLP, the component that clients use to locate services. User agents send broadcasts to service agents, or they use a directory agent if needed.

User Template   In NDS, a special User object that is used to assign defaults when a new user is created. A User Template can be created for each NDS container, and you can change the property values of this object to provide defaults for new users in the container. The User Template does not affect existing users.

Values   The data that is stored in the *properties* of an NDS object. Properties can have one or more values. Some are required, and others are optional.

Wide Area Network (WAN)   A network that extends across multiple locations. Each location typically has a local area network (LAN), and the LANs are connected together in a WAN. Typically used for *enterprise networking*.

World Wide Web (WWW)   A term used for the collection of computers on the Internet running HTTP (HyperText Transfer Protocol) servers. The Web allows for text and graphics to have hyperlinks connecting users to other servers. Using a *Web browser*, such as Netscape Navigator or Microsoft Internet Explorer, a user can link from one server to another at the click of a button.

Index

Note to the Reader: First level entries are in **bold**. Page numbers in **bold** indicate the principal discussion of a topic or the definition of a term. Page numbers in *italic* indicate illustrations.

Q

R

NETWARE® 5 CNE®
STUDY GUIDES FROM
NETWORK PRESS®

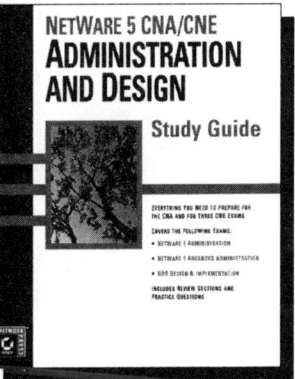

NetWare® 5 CNA℠/CNE®: Administration and Design Study Guide	**NetWare® 5 CNE®: Core Technologies Study Guide**	**NetWare® 5 CNE®: Integrating Windows® NT® Study Guide**	**NetWare® 5 CNE®: Update to NetWare® 5 Study Guide**
ISBN: 0-7821-2387-2	ISBN: 0-7821-2389-9	ISBN: 0-7821-2388-0	ISBN: 0-7821-2390-2
864 pp.; 7½" X 9"	512 pp.; 7½" X 9"	448 pp.; 7½" X 9"	432 pp.; 7½" X 9"
$44.99, Hardcover	$44.99, Hardcover	$39.99, Hardcover	$39.99, Hardcover
Covers:	**Covers:**	**Covers:**	**Covers:**
NetWare® 5 Administration (the CNA test)	Networking Technologies	Integrating Windows® NT®	NetWare® 4.11 to NetWare® 5 Update
NetWare® 5 Advanced Administration	Service & Support		
NDS Design & Implementation			

www.sybex.com

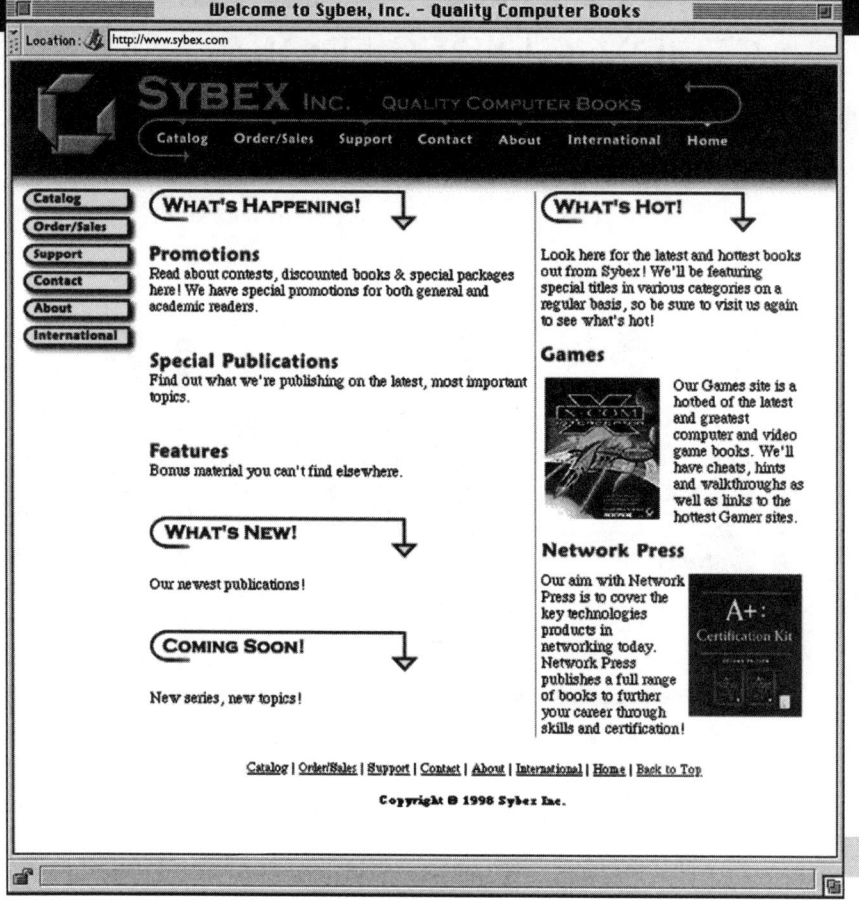

CISCO® STUDY GUIDES
FROM NETWORK PRESS®

- · **Prepare for Cisco certification with the experts**
- · **Full coverage of each exam objective**
- · **Hands-on labs and hundreds of sample questions**

ISBN 0-7821-2381-3
768 pp; 7½" x 9"; $49.99
Hardcover

ISBN 0-7821-2403-8
832 pp; 7½" x 9"; $49.99
Hardcover

ISBN 0-7821-2571-9
704 pp; 7½" x 9"; $49.99
Hardcover
Available April 1999

**CCDA: Cisco Certified Design
Associate Study Guide**
ISBN: 0-7821-2534-4; 800 pp; 7½" x 9"
$49.99; Hardcover; CD
Available May 1999

**CCNP: Cisco Internetwork
Troubleshooting Study Guide**
ISBN 0-7821-2536-0; 704 pp; 7½ x 9
$49.99; Hardcover; CD
Available May 1999

**CCNP: Configuring, Monitoring,
and Troubleshooting Dial-Up
Services Study Guide**
ISBN 0-7821-2544-1; 704 pp; 7½" x 9"
$49.99; Hardcover; CD
Available July 1999

SYBEX
www.sybex.com

From the Experts...

Who bring you Mark Minasi's #1 best-selling *Complete PC Upgrade & Maintenance Guide,* Sybex now presents...

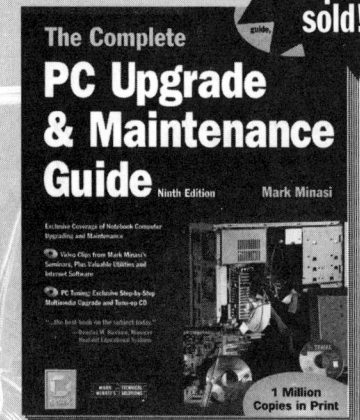

A+ TEST PREPARATION FROM THE EXPERTS

Sybex presents the most comprehensive study guides for CompTIA's A+ exams for PC technicians.

Visit the Sybex Web Site for the NetWare 5 CNE

Go to *www.sybex.com* for additional tools and information to help you prepare for the new CNE exams. On the companion Web site for this book, you'll find:

■ **Test Updates**

Tests and test objectives can change. We'll provide the information you need to stay up-to-date as you prepare for the tests.

■ **Online Testing Engines**

Test your knowledge with our exclusive online testing program from The Edge Group. Simulate the test-taking experience with challenging questions like those you'll encounter on the NetWare 5 CNE tests.

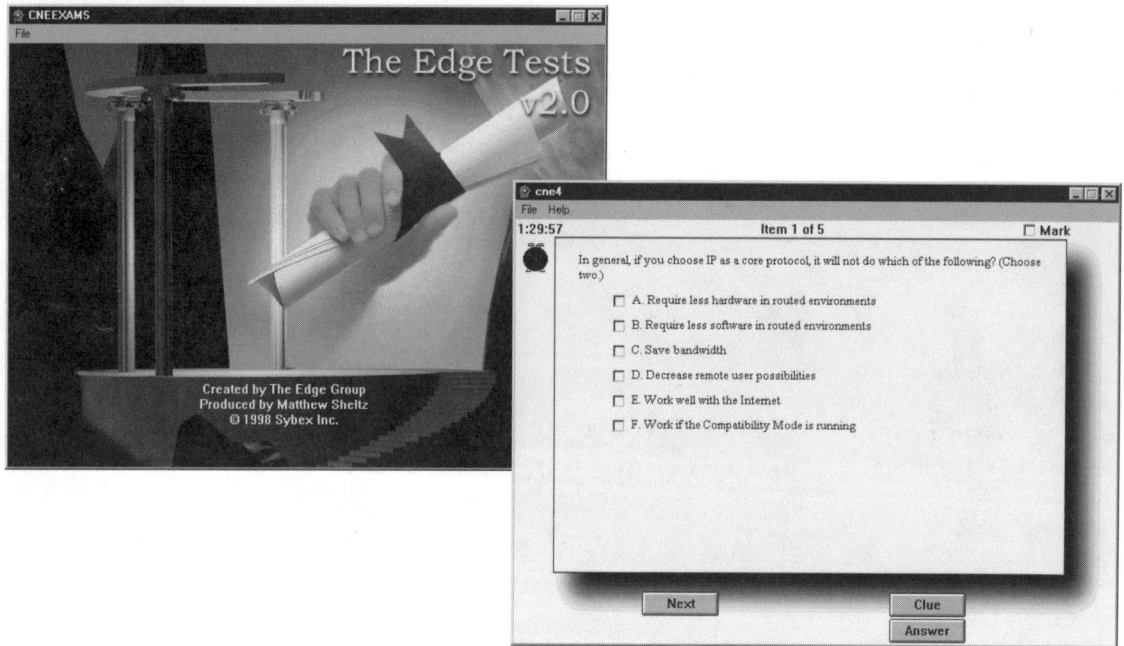

■ **Information on Other Certifications**

At Sybex's Web site you'll also find information on numerous other computer industry certification programs—MCSE, MCSD, A+, Java, Lotus Notes, Cisco, and more—together with details of Sybex books that will help you prepare for the certification exams.

 To get to the companion Web site for this book, click on the Catalog link on the Sybex home page (www.sybex.com), and then enter the title of the book in the keyword search box.